Merging Lives

This is a work of fiction. Any resemblance to any real person, place, or entity is purely coincidental.

ISBN: 1-4392-1346-1
ISBN-13: 9781439213469

Visit www.booksurge.com to order additional copies.

Merging Lives

Donna Pagano

Acknowledgements

From the bottom on my heart, I thank my good friend, Teddi Davis for her undying support, expertise, encouragement and talent. I couldn't have done it without you! To Chris Madden, big hugs for all your help, excitement and positive energy. Robin Downes—graphic artist extraordinaire, you are a delight to work with and I so appreciate your artistic eye. My children, siblings, and friends have also been thoroughly supportive, and to them, I say a sincere THANK YOU. Especially to my sister Brenda, I greatly appreciate all your efforts and incredible talent. To Mandy, thanks for your patience—you captured my girl, even before you knew her! I appreciate Dr. Alison Smith and Susan Barry for showing me so many things, especially the world of hypnosis and it's endless possibilities when dealing with the human psyche. And to my husband *Sam*, it's lovely to be with you again. The beat goes on with our karmic dance and life is our constant dance floor.

Mandy Thody is a painter and sculptor living in St Croix, US Virgin Islands. Originally from England, she has lived in South Africa, on several Caribbean Islands, the US, and on a sailboat for 20 years. Her work is mainly concerned with the human face and form in all its variety, and with the mythologies of different peoples, as well as flora and fauna of the Caribbbean. More works can be seen on her website at www.athodyarts.com, and in galleries such as Mango Tango (St Thomas, USVI) and Bajo el Sol (St John, USVI).

Foreword

The subconscious mind holds a wisdom which, when tapped, can illuminate the true reasons behind challenges we experience throughout our lifetime. Deep within are answers to the questions of our existence—Who am I? What am I doing here? Why do I feel so strongly about that person, place, or thing? The answers may be as recent as last week or a childhood memory or they may reside further back in the soul's memory.

By accessing the resources of the subconscious, the use of hypnosis has given many people therapeutic results in relief from fears, phobias and other forms of discomfort. Perhaps more importantly hypnotic regression puts willing people in touch with that eternal part of themselves—the soul.

Decades of research in regression have demonstrated that we each have patterns of experience, which we continue to play out until we learn from them, heal and grow. In my practice as a hypnotherapist I have witnessed remarkable transformations take place through regression work, whether it be current life or past life. There is no doubt in my mind concerning the eternal quality of the soul and its journey through human existence. It is my belief that we have worn many 'costumes' in our soul journey. We have been different genders, races and nationalities in many time zones and zip codes. The common thread is that we have been a soul having a human experience.

Merging Lives is a novel based on the author's actual past life regression work. It can be read as a good story and as an illustration of a portion of one soul's journey. Enjoy...and who knows? In the words of one of my mentors, Henry Leo Bolduc, you may decide to 'Go forward and regress.'

Susan Barry, M.A., M.Ht.
Cape Cod, MA

Part One

1760–1825

I believe I shall, in some shape or other, always exist; and,
with all the inconveniences human life is liable to,
I shall not object to a new edition of mine, hoping, however,
that the errata of the last may be corrected.

— Benjamin Franklin

Chapter One

1760

Wide rivers of mud-brown sweat streamed openly from the pale, bearded faces of the fiercely determined herders. The intensity of the round up had stunned the panicking animals to instant submission. Still the whip-wielders continued to work themselves into a merciless frenzy. The steamy night air came alive with swirling funnels of rock and dirt. There was no escape for the defenseless creatures.

She attempted to turn her head away. No longer could she bear to watch the terrified animals and their ruthless predators. The repugnant stench of fear invaded her nostrils. As she attempted to shield her eyes from the horrors before her, Pama was shocked to find that her hands were tied firmly behind her back. She tried to squirm free, but she was paralyzed—swollen with pain. For the first time in her life, she felt the strange star-shaped birthmark on her index finger burn with the intensity of a roaring fire. She had been told the mark was a symbol from the gods that she had 'the gift'. It had never caused her pain before.

As the sound of a solitary death scream penetrated her soul, Pama realized the beings around her were not helpless animals at all. They were her family, her friends, and all the people of her peaceful African village. Without warning, Pama's hands broke free. Her eyes blazed open. The essence of that scream was still reverberating in frozen caves just below her heart.

To date, this horrid vision was clearly the most painful of them all. Despite the hot, dry night, Pama felt as though she had been trapped under a chilling rain. Strangely, though fully awake, her finger still ached with the raw pain of an open wound. She placed the tender skin to her lips but felt little relief. Now drenched with perspiration, she reached for the comfort of her leopard skin, knowing she would have to re-live the horrible dream once more with the telling. The Chief would expect every detail.

Pama hoped the gut wrenching sound from her own throat had not disturbed her husband and young son. She looked in their direction. Thankfully, they seemed immersed in peaceful slumber. Pama's shoulders hurt and she turned gingerly, seeking solace in the soft moonlight. She then looked more closely at the star-shaped markings on the skin of her finger but could find no cuts or bruises. At last, the pain began to subside.

Why do I have to be burdened with these visions? What does it all mean? She mused.

Exactly twenty years ago to the day, Teshome, the village elder had passed through to the spirit world. During his long life, his dreams had served the people well. Whenever the visions came three nights in succession with building intensity, villagers learned to take heed and prepare against impending storms or whatever event had been brought to life as Teshome slept.

Sixteen years earlier, at the age of four, little Pama shared with her mother three identical nightmares about her friends becoming dreadfully sick after drinking from the nearby stream. Wisely, the young child's mother shared the premonition with the chief. Immediately, it was decreed that only rainwater was to be drunk, until further notice.

If only those thirsty skeptics had heeded that first warning, perhaps no villagers would have taken ill. Most did not live long enough to bear witness to foreboding truths, which, from that day forward, manifested themselves through the subconscious of the small girl. From the soul of her beloved maternal grandfather, Teshome, who had died within moments of her birth, Pama had indeed inherited, "The Gift."

This was the third night Pama had endured the raging nightmares and she knew what she must do. She watched her husband and son intently as the early morning light kissed their long dark eyelashes, waking them gently and unannounced.

"Good day, my Yondua, and my sweet boy, Zenebu." Pama smiled at her family as they sat up and stretched like lions lazing in the shade. Zenebu climbed into his mother's lap, snuggling about in her warmth, not quite awake. Pama stroked his back with her palm and looked over at her husband. He knew her well. Although her posture was composed and nurturing, her eyes told a tale of danger.

"I must talk to the chief right away. I had the nightmare again and it was even more horrible than the others." She looked deep into Yondua's eyes and realized they mirrored the terror she felt in her soul. "Why do I have to be the one?" she asked softly, looking up to the heavens. Pama felt the burden of her intuition and shuddered.

"You are the one because God has chosen you to be his mouthpiece, my love." Yondua gave his wife a reassuring smile and gentle hug. "Now, go. Tell the chief. The sooner he knows the sooner we will have a plan for our safety." He held his arms out to accept Zenebu.

"Yes, I know." Pama said reaching for the protective flap. "Please, feed yourself and Zenebu. I will return in a while.

The sweet smell of ripe corn and pumpkin enveloped her senses as Pama walked down the winding path to the chief's lodge. She listened to the early morning songbirds harmonizing in the tall Albeezia trees, which grew along the well-worn path. Pama loved her home. But if the forecast came to be, she could be taken away forever.

"Please Almighty One, let it not be true," she prayed. When Pama reached the chief's lodge she took a few deep breaths. She found herself drawing symbols in the dirt with her toe as she stalled the inevitable meeting. She disliked being the messenger of doom. "I hope I am wrong this time," she mumbled to herself.

The Tulu chief heard someone outside and opened the flap to extend a welcome. His warm, loving eyes gave her temporary assurance. "Excuse me, Chief, good day. I need to speak with you. I hope this is a good time, as it cannot wait. I am filled with fear."

"Of course, my child. Come in. Your son told me you were having these fitful dreams again. I had a feeling I would see you here today." The chief smiled with his whole being and Pama felt warmed by his compassion. He had great respect for her because she was the granddaughter of Teshome, and the chief knew the Tulu were blessed to have another one amongst them with the insightful gift.

"Yes, sir, it is true. I have had this same dream the past three nights. I must tell you what has been revealed about our people." Pama said, her voice trembling with fear.

"By the look on your face, it was more a nightmare than a dream."

"Yes, sir." Her eyes were big and round. "You are right. What I have to tell you is indeed a nightmare."

"Please, sit down. Tell me all that you can."

"We are going to be invaded by a wicked tribe of pale men who will kill many of us and enslave the rest." As Pama recalled the visions, they became all the more real with the telling. Once again her finger started to burn—that one finger with the star-like birthmark. She rubbed it against her skirt, hoping for relief. None came.

The chief stared at her with wide-eyed amazement. Her news took his breath away. She waited patiently while the information sifted through the depths of his reasoning.

"Wicked pale men?" his voice became weak and terror swam in his searching, dark eyes. Pama nodded, but did not speak. "We have heard about these invasions to other villages. I had hoped we would be spared." Brave and unflinching to a fault, the Tulu chief seemed visibly shaken by Pama's news. He looked deep into her eyes and saw the pain she had endured from her dreams. He too, felt the pain of his people. He so wished to protect them from the imminent horrors, which lay ahead.

Leaning toward the center pit, he gently pulled the smoke from the smoldering fire over himself, closed his eyes and took deep, calming breaths. When he was done, he motioned for Pama to do the same. Ordinarily, performing this tribal ritual made Tulus feel more centered, but unfortunately, the smoke did not ease the sense of impending doom. After a few moments, the chief spoke again.

"I will consult the elders immediately. In spite of the upcoming harvest, I suspect we should move up river tomorrow. If it is safe, we will send scouts back here to pick our crops."

Pama nodded. She was relieved that they might still be able to reap their bountiful harvest. The tribe had worked hard and the rains of the season had been plentiful.

"Please, child," the chief added, "do not speak of this to anyone. It would create panic and we need to be sensible. We will all leave together in peace."

For the moment, Pama's burden felt gently lifted. She smiled at her wise leader. Before leaving his lodge, he gave her a comforting hug but she could not help noticing his skin felt cold and damp.

That afternoon, the village men were working the grain fields as the women prepared the evening meal. Children's laughter mixed with the smells of sweet cardamom, cloves and spicy peppers. The hazy village was filled with the intoxicating sounds and fragrances of life.

The afternoon sun blazed with merciless heat. The air was steamy and thick. Pama felt her scant wrap clinging to her moist flesh. She wiped the sweat from her brow and tried to dry her hands on her skirt. *Things seem to be peaceful,* she thought, relieved. Looking up, she spied the crystal clear Konkoure River in the distance.

"I am going for a swim. Would anyone like to join me?" she asked the women in her work group.

"You go on, Pama. You know we are not as comfortable in the water as you are."

"I suppose you are right about that," she smiled. Pama was often teased for her natural ability to swim like the illusive fishes in the rivers and sea. Secretly, she considered it a grand compliment. "Has anyone seen my son?" she asked. "HE will want to swim with me."

"No, not since the morning. Last I saw, he was playing with the chief's boy and a few others," a woman replied.

"If you see him, please tell him I went to the river." The ladies nodded without looking up from their chores.

The surrounding fields presented a sweet, golden glow. Despite the beauty surrounding her, Pama could not help but relive last night's vision as she scampered along the narrow path toward the water. Occasionally, she peered pensively over her shoulders; half expecting to see hordes of terrifying white men leaping from the bushes, but all was calm. When Pama reached their swimming hole, she was surprised to find no one there on such a hot day. How unusual! Not a single bird or animal sought relief in the cooling waters.

It is true, I do love to swim, she thought, slipping out of her clothing and into the cool, calm refreshment. Their protected pool was located at a wide spot in the river. Huge boulders had formed a natural breakwater from the current. Pama plunged under the water, wishing it could wash away her looming fear. Floating on her back, she drank in the clear, blue afternoon sky as if it were an elixir, custom made by the gods to calm her anxiety.

Suddenly, a sense of urgency came over her. Within seconds, she was out of the water and dressed. Feeling less vulnerable with her cloth wrap in place, she began running back to her village along the well-worn trail. As she ran, she wished all the more that Yondua and Zenebu had joined her for the swim. They too, loved the water and Pama was proud of their son's swimming ability and fearless spirit. More importantly, she longed to have them at her side.

"ZENEBU!" Pama cried out. "Where are you? Zeeeneeebu... make a sound so I can hear where you are, little one!" Pama stopped to catch her breath. She was sure she would feel calmer once she located her family. *That boy is always off exploring somewhere.... just like his mama,* she thought, reflecting on their similarities.

"I am out here, Mama," his little voice cried out.

Instantly, Pama breathed a sign of relief. There he was, around the bend in the trail playing with several other children. But to her dismay, she realized they had a small Indigo snake trapped among them. "What are you boys doing to that creature?" Her voice echoed in disapproval.

"We were just playing with the snake. It likes us. It is not scared." Eager to change the subject, Zenebu jumped up and grabbed Pama's hand. He was trying to lead her down the trail towards the water. "Can I go with you and swim, Mama? Pleassse?" He was begging in his high-pitched, four-year-old voice. Zenebu was not allowed in the river without his parents and swimming was sure to upstage a snake, especially on such a hot day.

"Why are you whining about a swim, young man? Can you not see that I have already been in the river?" She gestured toward her wet hair, not at all distracted by the issue at hand. "You are scaring that snake by making it do what *you* want it to do. Shame on all of you! Do you all understand why I am upset?"

"Because we have taken away its freedom," the chief's son answered, somberly. "We will let it go now." Pama nodded her approval as the dazed snake darted away into the brush.

"Please Mama—take me to the river. After all, you are still covered in dust," Zenebu said. He was pointing toward the ground, so Pama looked down. It was true—her feet were grimy from running along the trail. "All right. We can go," she agreed, adding, "but only if your friends come with us!"

"Yeah! Yeah!" the children squealed with delight, jumping up and down. The little snake was long forgotten.

Pama began to hum a little tune: "Ay Ya Ay Ya, La La Ya Ya," and the children joined in with their sweet, young voices alive with harmony. They held hands and swung their slender brown arms back and forth as they paraded down the path to the river.

As soon as they arrived on the riverbank, the children jumped in the water but instinctively stayed close to shore. "Come! Swim with me to the other side!" Pama said, encouraging them to stretch their abilities. "The current is strong so you need to paddle hard." Pama stood where the water rushed against her body. "I know you can do it," she coaxed.

At last, their swimming hole was filling up with village women and children eager to escape the late afternoon heat. As a rule, the villagers did not go under water, but took to standing knee deep at the water's edge. Splashing their arms, they watched in fascination as Pama and the children played so fearlessly.

"Be careful! The water is dangerous!" scolded Soumana. Since she herself had never learned to swim, she kept her own children away from the deeper water. "Get away from the edge so you do not fall in!" she commanded.

"Soumana, let Mommy teach you to swim so you can play with us. It is fun." Zenebu called from across the river.

"Swimming is for fish!" She proclaimed, reaching down to splash water on her plump, meaty arms. "Bathing is for humans. I think you and your mother are part fish, Zenebu," Soumana said as her children snickered.

"We are fish, we are fish!" Zenebu, and his friends could not have been more delighted with themselves as they swam back and forth across the current.

After being in the water for quite some time, their fingertips became blanched and wrinkled. "Look Mama, we have skin like the elephants," Zenebu said. Now the children took to screeching and splashing each other with arms outstretched like the trunks of the elephants.

Pama relished the sun's warmth on her wet skin as she climbed gracefully onto dry land. She laid down on a big, flat rock to dry in the gentle breeze. Closing her eyes, she breathed in the distinct smell of wet earth. *I wonder if everywhere smells this sweet when it is wet,* she thought. With her eyes still closed, she listened to the comforting sounds of children's laughter and women's muffled gossip. At first, the children tried to coax Pama back in the water but she waved them off, drifting between worlds of consciousness.

As she dozed, a sordid dream invaded her reverie. She could see herself wearing short pants, which barely covered her upper thigh. Her scant shirt offered only thin shoulder straps. She was screaming in anguish while pacing the upper porch of a large, strange house situated right next to a clear, turquoise ocean. There was a man who appeared to be her husband, but he was not Yondua. He was attempting to take her children from her. There also was a woman by her side that had just put her sleeping child to bed, who attempted to soothe Pama. She stopped screaming long enough to look through the veil of time and right into Pama's soul.

"Every minute is precious. Hold Zenebu in your heart," she said. Her eyes were swollen, her face streaked with tears.

Pama awoke from her dream with a jolt and sprang to her feet, looking in every direction for her son. Thankfully, he was swimming nearby. She breathed yet another, sigh of relief, and scanned the area, all around, but saw nothing unusual. Still, she was tense and uneasy. The dream had left her with an even greater sense of urgency.

"Children, come! Let us return to the village." Pama said, glancing about her. Pama felt like an animal before a storm. By now, most of the children were drying off on the river bank, shaking water from their hair—except for Zenebu—who was still in the river. The laughter subsided as they gathered their things.

"Zenebu—get out of the water, NOW!" Pama screamed. She could hear the sound of fear in her own voice and she remembered the chief's desire to avoid creating a panic. In an effort to mask her feelings, Pama reached out and gave Zenebu a hug as he emerged from the water. She crouched low and held him tight, looking deep in his eyes. She could still see the images of her dream and protectively, she held him even tighter.

"Momma! You are squeezing me," Zenebu squealed and squirmed.

Pama released him. "Sorry, little man." She placed her hands firmly on his shoulders. "Stay close to me and hold my hand. Do you understand?"

Zenebu nodded. He knew his mother was serious.

They began walking with determination along the trail to their village. "Let us find your father," she directed in a firm whisper. "We must find him at once!"

Chapter Two

Once they returned to their village, Pama thought she saw movement in the bushes to her right. "YONDUA, YONDUA? IS THAT YOU?" she called out.

The words were barely out of her mouth when suddenly, hordes of bearded, pale-skinned men burst in to the village, surrounding the perimeter. The intruders were screaming in a high-pitched, foreign tongue, as they set fire to the huts. Pama's heart pounded in her chest like thunder as she scooped up her son and curled her body around him like a shield. Zenebu screamed and buried his face in his mother's chest. They heard the horrified cries of children and women all around them. Mothers clutched tightly to their babies, spinning around in circles, but there was nowhere to run. Pama and her people were gripped in horror as they watched the white men knock down their cook shacks and storage bins, destroying their home.

"AYAYAYAYAYAYAY!!" Pama cried, trying to see a way of escape through the smoke and dust, but there was not enough time. In a matter of minutes, the wicked men had corralled the women and children using ropes and whips. They chained them together with thick metal ankle cuffs. No one could run. They could barely breathe.

"Y O N D U A !" Pama screamed. Other women also called out for their men to save them. Having heard their distant screams, the Tulu men ran back to their village. Not knowing what to expect, some carried their farming tools along as weapons. Pama could not see through the haze but she could hear the white men yelling triumphantly as they clashed with their intended victims. It was clear, the Tulu had no chance against the rifles and clubs of the wicked captors.

"Mama, where is Papa? WHERE IS HE, MAMA?" Zenebu cried.

"I do not see him, baby. I am looking, but I do not see him," she answered as she leaned in toward her son. She longed to pick him up, hold him close to her heart. But tiny as he was, he had been shackled and chained, just as she was. Eventually, the noise and commotion grew less furious as the white ones masterfully went about their plundering.

Zenebu tried to stay near his mother's legs as the group was commanded to walk. Once they were away from the smoke and dust, Pama's eyes searched desperately for Yondua. She looked over the long line of people chained together, but she did not see him.

Gripped with sadness, Pama watched the white men as they gathered up just picked crops shoving them into their sacks. "Never again will we have this life, Zenebu." She whispered the dark declaration quietly so he could not hear. She looked into the frightened faces of her people. They were horrified beyond description.

Suddenly, a whip cracked next to her ear! Pama's group was being herded like cattle, forced to walk day and night for the next three days. She wondered if this living nightmare would ever end.

When Pama and her people finally reached the slave camp, they were weak and battered. She somehow found the strength to lift Zenebu up so he could catch a glimpse of his father ahead in the distance. Miraculously, Yondua and Pama had spotted each other earlier that morning. She tried to keep him within her vision at all times. Yondua looked gaunt and sickly and Pama was worried about him. "Your father is close, little one, do you see him? Over there, by the big tree," she said trying to sound reassuring. "Do you see him?"

"Yes, Mama. I do see him, but he does not see me. "P a p a," he started to yell out, but Pama reached her hand up and put it over his mouth to silence him.

"Ssshhhh," she quietly hissed with her index finger in front of her mouth. The star shaped birthmark caught her son's eye more so than the silent directive. He had always been mesmerized by the artwork of the gods on his mother's hand. "Be quiet, Zenebu. We are in danger and we do not want to draw attention to ourselves. Do you understand?" He looked into his mother's eyes and started to cry. "It is all right to be scared, but you must be scared, quietly." She squeezed his hand and he nodded, attempting a smile. "You are my brave boy, and we will join your Papa later, but you must be quiet for now.

After three days of endless walking, they had arrived in a place called Sierra Leone. Through swollen eyes, Pama saw the white man's village: a large, looming fortress perched high above the ocean and built into a cliff along the shoreline. The smell of human waste mixed with sweat stung her eyes even before they were forced inside the holding area. She lunged forward after being shoved down a long corridor and into a large stall with little ventilation. The Africans had raw, open flesh wounds from the iron bands rubbing against their skin. Pama looked in the middle of the room and saw the open hole in the floor, swarming with flies. *It must be the toilet,* she thought, gagging in utter disgust. Focusing her eyes to the dimly lit room, she saw Yondua, propped against the back wall. Feeling relieved by the mere sight of him, she exhaled. Sadly, he looked even frailer.

"YONDUA!" she cried impulsively. He looked up and saw his family across the dingy room, and motioned to them. "PAPA!" Zenebu tried to run across the room to his father, but could not for the shackles, which bound his feet.

Yondua moaned, reaching his arms across the room toward his son.

Pama inched her way through the crowd to Yondua. When she hugged her husband, she felt how weak he had become. "I am afraid for us, my love. I am especially afraid for you, my Yondua," she whispered feeling his arms and ribs. "You are quite ill." She looked into his eyes and felt his forehead. It burned like hot flames. "We need food and I need my herbs to make you well." She felt the back of his neck and knew he had a life-threatening fever. "Zenebu and I need you, my love. Do not let go of your life. Please, not yet. I cannot bear it if you leave me." Tears flooded her eyes and she gulped back sobs. He put his head in her lap and slipped from consciousness while little Zenebu curled up in his arms.

For the moment, she had her family, and Pama felt hope. "What is going to happen to us?" she wondered. "Mama, help us. Be our rescue. We need help from the spirit world. Please, help us," she prayed quietly to her mother's spirit as they fell into a restless sleep.

In the middle of the night, Yondua awoke to the sounds of riotous laughter. It sounded as though drunken men were stumbling down the hall. Just as he sat up, he saw three of them directly at their gate. One was fumbling with the key in the lock, while the other two were slapping each other about in dark-spirited glee.

"What do they want?" Pama whispered. Terrified, she clung tightly to her husband.

"Sshhh," he put his arm around his wife like a shield. Then, the gate to their stall opened. One of the men pulled a young female up from the group. Shaking his head, he threw the woman back into the throng. The drunkard continued combing through the remaining choices.

Yondua knew what they were doing and he moved his family back in the shadows, draping himself to cover them. He prayed the drunken men would find themselves other sex partners before they spotted his Pama. He exhaled his resignation when they finally disappeared with three shrieking women and did not return. He stroked Pama's sweaty brow, curled into her warmth, and slipped into a fevered sleep.

A glimpse of gratitude came with the morning light as Pama and her people were being assembled. Thankfully, they were to spend only one night in that wretched compound.

Not realizing the slave ship they were about to board was worse than the on-land stalls; Pama felt a brief sense of relief as they were whisked into the sunshine and fresh air. But fear soon prevailed as they were whipped with a cat-of-nine-tails, forced to walk up the gangplank and down into the bowels of the wretched slave vessel, *Camrita.*

Chapter Three

With an ailing husband and a trembling child, Pama was terrified as she huddled in a dark corner of the stifling hold of the ship. The air was thick with sweat, laced with fear, and it reeked with the stench of human waste. She looked into the frightened eyes of her fellow villagers as the full reality of their situation began filling her with terror. Pama shifted her weight against the creaking floorboards and her bloodied hands shook beyond her control as she drew Zenebu closer. Many children cried steadily, clinging to their mothers, but Zenebu remained silent, his large, terrified eyes breaking Pama's heart. Many men, and most of the women moaned in agony. They were all scared, cut and bruised and close to starvation.

At times, the ship rocked violently on the waves from passing storms. Whenever possible, Pama looked toward the daylight filtering through two small portholes. Sometimes a wave of salt water and a gust of cold Atlantic air would pour through the openings, leaving the villagers soaked. She longed to be on dry African soil again, breathing the fresh country air and feeling the sun beating warmth on her strong back. But today, as never before, she knew their lives would never be the same. Pama cried quietly to herself, wondering if she should be praying for a quick death. Was that not against the law of the gods?

Like a bolt of lightening, Zenebu jerked back into her arms. A large, hairy rodent with shining red eyes moved across the floor, skidding through a flow of vomit that had just spewed forth from several sick captives.

"What was that?" Zenebu asked, his voice full of fear.

"It was just a rat, my sweet boy. We have seen them down by the river, do you not remember?" Pama tickled her son in the hope of somehow lightening his mood.

"Yes, I guess so, but they were never *that* big!" He remained glued to her chest. "Tell me a story about Nana, Mama. Tell me she is with us on this boat." Pama's heart hurt as she listened to the tone of his small, unsteady voice.

"Of course, Nana is with us my little man. She is always with us." She kissed his head and cuddled him closer. "She wanted to go on many adventures, so I am sure she would not have missed this trip for anything."

"Why did she want to go to other places?" Zenebu asked. He needed to hear his mother talk about their family. "How did she know about them?"

"Because, she and my papa used to look at that beautiful picture book we have back in our hut, and they used to pretend they were going to travel to the places in the pictures."

"Where is your papa, Mama? How come we do not know him?" Zenebu asked her for the hundredth time. "Is he going to be where we are going?"

"I do not know where he is, my love. I never knew him. As I have told you before, his parents forbade him to be with your Nana because she was a young, black wash woman working in their house and my papa was from a wealthy, white family. They sent him away to be schooled in the country of *France,* and they threw your Nana out into the street before I was born." Pama sat up straight and held her head high, feeling her mother's indignation as her own. She felt tears forming in the corners of her bloodshot eyes and took a deep breath before continuing with her story. "But Nana did not care what color my papa was, because she loved him." Pama paused and Zenebu shifted in her arms. "My papa knew how to read. That is why he gave Nana that book—so she could learn to read it. But she never got the chance before she died. Someday, I want to learn to read and then I will teach you."

"What does that mean, *to read*?" Zenebu asked, his voice now heavy with exhaustion. "Whatever it means, I wish we could go home and read our big book right now." He stretched and yawned before cuddling closer to his mother.

"I wish we could, too, my little man. But, we have looked at that book so many times now, we can simply use our imaginations to remember all the beautiful pictures. We can even make up more stories." She tried to sound enthusiastic while answering his question. "*Reading* is when you know what the little black symbols on the pages mean and you follow what the story is about without having to make it up. When I was your age, my momma got that book out every night and we would pretend to go to those places in the pictures. But now, Nana is in the spirit world and my father is somewhere I will never know and we are here, going on this boat adventure together." Pama squeezed her son, hoping to help him feel safe.

"Why did Nana have to go to the spirit world, Mama?" Zenebu asked as he rubbed his eyes.

"Because, her body got too sick to carry her anymore. We do not need our bodies in the spirit world. Is that not wonderful? We can live forever there!" Pama answered, choking back tears. She rubbed his little arms to keep him warm. "Go to sleep now, my brave Zenebu. Dream about the cool, refreshing swim in the river we enjoyed the other day with your friends. I will join you there, my precious one." Pama fixed her gaze on her beautiful son and stroked his hair with her fingers until he fell asleep.

Each day, the Africans awoke to the sound of horrific waves crashing on the hull of their floating jail. Pama, Yondua, and Zenebu huddled together, finding small comfort from the mere touch of one another. The freedom of Africa felt like a lifetime away and now they were headed for enslavement in an unknown world. Pama could see the terror in her people's eyes. She too, was afraid but was determined not to show it. She began beating on the floorboards in a familiar rhythm, singing with her drumming and before long, the other slaves joined in. They needed something to bind them together and give them courage. Their native songs and drumbeat became that comfort, at least for the moment.

"STOP THAT RACKET DOWN THERE, for Christ's sake," their captors threatened from the deck. "Knock it off—NOW! Or we will come down there and KNOCK your heads off!" Pama closed her eyes. She took her time slowing down her lead before stopping the drumbeat altogether. She could only hope the sound would continue to resonate in their souls.

There was no doubt in Pama's mind that Yondua had malaria. She had seen people die from it over the years and she was terrified Yondua might do the same. His body shook with fever throughout each day and he became even more weak and frail. When he awoke each morning, Pama and Zenebu gave thanks to the gods that he had not been taken from this life during the night.

The conditions on the ship became more disgusting with each passing day and the slim rations they were given were a dismal, bland tasting mash lacking any essential nourishment. The white men did not share the harvested vegetables with the slaves. Instead, once a day, they were given a handful of potatoes and beans which had the consistency and taste of glue. When it was passed around, Pama scooped the mess with her hands and fed Zenebu, Yondua and herself anyway she could. The slave traders seldom calculated correctly the amount of rations needed on these journeys and there was not enough food to go around. Many Africans starved to death and daily, the malnourished, sickly black bodies, alive or dead, were pitched over the sides of the ship into the bottomless sea.

Despite her attempts to be strong, despair festered deep inside Pama's psyche as they sailed across an endless field of water to lives they did not choose.

Chapter Four

As they continued across the Atlantic, Pama watched her husband slip in and out of consciousness. *Clever of him to sleep through this unpleasant journey,* Pama thought, smiling to herself. Any relief he could get from this sordid experience pleased her. As she combed back Yondua's greasy hair from his sweaty brow, she felt her son fidget.

"Will Papa ever wake up, Mama?" Zenebu asked,

"I believe he will, son. He just needs to rest now." Oh, how she hoped it was the truth.

"Tell me about Papa, Mama. Tell me about how he got you for his wife," Zenebu coaxed. He seemed comforted by the sound of his mother's voice and the stories she told over their many hours at sea.

"All right. I will tell you about your Papa." Zenebu smiled and settled into his mother's embrace.

"Your Papa was the oldest of three children. He had two sisters who traveled to the spirit world before you were born. Your grandparents were never what you could call, *friendly*." Pama made a stern face and Zenebu laughed. "Your Papa grew to be the one the chief trusted most, because he is the wisest man in our village." Zenebu sat up and looked straight at his mother with his big brown eyes. He shook his head in delight. "Papa was the one who would suggest better ways to grow our crops. One time, when we were moving our camp to a new site, Papa knew just how to position our huts so that we could all enjoy the best breezes." Pama paused and reflected on that moment in time. "Your father is well respected, Zenebu. You should always be proud of him."

Zenebu looked at his father and then up at her and nodded again. Pama took her son into her arms and snuggled him close before she continued with her story.

"When I was nine years old, it was arranged by our families that we would marry when I turned fifteen. Your Papa is ten years older than me but he always told me he was content to wait for me to become his wife." Pama reached down and stroked her husband's sweaty forehead. "He told me he admired my energy and my beauty," she said lovingly. "I used to drive him crazy with all my wild ideas." Pama added with a gleam in her eye and Zenebu smiled.

"What sort of ideas, Mama?"

"Well, one day, I said to him, "Yondua, when we go to Bora Bora and I become Queen, that will make you King. Would you like to be a king?"

"Oh," your father said, "I do not think I would want such a difficult job as being a king, and I do not want to go to Bora Bora, either." Pama chuckled at the nostalgic memory.

With all sincerity, Zenebu asked, "Where is Bora Bora?" He did not comprehend what was so amusing.

"It is one of the places in our picture book, back in our hut," she said. "Your Papa loved our daydreams. In our discussions, we went everywhere together, exploring far beyond our village. He used to love to listen to me babble about places I had learned about and how anxious I was to go to as many of them as I could," she said.

"Did not my Papa want to go places, too?" Zenebu asked with wide-eyed innocence.

"No, baby. He did not, not really. I was always the curious one in the family—until you came along, that is," she tousled Zenebu's hair and hugged him tightly. Just then, Pama thought back to the dream she had experienced by the river. It struck her to cherish the present moment; tender times might well be fewer in the days to come. She fought back tears and tried to keep her mood optimistic for the sake of her innocent little boy.

"One time, I told your Papa we should make a boat from an old, carved-out tree trunk. Do you think we could do that, Zenebu?" She looked him in the eye to see if he was still paying attention.

"Yes, Mama, we should do it as soon as we get off this ship, so we can escape," he answered, sincerely.

"Yes! We could weave a sail from the reeds..." For a brief moment, Pama got lost in the fantasy, "... and when we are ready, we will set sail for distant shores! Papa will be the captain and you and I will be the crew. We will eat fresh fish every day and travel the coastline so we can go ashore often to pick vegetables." Pama could see that her son was enthralled. "And when we come upon new villages, the people will welcome us with open arms. They will be amazed we were so brave to have traveled so far and we will bask in the glory, as we tell them of our adventures."

Yondua had awakened just long enough to hear the last bit of her story. He shook his head and smiled at her optimism and energy in the midst of their horrible situation. "I do not know how to make a boat from an old tree, wife. How is it that you have this elaborate idea, my little sojourner?" He reached up to touch his wife's cheek. It was soft and smooth and oh, so warm... so lovely.

Pama smiled down at him and took his hand into hers and kissed it. "I saw a half rotted-out log floating on the river one day and I imagined it carved out and fashioned into a boat. We could do it! I know we could," she replied excitedly. "Together we can do anything because the power of three is stronger than one." She paused and saw that they both had their eyes closed. They nodded their heads in agreement. "Thank you for always dreaming with me," she said, reaching out to embrace her little family. "You two are my best friends—the only ones I trust with my whims. You listen to me without telling me I am crazy," she leaned down and added in a whisper, "like some of the women in our village used to."

"You scare them, my love," Yondua said emphatically. "Most humans are like the wild animals. They feel comfortable and safe being part of the herd and they have no desire to discover new lands and people. You, on the other hand, think of little else." Yondua curled into Pama's arms and they gazed up into the starry mid-Atlantic sky through the round porthole.

"Now, all I want to do is go home," she said with sad resignation. They were quiet for a few minutes. "Do I frighten you, Yondua? I would hate it if I scared you away from me." She paused before continuing. "I need you both. You are my true companions," she said with conviction, holding her family close. "Our souls are united on a deep level. I have always known this."

"Of course you do not scare me, my *strong one*. You intrigue me, when you are not exhausting me," Yondua teased. She felt encouraged by his steady, even breathing. "I also know that you and I are old souls. I have known this since you were very young."

Pama nodded slowly. He stayed tucked into her body as he drifted off to sleep. Zenebu could not follow what they were saying but he was comforted by the sounds of his parents' voices. Before long, he too, drifted off to dream and in his mind, Zenebu was back, splashing about in his swimming hole.

Pama, on the other hand, could not sleep. She was wide-awake with fear and amazement that their lives had been so altered in such a short amount of time. In the dim lantern light, she carefully observed the design of the ship. She thought the *Camrita* was an ugly vessel compared to the beautiful boats in their picture book. Those boats had carvings and fancy woodwork and plush, cushioned seats. This *Camrita* was being used for an ugly business. Shackles and chains hung from the ceiling, the sides of the hulls and they were mounted on the floorboards. Pama wondered how many times this boat had made this type of a trip. How many times had it been loaded with this kind of merchandise? Pama had no concept of the value of this living cargo, nor did she have any idea that those who survived the horrid journey were about to be sold at one of the biggest slave auctions in the Caribbean.

Chapter Five

At long last, the gruesome passage was over. *Camrita* dropped anchor in a picturesque harbor in the Caribbean Sea. Despite her pain and fear, the beauty of the island captivated Pama as she was brought on deck. With all the shoving and dragging, Pama lost sight of Yondua. After being rowed ashore, the Africans were contained in small pens, similar to ones used for livestock. Zenebu clung to his mother's side as they scanned the shoreline, hoping to see Yondua. Pama's legs were wobbly after being cramped up on the boat for so long and she was relieved to be walking on dry ground again. She and her group were eventually herded like cattle through a long walkway into a large fenced-in area with walls much too high to scale.

Without warning, a huge, bearded sailor came up from behind Pama and grabbed her, pinning her arms to her sides. She whirled herself around and kicked him hard in the groin. He howled in pain and temporarily let go of her. She curled herself over her son and ran to the other side of the holding pen. The terrified youngster clutched her frail neck and wrapped himself tightly to her waist.

The sailor hit Pama directly in the face with his scaly fist and began prying Zenebu from her strong, loving arms. She clung desperately to her son as her eye began to swell shut. Blood streamed from both her nostrils and her vision blurred. "M A M A!" Zenebu cried and clutched to her even tighter.

"PLEASE,—NOT MY BAAAAAAABBBY! NOT MY PRECIOUS BOY. . ." she begged in her native Tulu tongue, shaking her head back and forth. The French words she had learned from her mother came flooding back to her now and she pleaded: "S'il vous plait—me permettre de garde mon be´be!'" She kicked him again and ran back and forth to the corners of the corral with her terrified child dangling like a rag doll from her arms. In spite of her pleading, the sailor cornered her and ripped Zenebu from her grasp. He shoved Pama to the ground and stood above her with his hands on his hips. Then, he kicked Pama several times, and she curled up in a ball to protect her vitals. Beaten to a pulp, she still tried to get up, reaching for her son, but the evil man kicked her again. Before spitting on Pama, the sailor let out a spiteful laugh. He then grabbed the now hysterical Zenebu, and tossed him over his shoulder like a bag of feed.

Her son screamed loudly: "MAMA, MAMA, PAPA, MAMA, NO! NO! P a a a p a a a !" With outstretched arms, he was hauled away, where his parents would never see him again.

Pama crawled over and clung to the fence with bloody fingers. "Z Z Z E E N N E E B U U U," she screamed at the top of her voice. An agonizing wail emerged from the pit of her soul. "A y A y A y. O H ! SPIRITS OF RESCUE—COME TO ALL OF US! MAMA, COME TO ME! PLEASE HELP ME! Ay Ay Ay. O h h Ya Ya Ya. . . Z e e e e n e e e b u u u u. . . Ay Ay Ay—my b a a a b y. Y o n d u u a a a a. . .help us my love! WE NEED YOU!!! Z e e e n e b u . . . where are you? Where is my family? Please, come for me. PLEEEESE I BEG YOU! Don't leave me." Pama gulped air into her lungs between sobs. She lay on the ground, shaking her head in the dirt. "I cannot do this alone. I am not this strong. . . I AM NOT STRONG ENOUGH FOR *THIS*! . . . MAMA, HELP ME!" She got up and looked around like a mad woman, wide eyed and confused.

On bruised and bloodied legs, Pama paced around in circles, screaming and crying in anguish until a man came into the corral and whipped her quiet with a leather strap. Her eyes were opened wide with shock and deep sorrow; she huddled in the corner of the pen, whimpering softly. Her arms clutched her long, bruised legs to her chest and she rocked back and forth in a grief-stricken daze. Taking pity on her, one of the women took a gourd and filled it with water and washed Pama's wounds. They spoke volumes with their tear-filled eyes, but said no words between them. The woman gave her a gentle hug once she was finished and stayed close in case she needed her again.

Pama struggled to remain conscious as strange thoughts entered her mind. She was to learn a lesson of some sort now—a lesson necessary for her spirit to go on. She remembered thinking to herself, *how can anything persist in the midst of intolerable agony?* Commotion and noise were all around them, but Pama barely heard it. She stared with vacant, bloodshot eyes in the direction where her son had been taken, hoping he might return. Tears flooded down her face as she flashed on the memory that warned her to hold him close to her heart—that every moment was precious. *"I held him close"* she whimpered to herself, pounding her fist over her heart. "Please God, I held him *so* close. Bring my baby back to me, pleeezzzee. I am begging you—spirits, guides, Mamma! Come to my aid. PLEASE!" Worn out with grief, Pama collapsed in a heap, but she could not sleep.

That night, men brought fruit and rice to the women in her pen but Pama would neither eat nor speak to anyone. She kept to herself, anxiously looking about, listening for her family. As each endless day passed, she struggled to have hope.

Two weeks had gone by and several of the more robust women in the pens were well past irritation with one another. They had been confined to their crowded corrals, exposed to the blazing Caribbean sun and covered with dust and sweat. Seething with rage and fear, the more aggressive ones began acting out. Pama's sadness had fermented and she too, was impatient with their unbearable situation.

"Do not spill that fresh water," a trader said to his subordinate the morning of the auction. Indeed, fresh water was hard to come by on such a dry island. Three men were lugging soapy buckets with sea sponges afloat. There were only a few sack-type garments to go around. Many women were left naked. "Get those women clean so we get a higher price. And be sure to wash their hair—the lice are rampant!" he said to his men.

"If we are to be sold, then get on with it! We are not livestock!" Pama yelled in French. She could not stay quiet watching her African sisters being sexually molested by the men washing them.

One of them attempted to slap Pama across the face, but his colleague grabbed his arm midair. "Do not mar that pretty face anymore right before she goes on the block, you idiot! She is a beaut, that one. Feisty too! Should bring a pretty penny. Now, clean her up and NO lingering beyond the washing!"

As it had done countless times before, *Camrita* sailed across the world to the Caribbean ocean, arriving in the harbor of Top Haus, which was on the isle of St. Thomas. There, the harbor was the deepest in all the West Indies. It was a welcome hub for trade of all sorts, including sugar, molasses, slaves and rum.

Two additional ships had arrived the same week *Camrita* dropped her anchor. They too, contained slaves who were captured from villages along the western coast of Africa. The traffickers attempted to separate them from their own tribes, but with so many arrivals to deal with at once, some remained together.

Slave buying for plantations near and far took place at these auctions. The main activity took place at Market Square, a center of West Indian commerce. Occasionally, a second location would be assembled along the southern shore to accommodate overflow.

Pama was put on the block at the first auction of the week at the market square. Searching for familiar faces, she pretended not to notice the few she spotted, hoping that the same owner might purchase them all. She had not seen Yondua once since their arrival. As for her son, Zenebu, she constantly scanned the crowds and listened every day for the sound of his darling, little voice. All Pama could do was pray that their spirit guides would keep both her men safe and that someday, they would be reunited—if not in this life—surely in the next.

Chapter Six

Ramone Rodriguez, a young, blazingly handsome plantation owner, leaned his tall, slender body confidently against a stone wall at the square and surveyed his choices. He had plans to buy several slaves that day and wanted to get a good look at the inventory before the bidding began. His eyes scanned the dark live mass, studying the Africans huddled in groups against the back wall to the left of the auction block. He felt satisfied there were many healthy selections to choose from, and he started to walk away. It was then he noticed a tall, light-skinned woman standing alone in the far corner. Her skimpy shift was dirty and disheveled, yet she wore it well. The spark of determination gleamed in her eyes and she seemed daring and strong. Even in dreary clothing, bare feet and matted hair, she was far more striking and naturally beautiful than any of the other women on the block.

Ramone could not take his eyes off her. Eventually he caught her attention.

She stared back at him, holding his eyes with her own.

Determined to intimidate her with his steady gaze, Ramone shifted his feet and stood taller. His stylish clothes, made from the finest cotton and silk, draped his lean body with pride and elegance. He insisted this slave know that she had her place, and he had his. Such a strange feeling overcame him. His desire was beyond sexual. Never had he felt such unnerving rapture.

Still, she returned his stare intensely, with confidence.

Ramone knew he had to have her, and fidgeted nervously until she came up on the block. Before the auctioneer had the chance to ask for the first bid, his desire overcame his tongue and he shouted, "I will start the bidding with one hundred kroner."

After a few gasps and moans, the crowd grew intent. Ordinarily, bidding began at a much lower amount for a slave woman.

"I have an opening bid of one hundred kroner," the auctioneer bellowed. "Do I hear one hundred twenty-five?"

"One hundred fifty kroner," yelled Hans Kristoff, the elderly, wealthy owner of *La Grande Princesse* plantation on St. Croix.

Ramone had seen the old man before at the auction block. *A hard man to beat with all his money,* he thought. Ramone could also see that the man was visibly taken with the slave woman's looks, but Ramone was not going to let him have her.

Before he could make a bid, the old man bellowed again. "One hundred seventy-five," he blurted, bidding against himself.

The crowd snickered, but the auctioneer was determined to keep the momentum going.

"Two hundred," Ramone yelled.

"Two hundred fifty." The Crucian man stared at the slave woman, never taking his eyes off her save for a quick glance to his opponent.

Ramone could almost feel the sordid thoughts going through the old man's head. "Three hundred fifty," interjected Ramone, who now paced back and forth with determination. *Why did this man have to show up here today, of all days?* he thought. *She is not his, she is MINE,* he silently chanted to himself between bids.

"Four hundred," stated the Crucian, glaring at Ramone with the hint of a threat.

"Eight hundred kroner—final bid!" proclaimed Ramone. He had had enough of this relay.

The Cruician's shoulders dropped and he stepped back. No doubt, he was angry, but he held himself in check. Ramone overheard him talking to his foreman, shaking his head dismissively. "I wanted that strong woman, but I have my limits and eight hundred is well beyond reason. We have other purchases to make. Spending that much on one slave is ridiculous."

"We have eight hundred as a final, bid," the auctioneer shouted. "Eight hundred, going once... twice... gone to Senior Ramone Rodriquez from *Palmas Ondeando* in Martinique."

Ramone had purchased her for eight times the money a slave woman usually sold for. He knew that others were laughing behind his back but something beyond reason was driving him.

"Ramone, you should bid with your head and not your cojones," someone yelled from the crowd. "It is always more expensive when we make decisions with our lower extremities."

The men grabbed their genitals for emphasis.

"I *am* thinking with my head, gentlemen," Ramone replied haughtily. "This one is worth more than that price, if she keeps my foreman well satisfied. We all know how imperative it is to have happy overseers, do we not? As for me, I have my own Spanish tart to keep my fires lit." Before he made his way out of the auction hall, Ramone glared at his expensive new slave woman.

Just as intently, she stared back at him.

Walking to the door, Ramone stopped, gave her a serious look and mouthed in Spanish, "you had better be worth it." He sensed that she did not understand his language, but surely she could pick up his attitude and voice as a stern warning.

Still, she did not seem afraid of him. Something rare and raw and reckless was afoot. Perhaps for the first time in his life, Ramone felt somehow out of his element. Was he being challenged by an insignificant slave? How ridiculous!

Pama continued to stare back at him. Despite the grisly circumstances, she could not help but think he was quite handsome with his wavy yellow hair like spun gold blowing in the breeze.

Even from across the marketplace, Pama could see that his eyes were as blue as the Caribbean Sea.

I wonder if my father looked like that? She wondered. Her mother told her he had yellow hair. The plantation owner's full lips formed a smirk, and Pama could see his perfect, white teeth when he spoke. As she watched his body language, Pama sensed the man was quite impressed with himself. Ramone shifted from one leg to the other with an air of arrogance, the likes of which Pama had never before witnessed in a man. Was he trying to intimidate her with his steady gaze? He would soon learn that Pama was not someone who backed down easily, even when confronted by someone who had the ability to bring her harm.

Ramone bought a total of fifty-two slaves at the Top Haus auction that day—six of them were from the same village. The confusion from three different boats arriving together worked in the slaves' favor and thankfully, a few friends and relatives from the Tulu village were grouped together.

Summarily, the Africans were loaded on Ramone's ship, which was named *Mariah.* Smaller than the *Camrita,* it was a much more handsome vessel. Ramone looked his new slaves over and could plainly see most were weak from their trip across the Atlantic.

"I want these people in the fresh air during the day," he commanded his crew. "Shackle their legs and have them stretch their upper bodies. I want them healthy and ready for work when we arrive home."

"Yes, sir. Come on, you heard your master. Move those arms around. Come on; stretch out for Christ's sake! Take advantage of the fresh air, you idiots," the deck hand ordered the Africans who could not understand a word of his Spanish.

"YOU, Eduardo! Go and get some food—whatever you can find. These slaves need nourishment. "Go on! Get as much fruit as you can carry." Ramone ordered.

"Yes sir. I will fill up the cart with mangos. They are plentiful right now." Eduardo responded as he started down the road. Under his breath he grumbled, "Get your own damn fruit, you Jack-ass!"

With so much work to do on his plantation, Ramone planned on riding these slaves long and hard. *Best to fortify them on the sail home, rather than chaining them down below,* he thought to himself. Ramone could tell the Africans were relieved to be breathing in the sweet smells of the Caribbean. Within just a few hours, many of them looked markedly better than when they had been purchased.

Once they were under way, Pama pleaded with one of the sailors, asking if he knew the whereabouts of her family. The man did not understand Pama's African language and was shocked at her boldness. He backhanded her across the face, knocking her to her knees.

"PUTA! Shut up and get down below. How dare you be so familiar with me," he screamed in Spanish, leaving Pama in a shackled heap.

The *Mariah* sailed around to the next bay on the southeast side of St. Thomas. Ramone found his foreman, Enrique, who had attended the other auction, where he had purchased eighteen additional slaves on his behalf.

"Well done, my man. Chain these slaves down for the night and let us go to the pubs to celebrate. I feel a 'rum squall' coming on and I saw plenty of whores downtown!" Ramone patted Enrique on the back and they both broke into riotous laughter.

Once they were chained down for the night, Pama's eyes adjusted to the dim light. She looked around and tried to focus on the faces of the other captives. Her heart skipped a beat! At last! In a dark corner, she had spied Yondua leaning against the side of the hull. Obviously, he had been able to look acceptable enough at the auction so as to avoid being left to die with the sick. Pama stared at him with tears of disbelief. She did not dare speak his name for fear the overseers might hear her. It must not be know they were even acquainted. Instead, she willed him to look at her as she sent energy in his direction.

Eventually, Yondua saw her. He sat up, reaching his shackled hands out to his wife. He wanted very much to touch her and put his head in her lap so she could stroke his fevered brow. "Where is our boy?" he cried, silently mouthing the words. Pama responded with grief, shaking her head side to side. Yondua struggled to sit up. His hands were clasped around his frail legs, which were pulled to his upper body in a fetal position. Not having the strength to remain upright, he leaned against the wall and stared at his beautiful wife. He thought she had been lost to him forever and now, here she was. Shaking his head back and forth, he quietly cried his son's name like a mantra, over and over and over until finally slipping into the dark comfort of unconsciousness.

Chapter Seven

Exactly five years earlier, Ramone Rodriquez, second son of a wealthy merchant, was in Paris visiting his favorite brothel. At that time, the focus of his life was on proving his independence from his parents and older brother.

Sitting at the gambling table, Ramone carefully eyed his last opponent, a fat, sweaty Frenchman named Jean Baptiste. Lifting a stack of poker chips, Ramone casually leaned back in his chair, never once losing eye contact with the unfortunate Frenchman. "I raise you," he said with absolute confidence.

Baptiste wiped his forehead with his hairy forearm and studied his cards. His beady eyes shifted back and forth from the cards to the huge stack of poker chips in the middle of the table. It looked as though Baptiste had finally dug himself a very, deep, debt-filled hole.

Ramone smiled inwardly. This game would have normally been out of his league, but the poker gods were smiling on him this night. He was on a winning streak and had remained in the game into the early morning hours.

Baptiste nervously reached into his pocket and withdrew a piece of yellowed parchment. His hands shook as he unfolded it and reluctantly laid it on the table. Apparently, it was some kind of deed.

"What is this paper?" Ramone glanced at it, noticing only that it was written in French. He got up and began to pace back and forth behind Baptiste. "What are you trying to give me, here?" Baptiste cowered in his seat as Ramone leaned down and grabbed him by the front of his suit. "Do not tell me you are out of money, old man."

"I am out of funds, per se, but I have this deed to my plantation in Martinique which I am offering you instead. It produced several tons of sugar for many years and was quite a prosperous place. Its potential is worth far more than the amount I owe you." Baptiste looked up at Ramone, who was inwardly intrigued but showed nothing but contempt. He continued. "In the long run, you will make out much better than if I were to give you mere cash," Baptiste reasoned.

"If it is such a valuable plantation then why are you not there working this place yourself?" Ramone asked him. "People do not normally abandon property if it is doing all that well."

"Well," Baptiste continued nervously. "My wife became quite ill and we had to return to France to get her proper medical attention. After our return, she lived only a year. Her funeral should have been mine as well. I no longer had the strength to work the plantation. It was my wife who truly loved it there. I knew I could not manage it without her. However, it is an ideal endeavor for someone young and adventurous, like yourself."

Ramone shook his head in feigned disgust, grabbed the deed and shoved it into his pocket. "You had better pray this farm of yours is what you claim it to be," he shouted, pointing his index finger squarely in Baptiste's face. "I mean it, old man! I will come back and find you if it is not! You can bet on THAT." Ramone stormed out of the brothel feeling somewhat foolish for agreeing to take an old broken down, forgotten plantation at the other end of the earth.

The next day, Ramone packed his bags and returned to Spain. As usual, once he was back home, he was bored within a week. Clearly, he needed something stimulating, entertaining, and far away from his family.

"When are you going to settle down and take a wife, Ramone?" his mother nagged. "You need to find something substantial that interests you, son. Your father and I simply cannot continue to cover for your reckless life, you know?"

"Well, actually mother, I do have something worthwhile I am about to do if you must know. I have recently acquired a plantation in the West Indies. It is on the French island of Martinique. I am going to go there soon and run the place. I am not completely useless, you know."

"Of course you are not useless, Ramone. I am merely concerned for your welfare. I do not even want to know how you acquired such a piece of land, but I am sure you could do quite well there." His mother could not help but feel relieved Ramone would be away from Madrid for a while. She only hoped her youngest son would grow up and learn to deal with responsibility. Perhaps this French plantation would be the perfect answer.

The next day, Ramone began planning his first voyage to his new farm. He saw this as a chance to add a new dimension to his life, perhaps even make his parents proud. Ramone also hoped to show his fortunate, older brother what success was really about—how to earn wealth, rather than sit back and inherit it. These were foreign concepts to someone as spoiled as Ramone, but he was willing to explore the possibilities.

Chapter Eight

After three weeks of rough, stormy sailing, Ramone finally arrived on the lush green island of Martinique, grateful to be on dry, solid ground again. With deed in hand, he was eager to see his winnings. As they jostled about in a make-shift carriage, Ramone and his entourage finally turned down a long, curved driveway. Instantly, Ramone was mesmerized by the overgrown pink bougainvillea, intertwined with Bird of Paradise, along a corridor of tall, stately royal palm trees. Sweet, honey-like scents filled the gentle breezes. Ramone had never seen such beautiful flowers, or palm trees as grand. Even in it's over grown state, the gardens around the house were magnificent. "Enrique will know how to put these grounds back in order. How lovely it will all look once it is attended to!" he declared to himself.

As he rode further down the driveway, the plantation's great house came into view. To Ramone's dismay, he realized Jean Baptiste had embellished upon the description of the house. It might have been grand in its day, but through years of neglect, it had gone to ruin. While walking through the lower rooms, Ramone admired the mahogany woodwork. He appreciated the smooth sensation of the carved teak banister under his hand as he walked upstairs. Apparently, many hands had gone into making the wood flawless, and for a brief moment, he wondered about

Jean Baptiste's life. Ramone remembered the look of despair on Baptiste's sad face as he relinquished the deed on that fateful night in Paris.

While rambling around inside his worn-down dwelling, Ramone noticed much of the spacious square footage seemed to honor outdoor living. Planter's chairs, made of carved teak, with extended arms were positioned by the door. There, boots could be removed before the hard-working owner walked inside. Along the verandah, rattan rockers and tables with simple wicker chairs were cleverly arranged. The house had an airy, informal style, strangely appealing to Ramone, who was the product of a more formal household.

He was glad he had thought to bring along his carpenter, Enrique, when he saw the broken window frames, cabinet doors, and numerous pieces of furniture, all in need of repair. Walking along the verandah, he couldn't help but admire the trellis, a thick mass of peach, white and crimson colored bougainvillea. "I wonder if this maze is hearty enough to ward off the rain," he said out loud. As if on cue, a light rain passed over and Ramone was pleased that the mature, interwoven plants did indeed keep the drops from coming through. "Amazing," he murmured.

He took his time examining his new home, paying attention to every detail. Ramone had never before owned property and it gave him a sense of pride to be the master of such a place. In his opinion, the dwelling was a perfect size: neither too large, nor too small. The roof was a gently sloping design and open beamed on the inside exposing deep, red mahogany. A tree had fallen on the corner over the front entry and Ramone could see daylight through the ceiling in the foyer. He was pleased with the impressive, sweeping staircase. The bottom stairs fanned out wider than the top, like welcoming arms, and the railings were the same carved teak as the inside banister although not nearly as smooth to the touch. The sun had bleached them out, making them brittle. *Enrique will need to fix this right away,* he decided to himself.

Inside the house, the rooms were laid out in an open design with louvered windows on either side of the numerous pairs of French doors, which opened to the outside.

The living room was lower than the rest of the first floor, with four, wide plank mahogany stairs leading down into it on two sides. Ramone looked for a fireplace, and then realized none was needed on this balmy, tropical island. The built-in cabinetry in the dining room reminded Ramone of the woodwork at the brothel in Paris where he had won his estate. It had panes of beveled glass and gingerbread trimming along the top where it met the ceiling.

Upstairs, Ramone discovered five bedrooms. "Well, there is plenty of room for my parents, should they ever decide to grace me with their presence," he mumbled to himself. He was quite sure they would never make the arduous journey, and that initial thought actually gave him a feeling of relief. *Finally, I can be myself without them breathing down my neck.*

The bedrooms were accessible by entering a common balcony, which ran the full length of the house. The railing around the balcony was the same decorative wrought iron, which graced the down-stairs. It was horribly rusted, but Ramone felt Enrique would know how to refurbish it.

Ramone was used to marble and tile but he was intrigued by the floors in his new house, which were fashioned from wide planks of red mahogany. The windows were arched and had chipped, light blue shutters that closed and latched from the inside. Ramone wondered if they were designed to protect against the severe tropical storms he had heard about. *Certainly, it cannot be to protect against thieves way out here,* he thought. Indeed his plantation was far away from the closest town.

As Ramone sat at the top of the sweeping front staircase looking out over his new estate, it was apparent the grounds around the house had once been lovingly landscaped but had grown wild over the years. "I would be willing to bet Baptiste's wife planted these gardens," he said aloud. He recalled Baptiste claimed it was she who loved it there. The fields were surprisingly rich with thriving sugar cane, and in spite of the neglect, he hoped they would produce impressive yields once again. Ramone breathed in the sweet smells of gardenia and jasmine and watched the royal palms that lined his entranceway swaying in the breeze.

"*Palmas Ondeando*," he said out loud with profound satisfaction. "That is what I will name this plantation!" he shouted the name out as he stood at the top of the stairs. He held his arms out wide, as if attempting to measure it all. "This is *Palmas Ondeando*—soon to be the finest plantation in the West Indies!" Exhaling deeply, he felt a surge of confidence. *Swaying Palms* would be just the thing to prove to his parents, and his only brother, that he was not the failure they thought him to be.

Ramone looked over and saw numerous outbuildings beyond the slave shacks. They were situated down a small hill, which he had not yet noticed. As he walked down to investigate, he was pleased to see the many tool sheds, and drying shacks. To Ramone's inexperienced eye, they looked somewhat sturdy, although some obviously needed new roofs. He continued to explore the lush, adjoining hillsides, imagining them filled with grazing livestock. The barns were large and offered many stalls and pens for cows, chickens, pigs, horses and oxen. Grateful that his parents had given him generous funds for initial expenses, Ramone envisioned the barn filled with fine horses—Spanish Normans—perhaps—maybe a few Arabians. Determination flooded his senses. *Palmas Ondeando* would become the showplace of the Caribbean.

True to his dream, in three years time, Ramone had turned his estate into a roaring success. He had purchased two hundred slaves, which far surpassed the plantation's original holdings. The land mass was a total of a hundred acres when he first obtained the plantation. Within the first year Ramone bought an additional hundred acres directly adjacent to his property.

As the horses pulled the wagons full of Africans down the long, palm-shaded drive, Pama could not help but admire the lush landscape and the delicate aromas offered by the steady breeze. It was a seductive mixture of salt and flowers with a hint of sugar and coffee. Her home in Africa did not have the variety of beautiful flowers or fragrances that she had experienced since arriving on Martinique.

Once they had disembarked the wagons, the slaves were herded, single file, to the shacks. Even though it was difficult to walk with shackles on her ankles, Pama was relieved to once again be using her legs after the four-day sail from St. Thomas.

Yondua was placed with a fellow Tulu man named, *Sabuti*. Coincidentally, he had grown up in Morocco and had once been acquainted with Yashika, Pama's mother. When Enrique's back was turned, Sabuti whispered to Pama, "I will look out for him. Do not worry." Pama was comforted and she quickly kissed him on the cheek.

Within minutes, Pama felt someone grab her arm. "Come with me, you enticing piece of ass," Enrique barked while fumbling with the keys to her ankle cuffs. The man had a firm grasp on her arm as he pulled her along toward the great house. Once they were out of sight from the others, Enrique turned around and faced Pama so he could leer down the front of her garment. He rubbed his hands over her body, resting them on her breasts.

"You will end up in my bed eventually," he slurred in Spanish. Pama was becoming familiar with the smell of alcohol since her capture and she detected the stench of rum on his breath. He disgusted her almost as much as he frightened her. Even though she understood nothing of his native language, Pama knew he was a vile man and she was not safe in his presence.

As she entered the great house, Pama was astounded at the overall grandness of the place. *This is just like the palaces in my book,* she thought to herself.

"Stay here while I go and get your master," Enrique said sarcastically, stumbling out of the room.

He left her standing alone in the living room. Separated from the others, she felt vulnerable and frightened. *What do they want with me,* she wondered even though she knew the blond master wanted her sexually. She felt his intensity the moment he set his eyes on her. Now, when he came down the stairs and looked at her in her shabby garment, she could still feel his interest. Something intensely exotic was connecting with her spirit—something beyond her control. What in the world was happening here? Despite her humiliation and physical pain, Pama felt somehow euphoric.

"You are to live in these quarters," he said in French as he motioned her toward the kitchen building. "This was another woman's room, but now it is yours." Ramone continued, opening the door. "The closet is filled with suitable clothing and I want you bathed and changed at once. I am told you speak French," he said, walking into the room. "How is this possible?"

"My mother was raised in Morocco and worked in a French household. My father was a white Frenchman, although I never knew him," she answered.

"That is fine. At least I do not have to start from ground level. You will be schooled in etiquette and deportment, immediately," Ramone told her. "You will learn proper manners and I want you fluent in Spanish, as well. The sooner you get rid of that African gibberish, the better."

"Excuse me, Master. Will I also learn to read and write?" she asked coyly.

"Perhaps, if you grasp what you are being taught quickly. I sense you are smart and will learn easily." He gave her a smirk before adding, "I have plans for you, Pama. I need you to pay attention around here -pay attention, obey me and keep me satisfied. These are your jobs."

"Yes, sir. I will do my best." Pama was both fearful and elated by her master's words but she tried her best not to show it. Instead, she curtsied and looked him squarely in the eye. *Perhaps I have unnerved him,* she thought. What an extraordinary concept! Keeping him satisfied might not be all that unpleasant, even if it was against her will. He was a fine looking man, to be sure.

Claudita, Ramone's previous concubine, had occupied the bedroom, which Pama was assigned. Originally from Argentina, Claudita had been living in Spain before coming to Martinique. Ramone met her in a pub one night in Madrid and had talked her into making the long journey with him to Martinique. Ramone thought she was beautiful with her long legs, blonde hair, green eyes, and body so hot, his fingers sizzled when he touched her. He needed to have his sexual needs met with regularity. But over time, Claudita had become a possessive shrew.

"I will make your life a living hell for as long as you are fucking my man, you African Puta!" She was screaming in Spanish at Pama while she packed her belongings from what had been her closet.

Pama did not understand her words but could tell she was someone to avoid.

"And do not get too comfortable in my room, either! Ramone will move me back in here once he realizes what he is missing. Now get out of my way," Claudita commanded, pushing past Pama. She held her head high and stormed down the path to the employee quarters, her few personal possessions dangling from her arms.

Ramone was coming around the corner just as Claudita marched by and she spit on the ground as she passed. Ramone laughed and felt relieved to be rid of her. *Pama is my property, and I will do with her as I please, with no back talk,* he thought. *I will give*

Claudita to Enrique to enjoy for a while. He has never been shy about his desire for her. He felt proud of himself for coming up with such a workable solution. Ramone knew he could not afford to have a disgruntled overseer on his hands, particularly with so many slaves to keep under control.

Over the course of the next several months, Ramone worked hard at turning Pama into a proper lady—one he felt proud to have in his life—and one he could control. She learned social grace and style appropriate to his background. However, deep in his heart, Ramone knew he could school her all he wished, but though she was light-skinned, she would never be appropriate in his Spanish world where fair skin was proof of purity of the blood. Fortunately, Ramone was not in Spain anymore and his parents would never have to know about Pama. "She is my own island lady, and I do not have to justify her to anyone," he muttered aloud one day while watching Pama walk gracefully up the stairs. *After all, Martinique is my island of fantasies,* he thought happily, as he followed her up to his bedroom.

Never the fool, Pama was obedient and did as she was told. She obliged Ramone sexually, which was not altogether an unpleasant experience. Despite her guilt, Pama felt a sense of belonging with Ramone—a familiarity she could not explain. Unlike Yondua, Ramone was an experienced lover and knew how to pleasure her in ways she had never before experienced. He was usually quite tender—except when he had been drinking. Pama played along physically, but told herself she was not in love with him. Her heart was always with Yondua. Ramone was simply her master, and she was his slave. When they had sex, Pama found herself pretending she was not with Ramone. If she fantasized about Yondua touching her the way he touched her, she could participate playfully.

Ramone interpreted her sexual cooperation as love. The unlikely situation only caused him to become more deeply obsessed with her.

Ramone left *Palmas Ondeando* often, giving Pama the opportunity to change into colorful shapeless, wraps, kick off her shoes, and run like the wind to her people in the slave shacks. Except for Yondua, Sabuti and Soumana, they were not Tulu people, but they were her Africans, nonetheless. She told their fortunes, sang songs, danced their dances, calmed their fears and listened to their longings. Pama found herself elevated to a priestess among her people. Her living situation had changed but her calling had not. She was often asked to formulate and administer potions, which she had learned from the Tulu medicine man. The elixirs were taken by some of the pregnant slave women who could not bear to have their babies born into slavery. It saddened Pama to eliminate life but she understood why the woman could not bear the pain of having their babies ripped from their arms and sold like her darling Zenebu.

Ramone was well aware Pama was enjoying her little freedom jaunts down in his slave village. But he did not know she also went to be with Yondua. Ramone admired her curiosity and knew she explored the vicinity around the plantation, reporting her findings to her people, since they had no freedom to roam about. In part, Ramone found himself tolerant of the situation because he was proud of his estate and glad she found it pleasing. Her favorite spots seemed to be down on the beach and up into the mountains at the waterfall. Occasionally, Ramone enjoyed spying on her when she was swimming. He loved to watch her remove her clothing and dive into the water. Once, he surprised her by quietly slipping into the mountain pool. He surfaced directly behind her, grabbing hold of her naked body in a tender, playful manner.

"Oh, forgive me Master. I needed to bathe," she said shyly. Any time she wanted, Pama could have the downstairs slave woman draw a warm bath for her, but she preferred a freshwater swim, instead. Pama hoped she would not be punished for taking such liberties, but her fears were soon calmed as Ramone played with her in the refreshing, cool water.

"I need to bathe, too," he teased. He splashed her and dove underwater, surfacing behind her and tickled her gently. After their swim, he stretched out on the big, flat rock that hung over the pool and dried his body in the warm, afternoon sun. Ramone watched Pama stand under the full force of the waterfall, laughing out loud in answer to its sheer power. She was the most beautiful woman he had ever known, and he had known more than a few! He marveled at her free spirit, despite her captivity and was enchanted by her mix of innocence and wisdom. It was not until the sun had set that Ramone and Pama headed back to the great house together.

That night, Pama dreamed of that magnificent waterfall. She was on the plantation with Ramone, but they were dressed in much different clothing from what they had worn. She had on short pants, and a scant, tight-fitting blouse. Her feet were clad in a white, sponge-soled shoe with strange cloth uppers that laced in the front. Ramone was dressed in the same type of short pants. His short sleeve shirt had only three buttons by the neck. But, his shoes were much more elegant: a soft brown leather polished to a bright shine—a slip-on style with no laces. She was coaxing him to come with her to the waterfall for a swim, but he refused to get his shoes muddy. His attitude was smug and aggressive. All around them, the plantation was in ruins, as if it were abandoned. Pama ran up the trail to the pool, and stopped to catch her breath when she reached the bend where she could hear the waterfall. She looked straight through the veil of sleep and a strange spirit appeared. It was a dream-like version of herself. The spirit woman stared at Pama and said: "He aims to envelop you because you are his obsession. You are learning a lesson about misplaced power. Take heed." The ghostly presence gave a confident nod and a wink before disappearing into the mist.

Pama awoke feeling thirsty after her strange dream. She got up and went to the basin for some water. With glass in hand, she wandered out on the verandah. In the full moon's light, Pama saw that the plantation was indeed intact and Ramone's muddy boots were right by the door where he had left them earlier that evening. Shaking her head, she finished drinking her water and went back to bed.

Even though it was hard to adjust to being a slave, Pama was exhilarated in this new tropical place. The other slaves told her they longed to return to Africa, and she, too, longed for the life they once had. But, she did not miss the dryness of the place they had called home. The balmy, Caribbean air agreed with her and she liked the humidity on her skin.

"Yondua, I do not miss the hard, parched African soil, do you?" she asked him one morning. "This place is a paradise with all these flowers," she said, gesturing at the gardenia behind her ear. "And I love the steady breezes off the ocean." She took a deep breath, appreciating the smell of the salt air. "This is like one of the places we used to pretend we'd go to together! But, we never imagined we would go as *slaves,* did we, my love?" In spite of how hard it was to endure the many changes in their lives, Pama enjoyed being somewhere so different and beautiful!

"No, my precious wife, we were too innocent to have imagined such horrors. But yes, we did dream of many adventures. Actually, you conjured them up and I imagined them with you!"

"Even though we are slaves and have suffered many hardships, I am thankful to the Great Spirits. My heart aches for our son and every day, I wish I could hold him and show him the beauty of Martinique," she stated. "Sometimes, when I am up in the waterfall, I pretend we are swimming together. He was such a strong swimmer . . ." As she reminisced, her voice grew softer. "I dream of our fellow Tulu tribe members looking after Zenebu, wherever he is. Perhaps our boy is on an island even more beautiful than this one. I hope he is."

Yondua let out a long exhale but remained quiet. Pama looked him in the eyes. "This is how I deal with our loss. We go on with our lives because we must."

Yondua nodded. "Yes, my *strong one,* we must go on—and you must get back to the great house before you are missed." He patted her backside and hugged her tightly. "I love you—now and forever."

She touched his cheek. "I love you forever, as well." Then Pama turned and ran down the path to meet her master's many needs.

Chapter Nine

Ramone met Enrique in a taverna in Madrid back in his wilder days. "Bartender! Give my new friend here another drink," Ramone slurred. "In fact, hand me his tab. We will be adding more drinks to it before the night is through!" Ramone had been drinking steadily for well over an hour and he was already quite drunk. "So, what the hell do you do with yourself when you are not in here getting sauced with me?" he stammered, passing Enrique his drink.

"Well, when I am sober, I am a craftsman mainly, but I'm a fast learner and I have a good, strong back. I could do just about anything you needed me to." Enrique said as he puffed out his chest and sat straight on his stool. He was a man in dire need of a job and some quick cash but he knew better than to appear desperate. His trade was carpentry and he was good at it, but he could never seem to work steadily enough to get ahead. Money had a way of slipping through his fingers, and he was continually in debt.

Over several more glasses of wine, Ramone bragged about his plantation in Martinique, his new home he had not yet seen. "There will be a lot of carpentry needed, no doubt. The place is grand but it has been abandoned for several years. I could use a skilled man such as yourself," Ramone said slapping Enrique on the back. "I am offering you employ in the West Indies, if you want it, my man! What do you say to that?" Ramone grasped his tankard and slammed it into Enrique's as a toast to finalize his offer.

Enrique was not the adventurous type and would not usually have considered leaving Spain, but he was drunk and Ramone's offer was both generous and intriguing. The promise of a future in a warm, beautiful place was hard to pass up.

"I would be a fool to turn down a job and an opportunity to travel all in one night!" Enrique laughed, clicking his own glass toward Ramone's in response. "Agreed! I shall go with you to the West Indies. Spain will be here waiting should I decide to return."

"Yeah, sure! Anxiously awaiting, to be sure." Ramone slurred. "Hey! Here is an idea! You can be my overseer."

Typically, overseers were cruel and relentless and Ramone felt Enrique could most likely handle the job. He was too drunk to see that Enrique was not much of a leader but Ramone appreciated his smooth talk and slick demeanor, qualities much like his own. Even in his inebriated state, Ramone was certain Enrique could handle carpentry duties and manage a field full of Negroes on his Caribbean plantation.

"Right you are, Sir. I will get those *baboons* whipped into shape," he stammered as they stumbled on their stools. Then they saluted each other and burst out laughing again.

"We set sail next Thursday morning. Meet me on the docks Wednesday afternoon and bring your gear. The islands await, my friend! This is going to be a whole new life for us!" Ramone paid the bill and they each went on their way.

Even through the dense fog of the following morning's hangover, Enrique found himself looking forward to the trip and he congratulated himself for being chosen such a worthy assistant.

Over the three weeks it took to reach Martinique, a genuine friendship between Ramone and Enrique developed. Having been raised in the Spanish caste system, Ramone was initially uncomfortable befriending Enrique this way. Their boundary of employ was sure to get muddied. Ramone remembered his mother used to chastise him for playing with her servant's children after school when he was a boy.

If you mix with them, there will be anarchy, Ramone! He could hear her voice nagging in his head. *They're not like us.* But now, Ramone was lonely for male companionship. The hell with propriety! He considered Enrique an invaluable friend. During those first two years operating the plantation, the two of them often went carousing after a long week of work.

As it was with many plantation owners, Ramone had his way with whatever slave women he wanted and often, he would pass them onto Enrique when he was finished. Keeping him sexually satisfied aided in insuring his commitment to the plantation.

"When you tire of that new one, feel free to pass her on to me for a while. She has got one hell of a body on her. Damn!" Enrique would always punctuate his remark with a lewd gesture, like grabbing his genitals. He could not wait to get his hands on Pama, and he assumed he would get his turn with her soon enough.

But to his surprise, Ramone sternly cautioned, "You keep your hands off of her. That one is my property exclusively and she is off limits to everyone but ME! Understood?"

"Yes, sir. Whatever you say." Enrique was a bit taken aback at Ramone's possessiveness, but accepted it, as he should. "She is a beaut, that one. No question about that."

Much to Enrique's amazement, Ramone had yet to tire of Pama. To the contrary, it seemed he was becoming more obsessed with her with each passing day. Not wanting to seem unreasonable,

Ramone gave Enrique permission to have his way with Claudita. She was like an old pair of boots he did not need anymore. From time to time, Enrique resented being handed Ramone's leftovers, but he did enjoy Claudita especially when rum made her more pliable. After spending time with her, Enrique learned that she festered with hatred toward Pama for taking her place in Ramone's bed. Her drinking masked the pain of rejection, but inside she seethed with jealousy. He knew Claudita only accepted his advances because she had no money to leave the plantation. In her many drunken stupors, he heard her scheme about doing away with Pama.

Truth be told, Enrique also seethed with jealousy and resentment toward Pama. He was well aware that Ramone sought her wisdom about certain matters regarding the plantation, rather than discussing it with him. He hated how she seemed to know intelligent solutions to problems that should be reserved for his expertise alone.

One evening after an early dinner, Pama insisted on taking Ramone to an upper field that had recently been terraced up the mountainside. "I have been wanting to show you this retaining wall for over a month now. We have had some hard rainfalls since you were last on island, and I feel this wall is ready to burst. It will likely happen the next time we get steady rain and if this flow is not redirected, we will lose the cane in the lower fields."

"Have you mentioned this to Enrique?"

"Yes, sir, I did. He slapped me and told me to keep quiet." Pama did not miss an opportunity to intimate Enrique had overstepped his bounds.

In the soft moonlight, the wall looked strong enough to Ramone, however he decided to bring Enrique to the site the following morning to look it over.

"These damn women will run you ragged if you let 'em," Enrique said, laughing off the situation when Ramone told him how insistent Pama had been about redirecting the run-off. He made a feeble effort to check it over and decided it looked fine. "That wall will out live us both," Enrique said, patting his boss on the back as they walked back to the barn. Knowing nothing about construction, Ramone assumed he was right.

Two days later, after a short but powerful rainstorm, a field worker ran into the great house, screaming.

"Excuse me, sir, but we got a river running through the cane in the lower fields! The wall burst wide open and we cannot stop the water, master." Enrique shot a fiery look across the room to Pama before he and Ramone ran out of the house. He was furious! *Is that woman a demon? A witch? That is it! She must be possessed! I must save the master from that devil woman!*

One hot summer afternoon, Enrique sneaked quietly behind some slaves working in the cane fields and overheard them talking amongst themselves." He strained to listen carefully because their Creole language was hard to understand.

"It be hard on Yondua wid his wife in da bed wid da mastah. He too sick to be vexed bout it na mor. Don do no good, no how. We ave na cantrol of life na mor."

"True, true. All de same, it be hard fa de mon, havin' his wife fuckin' de dam mastah," the other man replied flatly. They both shook their heads in agreement of the situation.

Enrique smiled at this juicy piece of news and began scheming about how to use it to his advantage. If Ramone knew Pama was married to Yondua, he might have Yondua shot, or at the very least, sold. Hours later, at dusk, Enrique literally ran into Pama along the path from the vegetable garden and caused her to drop the harvest she was carrying in her apron. As she leaned down to pick up the scattered vegetables, Enrique spat out the evil dialogue formulating in his mind.

"I have learned something valuable about you today, Missy—something I am sure you and your *HUSBAND* had hoped would remain a secret."

Pama cringed with fear, but prayed to God she had not shown it. She held her hands steady and continued picking up the vegetables with a careful rhythm.

"That is right, *sweet thing.* I know Yondua is your husband." Enrique paused to illicit an air of suspense and Pama began to sweat uncontrollably. "I also know what Ramone would do if he knew this." He paused long enough to intensify Pama's terror. "Now then, if you want me to keep quiet about this to the master, we will have to strike up a little bargain, you and me." He leered down her dress as she remained bent over and reached into her plunging neckline to fondle her breasts.

"And what kind of bargain would you be wanting to strike with me, sir?" Pama asked with an even voice. No matter what else might happen, she could not bear for any harm to come to Yondua.

Enrique kept his filthy, calloused hands cupped over her full breasts, and rubbed his protruding groin up against her. "Well, the deal is this: YOU accommodate ME whenever I want you or I tell Ramone your little secret. I am sure you realize the consequences should this information reach your owner."

Pama looked into Enrique's eyes. She longed to spit in his face, but refrained from doing so. "Of course I will oblige you, sir, when I am not with my master."

"You are as smart as I thought you were. Now, get those vegetables into the house and then bring that sexy body of yours to my quarters. No time like the present to consummate our new arrangement," Enrique said with a cynical laugh as he pinched Pama's cheek and undressed her with his bloodshot eyes. She curtsied and went into the great house with her apron full of soiled produce.

After placing the vegetables on the kitchen table, Pama went to her room, slammed the door behind her and collapsed on her cot. She let out a gut-wrenching cry so loud it brought Soumana, her lifelong Tulu friend, knocking on her door. "Pama, it is I, Soumana. Are you all right?"

Pama reluctantly unlocked the door. Doors could be so forgiving—and so inflexible. "Yes, thank you, Soumana. I am in a foul mood, that is all. I am all right," Pama replied, gathering her wits about her. Soumana smiled and nodded. Pama could not bear the humiliation or the danger in discussing what she was about to submit herself to.

"M a m a, can you hear me? M a m a! Hear me! Please give me strength, Mama. Help me endure more abuse. . . help me great spirits, oh, please help me endure it." What lesson is this, oh Great Spirit? Please let this agony be gone from me. Give me strength.

Pama got herself together and slowly walked the short distance to Enrique's quarters, dreading each step that took her toward her doom. She had no choice but to let Enrique rape her repeatedly. Unlike Ramone, Enrique had no skill when it came to sex and Pama lay motionless on his bed until he was finished with her.

At first, Enrique tried slapping her around to make her participate, but he could not afford to bruise her. If Ramone knew he was forcing Pama to have sex with him, Ramone would fire him—maybe even kill him. It was a dangerous game he was playing—delicious and dangerous!

"I know you participate for Ramone more than you ever give me. I can always tell by his stupid, freshly-fucked grin," he spat in her face, one afternoon, shaking her. "You'd better start cooperating or I will tell Ramone about Yondua. I might as well be fucking a dead woman!"

"Yes, sir. I will try to do better." Pama replied in a monotone voice, knowing there would be no better performance, ever.

Chapter Ten

Yondua never fully recovered from his bout with malaria. As time went on, he clung to his life by a thread. Whenever possible, Pama made him herbal elixirs that gave him temporary relief, but the herbs could not eliminate the virus entirely and Yondua eventually slipped into an advanced state of weakness. No longer able to do much around the plantation, his friends covered for him by doing his chores. To flaunt his power, Enrique enjoyed whipping Yondua periodically—especially in the presence of Pama, and he took great pleasure in terrorizing the powerless couple about being married.

"Sabuti, it grieves me so to watch my beautiful Pama be used by these men. None of us have choices for our lives anymore . . . " Yondua rambled on to his workmate and roommate one evening as they sat on the porch of their shack. "God knows, I do not have the energy to comfort her anymore." Yondua sat down and thought about his dearest love. "I have always adored Pama for her energy and enthusiasm, but sometimes, just being in her presence tires me. I hate to admit it, but it is true." Sabuti nodded with a tender air of understanding. Yondua took a deep breath and closed his eyes in thought.

"I am glad she lives in the big house," Yondua said submissively. "Pama is better off. She is my queen and she deserves to be comfortable."

Sabuti nodded again and took a deep drag off his pipe before handing it to Yondua. "The Spirits know how to turn things around, my friend. Perhaps not in this life, but surely in the next."

Yondua fell silent. What else could possibly be said? A next life—a better life?

Exactly two years to the day after they had arrived on Martinique, Yondua finally passed into the spirit world. During his last days, he became uncharacteristically talkative and needed Pama to hear him.

"You will run Palmas Ondeando one day, my love," he told Pama. "The decisions will be yours and all of us will benefit from the success of the crops. It will be up to you to free our people. This is important, Pama. LISTEN TO ME! This is important! You are the *Strong One,* just as your name says. You will have the power . . ."

Pama knew her husband was walking the border between life and death and his insights carried deep wisdom. Eventually, Yondua slipped into a coma. She sat with him late into the night and came back to his shack before Ramone awoke, but her Yondua never again opened his wondrous dark eyes.

For the first time in her life, Pama was truly alone. The realization of this gripped her heart and she fell into a deep, sorrowful depression, unable to cope with daily life. Her losses had rendered her incapacitated.

Fortunately, Ramone was off island.

Chapter Eleven

For the first week after Yondua's burial, Pama succeeded in avoiding Enrique. He passed the word through the household that he was giving Pama time to grieve, but she knew it was part of a ploy for her to keep silent about their arrangement.

She cried each day as she realized her best friend and confidant was gone. How would she get through the rest of her life without her sweet, compassionate Yondua? He had been the balance and comfort she needed in her life and now she felt alone and angry that he was gone. He struggled so hard to stay alive during his last years and as she recalled the injustices he had suffered at the hand of Enrique, her angered soared. After five days of mourning, Pama went looking for their illustrious overseer.

"Soumana, have you seen Enrique around anywhere?" she inquired when passing through the kitchen.

"No, Pama. I have not."

"If you do, let me know immediately." Pama's manner was curt and impatient.

"I will." Soumana replied obediently. Pama's rage filled the room and she rushed out the door, leaving it to slam behind her. Soumana sensed Pama's fierce determination and hoped she would not do something she would later regret.

That same afternoon, Pama learned that Enrique was with two slaves in the barn, attending to the horses. Anxious to do what she must, while she had the nerve, she marched to her mission. Her explosive energy blasted in before her, causing the horses to rear up and the chickens to squawk. With eyes blazing she was intent on burning fear into the soul of her enemy. Her skirt swooshed violently as she paced back and forth. Never once did she lose eye contact with her prey.

"Leave me alone with this man!" she ordered. The slaves looked to Enrique for guidance, but their overseer looked as though he had just seen Yondua's ghost. At that moment, Enrique was far from the pillar of authority the slaves knew him to be. Confused as to who was now in charge, they remained in the barn.

"GET OUT!" Pama commanded, pointing to the door. They raised their eyebrows in silence, not knowing what to do, and Enrique motioned for them to leave. "Close those doors behind you!" Pama commanded. As the slaves hung their tools and dutifully latched the stall doors, Pama continued to pace back and forth like a hungry lion. The only sounds in the air were the *swoosh, swoosh* of her skirt as she spun around.

"ENOUGH OF THAT! GO!" One of the slaves dropped the shovel he was carrying and they both scurried out the door. Pama thought of using the shovel to kill Enrique, but for the moment—she settled for the sheer delight of watching him squirm.

"If you even so much as *look* at me, I will tell Ramone everything." He started to react but quickly changed his mind. "I assure you, Ramone will believe ME over you." Pama raged on as Enrique stood stone still, the impact of his situation sinking to the deepest parts of his psyche. "Do not come anywhere near me. Not ever! And while I am at it, you ease up on my people! THIS IS YOUR ONLY WARNING!" She grabbed her skirt, whirled it around, and boldly stormed out the door with her head held high.

Once she reached the great house, Pama laughed out loud, as she recalled his terrified expression. "You should have seen him, Soumana!" Pama said, recounting the situation to her friend. "He looked as if he might soil himself!" The two women laughed so hard they had tears running down their cheeks. At last, the tide had turned. With his passing, Yondua had freed his love from the clutches of their enemy.

Standing limp and alone with his mouth agape, Enrique realized Pama now held the power. How could he have let this happen? "Damn! I had better steer well clear of that bitch," he muttered to himself. Ramone was a fiercely jealous man when it came to Pama and Enrique was suddenly filled with trepidation. Ramone had just returned from his travels and knew nothing of what had transpired, yet.

Over the next several weeks, he was considerably easier on the slaves and he stayed away from Pama. Initially, she was pleased her threats had worked. All the same, her new power did not give her quite the elation she thought it would. Instead, she withdrew deep inside herself in an attempt to feel more secure. After the sexual abuse and the losses she had experienced, Pama was numb, and no longer the free-spirited woman she had always been.

Almost all of her playful, physical cooperation in the bedroom had ceased with Ramone and her distance made him uneasy. No longer did she romp along the beach or run with the wind in her hair. Little by little, the magic of her life was replaced with depths of despair. Sadly, she did little more than sleepwalk through each day, anesthetized from all she had endured.

Chapter Twelve

"DAMN IT, Pama! Where do you go with your soul? The distance is unbearable! Why are you no longer close to me?' Ramone was heartbroken after yet another night of cold, meaningless sex. "I do not understand why you will not love me. You obey my every word, yet you feel so detached from me. Can you not feel how much I want you? Do you not know how much you consume me?" Ramone gulped down his glass of wine and slipped deeper into a drunken stupor. "Do you no longer think of me when I am not here?" he slurred. Her emotional unavailability made him insane with frustration.

"We all pray for your safety each time you leave the island, sir," she replied, her voice filled with apathy as she walked over to the washbasin to clean up.

"Is that so?" he stammered while lunging at her. "Get over here and show me your concern!" he yelled. He grabbed her hand and placed it on his swollen crotch.

As the years passed, Ramone became more obsessed with Pama, yet she remained aloof. He had temper tantrums with displays of physical violence to others, but as frustrated as he was, he never struck his magnificent Pama. He had blatant sex with other female slaves so Pama would find out but his plan backfired. He was crestfallen when he finally understood and was livid when she was not the least bit jealous.

"Why does she no longer need me as I need her?" Ramone shouted, shaking his fist to the sky one morning while walking along the beach. "Does she not see how much I love her? Why does she not realize how much better her life would be if she would just let me get closer?"

"What can I do to make you love me?" Ramone confronted her straight on one night after yet another round of cool, calculated sex. Never before had a woman so consumed his soul. Despite her frigid demeanor, he was gripped by rapture. "I want all of you, my darling, not just your obligatory obedience." His voice reminded her of a spoiled child's.

His obsession bored her. *Why does he not fall in love with some hot-blooded Spanish lady?* Pama got out of bed and went downstairs. When she reached the bottom step, she had another thought. Ramone was leaning over the banister. His eyes were drinking in the vision of her body, which was silhouetted and backlit by the moon.

She hesitated at first, and then looked up at her master. "You want to do something for me, Ramone? Find my son and buy him back for me. That would make me whole again. Perhaps then I could truly love you," she lied, walking toward the front door.

"You cannot be serious, woman. That boy could be anywhere in the West Indies. . . perhaps even America. I could never find him! And, even if I did, his new owner would not likely sell him, especially if he has your fiery spirit," he added with a spiteful laugh. "Healthy children are prized slaves because of the many years they have ahead of them. You know that! Now, get back upstairs! If it is a baby you want, then I will make you pregnant" he announced, devouring her with his eyes. He was aroused again from having watched her float through the moonbeams in her flimsy nightgown and his ego swelled at the suggestion of starting a family with her. To hell with his parents' prejudices! This was another world—another time.

"I do not want another baby, I want my own son back," Pama whispered softly under her breath. She did not want to nurture a child made with Ramone but she dare not let him know his idea was not brilliant.

"Come up here this instant, and I will give you *my* baby," Ramone ordered.

Why is he not on one of his many journeys? Life is so bearable when he is away, she thought. Pama took a deep, jasmine scented breath and looked over the fields of sugar cane swaying in the breeze. "That is what my Zenebu is doing right now—dancing with the cane in the moonlight… somewhere," she whispered before climbing the stairs to Ramone's bed.

Whenever the opportunity presented itself, Pama wandered along the beach. When he was on island, it was virtually the only place she could get away from his constant groping. Often, she looked out over the sea wishing she were not on an island with no means for escape. The two neighboring islands were Dominica and St. Lucia; both could be seen in the far distance. Unfortunately, each was too far to swim to. She closed her eyes and imagined herself being escorted across the rolling sea by majestic dolphins, reaching the foreign shore as a free woman.

These days, Ramone was taking her to bed more often than ever before. He reasoned that if Pama became pregnant, she would finally give him her love. But, after three months of twice-daily intercourse, she had still not conceived. Her distant attitude made Ramone feel lonelier than ever. He craved deep, meaningful connection with Pama and he grew more delusional about the possibility.

To vent his frustrations, Ramone began to gamble again. He made risky business deals, which sometimes caused him to be away. *Perhaps new adventures will soothe my aching soul,* he thought. *At the very least I will not have to look at Pama's beautiful face every day of the year.*

Shortly after Ramone left on a gaming jaunt, Pama feared that he had indeed accomplished his mission. "Please God, start my cycle again. Do not put his child inside my womb," she begged before going to sleep. "DAMN HIM!" she shouted one day while hanging the laundry on the clothesline. Weeks had gone by, and still, no blood.

On numerous occasions, thoughts of mixing up an elixir to eliminate her baby crossed Pama's mind, but she could not bear to do it. She remembered how elated she was when she first learned she was pregnant with Zenebu and how it felt once he became large enough to move and squirm around inside her belly. She could feel herself bonding with the life that grew inside her. Back then, it seemed her life held more significance because it was housing the life of another. Gradually, Pama warmed to the possibility that another child might fill the cold, gray void in her heart. Perhaps it would reconnect her to the joy she once had, so very long ago.

Pama was a full six months pregnant by the time Ramone finally returned home. Intuitively, he felt a sense of rejuvenation in the air. "What is going on around here, boy?" Ramone asked when he arrived at the barn of *Palmas Ondeando.*

Shyly, the stable boy answered, "Well, sir, Miss Pama . . . she is with child, sir."

"Well, well! Is that right?" Ramone puffed his chest out and the boy nodded. He dropped everything and darted up to the great house. "Bring my things to the house after you attend to my horse," he shouted back at the boy. Scaling the entry stairs two at a time, he burst through the front door. "PAMA! PAMA! Where are you?"

She was outside weeding the vegetable garden with Soumana when she heard his voice. "Damn! Why did he have to come home?" Pama whispered and they both giggled. She struggled to get her bulging body upright and then brushed herself off. She could tell Ramone was frantic for her to come to him but she took her time. She had not been looking forward to his return. What a sight he will be now, strutting around like a brazen peacock once he discovers his achievement! "Now, we have to endure three months of his cocky bragging about his *son*," she whispered to her life-long friend. The women both chuckled, conspiratorially.

When Ramone found her, he scooped her up in his arms and kissed her everywhere. Tears welled in his bloodshot eyes as he touched her belly. His child was growing inside of her and for the briefest of moments, Pama felt a slight sense of fondness for him. It was rare to experience his sensitive, tender side out in the open and she smiled up at him. "Well, hello, Master. Welcome home. It is nice to see you, but would you please put me down?"

"Oh, of course. I do not wish to make you dizzy. How do you feel? Does he move around a lot?" he asked, placing his hands on her belly.

"Yes, *she* does kick and squirm quite a bit," Pama replied with a little smile. He smiled, as well.

"You should no longer be working in the garden in your condition," he said with genuine concern. "Soumana! I want you doing all of Pama's chores until my son is born. Nothing can happen to him while he is being formed," he exclaimed proudly. "He must be perfect in every way." Soumana nodded compliantly.

The father-to-be continued to crow. "When our baby is born, I will be the head of our family and you and our son will obey me. I know what is right for my woman and I will know how to be a father when the time comes."

Pama shook her head but said nothing. *Perhaps being parents together will finally convince her to give me her heart,* he secretly hoped.

Later that evening, Pama was sharing her evening meal in the kitchen with the household slaves when the door to the formal dining room burst open. "Come and eat with me, my lovely." Ramone extended his arm to help her up and she gathered her plate and obediently followed her master.

Once she was settled in her dining chair, Pama could see Ramone was in his cups. "Our child will very likely have off -white skin, or at the very most—a light shade of tan, would you not agree, my darling?" he asked while pouring himself another glass of wine. "After all, you are very light skinned, and I am Caucasian. Our child will be a delicious blend of both our skin tones, I would imagine," he boasted. Ramone sat back in his chair and took a long sip from his full glass. Of course his child would be light in color! He could not tolerate the thought of his baby being *black*.

The combination of Ramone's arrogance and alcohol was more annoying than usual. Pama was tempted to fling his wine across the room and tell him to not be fooled by her light skin, but she remained quiet. She was thinking about her grandfather, Teshome. His skin was so black that when her mother was young, she thought her papa was dark purple! Ramone had never bothered to ask about her family, and now, all he seemed to care about was the white skin in her lineage. "I am quite sure our child will be beautiful, Master, whatever skin color it has."

Over the next three months, he behaved like a doting father, hovering over Pama as if she were an invalid. He was driving her crazy and she felt more claustrophobic than ever. "You are acting like my servant and treating me like the master," she told him one day with a sheepish grin.

Ramone smiled, "I only want you rested for the delivery of our son."

I wish he would go away on one of his jaunts, she thought. "I am rested, Master. Actually, I am strong as an ox. It is healthy for me to keep moving. Exercise is important for pregnant women. You must allow me to roam about the plantation so I do not get stiff and lazy." She had not been to the slave quarters in weeks and she missed spending time with her people.

"All right my dear. Get your exercise, but make sure you do not overdo it," Ramone conceded.

During Pama's last month of pregnancy, a large grinding wheel on the plantation sugar mill fell into critical disrepair. Ramone learned that someone in Fort Royal had recently purchased some quality equipment from a farm that went out of business in the mountains above Kingston, Jamaica.

"I am afraid I need to go to Jamaica right away and purchase another grinding wheel. I cannot wait or we will lose the entire crop.

He tells me this as if I should grant him permission, she thought. Pama was well aware that without the wheel, sugar production would stop and Ramone could not afford the loss.

In all sincerity, he said, "I hate to leave you now, my darling, with our child so soon on the way. I would avoid this situation if I could." Ramone got down on one knee and took her hand in his. "I will return as soon as I locate this farm, purchase the wheel, and load it on my ship."

Pama laughed at his gallant display. "It is fine, Master. The plantation is the important thing. You go on. I will be in good hands with the mid-wives." It wasn't difficult for her to sound convincing. "Now, go take care of your business, and when you return, you will be a father." Truth be told, she wanted him gone so her baby could be born in the presence of her own people.

"*This is my baby,*" Pama said to herself after Ramone had left the room. "You are too selfish to know the first thing about being a father," she muttered under her breath.

Exactly thirty days later, Pama went into a long and difficult labor. It was two days before their healthy, nine-pound daughter finally arrived. The infant was good natured and lovely and Pama was delighted by her uniqueness. In spite of her parents' light complexions, their baby was dark-skinned with blue eyes and smooth, red curly hair. "Where does your amazing red hair come from?" she asked her little girl one night as she was nursing her. "Perhaps it was someone in my father's family," she reasoned.

Ramone had never spoke about names for their child, so Pama took the liberty of calling their daughter Ruby as a tribute to her dazzling hair. The ache in her heart from the loss of Zenebu seemed to lessen since she now had her little girl.

"You have a big brother, Ruby. His name is Zenebu and he is strong and brave. I believe he lives on an island even more beautiful than ours. "One day, we will all be together," she promised. Each evening, Pama told her daughter stories about her brother as she put her to sleep.

Ruby grew fast, and she was almost a year old when her father finally returned.

In spite of Ramone's excitement about becoming a father, he had still managed to get sidetracked in Cuba for several months. After locating the grinding wheel he needed for Palmas Ondeando, he ran into a ship captain one night at a pub. The man was planning to leave Jamaica and was going right past Martinique on his way to St. Lucia.

"I will pay you handsomely if you will take a large grinding wheel to my plantation and get word to my overseer that I will be detained a while longer." Ramone slurred. "I have several parcels in my room that also need to be delivered," he added.

"I do not see why not, Senior Rodriquez. I am always interested in a little extra work—if the price is right," the captain emphasized. Ramone nodded affirmatively and shook the captain's hand. "I sail day after next. Have your cargo delivered to the docks tomorrow afternoon and I will have them at *Palmas Ondeando* within the next few weeks. I have a stop to make on St. Croix first."

"Grand! I appreciate it. This takes a load off my mind." Ramone breathed a sigh of relief.

Later that night, in a different little pub by the docks, Ramone met a gentleman who had just arrived from Martinique. The man had been a visitor on a neighboring plantation and was privy to the local gossip from *Palmas Ondeando.* "I heard your woman had a baby girl," he told Ramone over a few tankards of ale. "She had a hard time of it, I guess, but everything is fine now, and the girl is healthy and normal. "They call her Ruby, because she has beautiful, soft red hair."

"A girl, eh? Well, that is just fine," he said flatly. *She must have my mother's red hair. . . the child must be white. After all, Negroes have black, kinky hair,* he thought. Ramone wanted to ask the man about the baby's skin color but he feared the answer.

He was glad Pama was all right, but a daughter was nothing to rush home for. He had been invited to attend a huge celebration in Cuba hosted by people he had met in Jamaica and he was tempted to accept.

"How can I pass up such an invitation?' he asked himself aloud. "I cannot wait to socialize in my native language again and we Spanish people know how to dance and enjoy life much better than the French!" he said, laughing to himself.

Indeed, Ramone found his new Cuban compatriots grand and gracious hosts. One of several Spanish-speaking guests, he was treated to exquisite mid-day meals each day and nearly every evening there was a spectacular gathering to attend. Before he knew it, months had turned into a full calendar year before Ramone finally returned home to *Palmas Ondeando.*

Chapter Thirteen

As Ramone neared *Palmas Ondeando,* he felt excited and anxious to see his new family. He missed Pama and was also looking forward to finally seeing his new daughter. When he reached his plantation, Ramone rushed in the house to see his two girls. He was delighted and not at all surprised to see that motherhood had made Pama more radiant than ever before. He had been with numerous women over the past year, but not a single one was as magnificent as his Pama.

"Let us go upstairs where you can give me a proper welcome," he cooed, nestling his face in her neck to breathe in the smell of her. "I have longed to ravage every bit of you." He felt the tightness in his groin and took Pama's hand and rubbed himself. He hoped to arouse her as much as the very sight of her had done to him.

Just then, a dark-skinned child toddled into the foyer with her red curls bouncing and her plump little arms extended. Soumana was just behind her. So what was this? Ramone was horrified when he saw the negro child was actually running toward him. He backed up against a table with the full force of his prejudice and knocked it over with a crash. Ramone was not about to hold the child, much less acknowledge she was his daughter!

The baby started to cry and Pama quickly scooped her up so she would be silent.

"Take that creature down to the slave quarters at once and keep her there!" Ramone commanded Soumana. Feeling the tension, Ruby exploded into a full screaming, kicking fit. Ramone turned his back and stared out the window with disgust. Soumana came over and struggled to take the now hysterical Ruby out of Pama's clinging arms. Their eye contact gave Pama assurance that she would keep Ruby safe. Soumana left the room with Pama's frightened little daughter, flailing about in her arms.

This is a nightmare, Ramone thought to himself.

" M A M A ! M a m a! ma a a m m a a!" Ruby's cries grew fainter as she was taken away.

"PLEASE, Ramone! I BEG you," Pama pleaded as she looked out the window at her daughter disappearing down the path. "Bring Ruby back so she can be with both her parents. She needs to get to know her Papa!" Pama begged. "DO NOT DO THIS, RAMONE, P L E A S E, DO NOT DO THIS!" The familiarity of the situation gripped her heart like the talons of an eagle and she knew she would do anything to get her daughter back. "Did you even look at her? She is a beautiful mix of us both, Ramone. Did you see her fine cheekbones and her beautiful little rosebud mouth? I am sure she carries many of your family traits. . . p l e a s e . . Ramone, I beseech you."

"SHUT UP!" he shouted, backhanding her across the face, knocking her to the floor. "YOU will be with me in my room, and that slave child will NOT live in this house! I do not know who else you have been FUCKING, but I am NOT the father of that child." Ramone straightened his collar and smoothed back his hair. "She is a NEGRO and she will live with the NEGROES. That is my final word on the matter!"

"I have not been with anyone but you, Ramone, I swear it. I had many dark relatives and Ruby inherited their coloring. Please, get to know her. She is bright, just like you and so very precious," Pama petitioned. "P l e a s e, I'm B E G G I N G you, Ramone."

"Such desperation coming from a woman of iron. This groveling does not become you, Pama," he said smugly, pouring a stiff drink from a nearby decanter. "You better NOT EVER fuck anyone else, woman! Do I need to remind you that you are MY property?" He pointed his finger at her and she shook her head. "Now, get up to my bed and wait for me! That child will live in the slave quarters with her people and I will not hear another word about her from you or anyone else! As far as I'm concerned, that child does not exist!" he emptied his glass with one immense gulp.

Pama's heart felt as though it was being ripped from her chest as she dragged herself up the stairs. "Mama, watch out for my Ruby. My babies are in your charge now. Watch over them . . . please," she whimpered between sobs. She could hardly believe this was happening to her again!

Ramone drained another generous pour of alcohol while pacing the length of the verandah. He pondered what to do about the child. Eventually, he calmed a bit as the alcohol took hold. He sat back in the planter's chair by the front door and called for the staff to remove his boots.

Barefoot and alone, he began thinking about Pama upstairs, naked in his bed and he grew dizzy with anticipation. "God, I have missed the very smell of her," he mumbled, feeling aroused, yet again. He attempted to strip off his clothing, but in his inebriated state, he struggled with the buttons on his white, billowy-sleeved shirt. At last, he pulled the shirt up over his head and threw it on the floor before staggering up the stairs to have his way with his ever-obedient slave.

Ramone kept Pama up all through the night. He fondled her body and responded to her touch well into the morning. She did everything she could to please him, hoping she might cajole him into letting her little girl come home. All Pama could think of was her darling Ruby and how scared she looked as Soumana took her away. *How could anyone care so much about skin color?* She asked herself. *Was this to be yet another horrifying life lesson?* She imagined her little one crying for her Mommy long into the night. It was almost three o'clock in the morning when Ramone finally fell into a deep sleep. Pama lay awake, scheming of ways to escape the island with her daughter, but she could not come up with a viable plan. Eventually, she wore herself out and drifted off in a deep, fitful sleep.

Within minutes, Ruby appeared to Pama in a vivid dream. Her daughter was being held in the arms of a slave woman. They were both waving goodbye to Pama as the ship they were on was sailing away. The boat bore the name: *La Grande Princesse* on the back transom. Pama was running down the dock, screaming, "R U B Y ! ! R U B Y ! ! COME BACK !" But they ignored her pleadings as the vessel continued to sail away.

"Wake up, Pama!" Ramone shook her until she awoke. "You were screaming the name of that child in your sleep. You are keeping me awake. God damn it! I TOLD you I never want to hear that name in this house again!"

"I am sorry, but I have no control over my speech when I am dreaming. Please, Master, I am worried about her. I dreamt that she was sailing away on a boat and I could clearly read the name. It was *La Grande Princesse.*" Pama was sitting up now. "Do you know this boat, Master?" she asked.

"Of course I know of no such a boat. It was a stupid dream, for Christ's sake! I am exhausted from my journey and need to sleep. Do not waken me again," he grumbled, turning over on his side. Pama stroked his hair away from his forehead and he fell back to sleep almost immediately. As soon as his breathing became steady, she quietly got up and ran to Soumana's shack. She was pleased to see her daughter curled into Soumana's warmth, sleeping soundly. Pama kissed Ruby's sweet little hands and her eyes filled with tears of love for her precious baby girl. Would Soumana be relegated to raising her? Would Pama have to steal away to share precious moments with her daughter, as she had with Yondua? Soumana had not awakened, nor did Ruby, and Pama slipped out as quietly as she arrived.

Early the next morning, before the sun, Ramone was wide-awake, fully dressed, and pacing across the verandah. What was he to do about this wild, black child? He felt there was only one sane solution: he would sell her. *The last thing I need is to have rumors getting back to Spain,* he thought to himself. His parents were now proud of him! After all, he was an upstanding, prominent land baron in the West Indies. What they did not know was that his older brother, Esquivel, was subsidizing Ramone. He had paid Ramone's gambling debts and kept the plantation going while his younger brother was busy having babies with black women and attending parties in Cuba. Living the deceptive life had become Ramone's specialty, and the snobbery of his upbringing ruled over his better judgment and his love for Pama.

We can try again for another baby right away, Ramone decided all by himself. *With mixed parentage, outcomes can have many variations. A light-skinned boy would be much more appealing. The odds are in my favor,* he thought.

Pama sprang out of bed with instinctive urgency. She needed to find Ruby immediately! After checking the porch swing, the verandah and the vegetable garden behind the house, she burst into the kitchen. "SOUMANA! WHERE IS MY DAUGHTER?" Panic was forming in Pama's chest as she struggled to breathe.

"I thought she was with you," Soumana replied, startled at the sudden eruption. Pama spun around, scanning the room with a wild look in her eyes. She felt the same terror she had the day Zenebu was ripped from her arms five years earlier.

"Ruby was sleeping in your shack a few hours ago, I saw her! I was there, watching her sleep. WHERE IS SHE?" Pama was frantic.

"I do not know where she is. I fed her breakfast early this morning. The master said something about you and he spending the day together with your daughter." Soumana now realized Ramone was up to something wicked.

"How could you have thought for one second he would have had such a change of heart?" Pama's voice exposed her raw terror and Soumana's eyes filled with tears. "I am sorry, Soumana." Pama put her arms around her dear friend. "This is not your fault. You could not have stopped him." They clung tightly to one another. Anguish flooded over Pama in an emotional tidal wave and she collapsed in a heap where they both stood. Soumana cradled Pama's head in her lap. She combed back Pama's disheveled hair from her tear soaked face and let her cry.

When she got herself together, Pama spent the rest of the morning wringing her hands while pacing the length of the porch—back and forth, back and forth. Her raging eyes were fixed on the palm-lined entry to the plantation. Every maternal instinct she had was honed by protective anger. Finally, in the early part of the afternoon, she heard Ramone's carriage rolling down the road to *Palmas Ondeando*. She bolted down the stairs and ran to meet him, hoping she would see Ruby sitting on her father's lap, waving at her with her small, chubby hands. But, unfortunately, Ramone was alone.

"Where is Ruby?" He sat smugly in his seat, refusing to respond. Without even a glance in her direction, he continued down the lane. Pama ran after him screaming angrily. "What have you DONE?" Ramone glared at her, clearly incensed by her boldness.

How dare she address me in such a tone, he thought to himself. He smirked and said nothing, continuing up the road toward the barn.

"WHERE IS OUR DAUGHTER, Ramone?" Still, Ramone kept silent, staring straight ahead. In exasperation, Pama picked up a rock and threw it at his rig, scaring the horses. "ANSWER ME, DAMN YOU! !" she screamed.

"GOD ALMIGHTY, PAMA!" he shouted, struggling to get his horses under control. When they settled, Ramone jumped off the carriage and grabbed her by the arms. He shook her, slapped her across the face, and then shoved her to the ground.

"If you must know, that black *animal* of yours has been SOLD—as *Negroes* generally are. She brought a surprisingly good price, too," he gloated, patting the jingling coins in his top pocket. "NE V E R strike out against me like that again," he shouted with his hands on his hips, veins bulging from his neck. "I refuse to hear anything of that dark beast again in my house. IS THAT UNDERSTOOD?" Pama lay bruised and bloodied, glaring at Ramone with hatred strong enough to kill him.

"God damn your soul STRAIGHT TO HELL, Ramone Rodriguez." She got up and spit at him before bolting off like an angry lioness looking for her young.

At first, Ramone started to go after her, but thought better of it. He had had a long day. The process of selling Ruby had taken more out of him than he thought it would.

"That woman will be at my beck and call from now on." Ramone declared aloud, recovering from the incident. "How DARE she be so aggressive toward me!" He brushed himself off before seeing to his carriage.

While the slave boy attended to his rig, Ramone walked slowly toward the great house. Suddenly, he remembered Pama's dream from the previous night.

"How could she possibly have known the child would be sold to *La Grande Princesse* plantation? I had not yet decided to sell her when she had that dream. Enrique was right! That woman is an absolute WITCH!"

Indeed, the overseer, from that very plantation, had purchased Ruby. He just happened to be leaving for St. Croix that same afternoon. The plantation's ship bore the same name. *It's ironic, considering how much the owner of La Grande Princess wanted to buy the child's mother, years ago,* Ramone thought. Pama must never know of this strange coincidence.

Pama ran as though she had been shot from a cannon. Her agony had given her super human strength and she ran up the mountainside, all the way to the waterfall without stopping to catch her breath. "A y y y y y A y y y y Y a y a y a y a y a y a y a y. My b a a a a a b y , my Ruuuuubbby. Bring back my baby... bring back my ba a a a b e e e e."

"I HATE HIM," she screamed as loud as she could, gasping for air. "I HATE HIM! I HATE HIM!" Desperation flooded over her like blood from a gaping wound. She thrashed in the water, screaming her daughter's name: "Ruuuuubbbbbyyyyy," until she was completely exhausted. She bent down on the huge warm rock by the edge of the pool, dropping into a fetal position.

"Oh Great Earth Spirit," she whimpered. "Why did you take both my babies from me? Why can I not be the mother that I am? WHY?" she screamed at the air above her. "OOOHHHHH Ayyyyyyyy, Ayyyyyyy, Ayyyyy."

The sky was now a delicate shade of pink streaked with red from the last of the sun's rays. Pama shivered in her wet clothes. She dragged herself upright and headed back to the new hell Ramone had created for her.

It was almost dark when she slipped in the back door. She was relieved to find him passed-out drunk. Her punishment would no doubt come soon enough. "Please, Spirits—bring my Ruby to me in the dream time. Let me see her again—please," she prayed in her room. "Mama, watch over your granddaughter. Be her protector... go with her... oh, my sweet Ruby, girl. How can this be happening? How can both my children be taken away from me, sold like livestock? How can this be happening to me, again? M a m a... the pain is too deep..." Pama rocked back and forth on her bed until she finally fell into a deep, dark, lifeless sleep.

From that day forward, Pama retreated deep into herself. Ramone's dreams of nurturing a family of light-skinned boys with the woman he loved were shattered. He realized that by selling Ruby, he had ruined any chance of Pama ever loving him. But neither could he live with having a black child.

Five years of hard times passed. Only Ramone knew that *Palmas Ondeando* was in deep financial trouble. He had been absent during much of that last half decade and when he did return, he was unkempt and largely out of control. His drinking was excessive and it was obvious his life was in serious decline.

He continued to take Pama to his bed when he was on the island and she obliged dutifully, stroking his ego like an obedient slave. She knew her place. But Ramone could feel her condescending tolerance and knew she would never really be his.

Pama could see that Ramone's stamina was waning. His drinking was clouding his judgment. He often mumbled about bad debts, bad decisions and the demise of his material world.

Just as Yondua had predicted before his death, Pama eventually took on the task of operating the plantation whenever Ramone was traveling. Enrique had died the previous year and the new overseer Ramone hired was yet another incompetent alcoholic. This new man knew his boss trusted Pama, so he began consulting her about the general operation of the plantation. Eventually, much of Pama's time was spent in charge of things while the overseer was passed out drunk. She sometimes went into town to take care of plantation business and it was obvious to the townspeople she was a woman of power and decision—much to the white people's dismay. As usual, they gossiped and giggled loudly enough for Pama to hear.

"Look at that uppity slave whore of Ramone Rodriquez, doing business like a *free* woman. He had better straighten her out when he gets back or he will never reign her in."

Chapter Fourteen

Being the eldest son in a wealthy family had its privileges, as well as its drawbacks. Esquivel Rodriguez was expected to live his life exactly as any firstborn son of his social standing.

He worked in his father's lucrative shipping firm, a business that he quietly loathed, and at the age of twenty-two, Esquivel married a woman named Isabel Ramierez. Isabel was the only daughter of a suitably, wealthy family from Barcelona. Their marriage had been arranged long before when they were each ten years old. Had Esquivel the opportunity to make his own choice, Isabel would not have been the woman he would have picked. She was a pleasant enough person, but Isabel lacked passion for life and held little excitement for the world around her.

Although Esquivel rarely exhibited it around his family, he was a passionate soul. His was a fire that burned deep. He was captivated by thoughts of the West Indies, although he had not yet been there. For years, he had lived vicariously through his younger brother's adventures. Of late, however, Esquivel had not felt a true thrill about much of anything. "I am choking from all this dutiful obedience. Please, God, help me feel alive, again... really ALIVE," he earnestly prayed. He felt numb inside and needed something to look forward to.

Esquivel lived on his family's expansive estate with more money and material objects than he knew what to do with. He never had cause to think much about his fortune one way or the other, although there was one possession he owned that he truly adored. It was a gold pocket watch his father had given him on the occasion of his twenty-first birthday. The skillfully crafted timepiece featured beautifully tooled carvings of a waterfall on the lid and it played the most enchanting music when opened. When Esquivel first received this present, he was mesmerized by the tune and he found himself pulling the watch from his pocket incessantly to not only check the time, but to hear the music. The tune stirred an intoxicating passion in his soul's memory.

"It is pitiful that a musical pocket watch is my greatest source of joy!" he reflected while walking alone through the rose gardens of his family's estate.

Esquivel accepted his fate, yet oddly, he found himself jealous of his adventurous brother, Ramone. Ironically, Ramone had always been jealous of Esquivel for being direct heir to the family fortune.

If Ramone only knew what a prison all this is, mused Esquivel.

Esquivel wished he could be more like his younger brother, but with their strict, conservative, controlling father watching his every move, he dared not risk losing his fortune. It was all he knew. Instead, he daydreamed about living in the West Indies and running his very own plantation.

Being a dreamer, while both awake and asleep kept Esquivel sane, although of late, his sleeping dreams had been repetitive and strange. In them, he was dressed in rawhide pants and fur-lined boots up to his knees. He lived in a northern, sparsely populated, French speaking place, wild and untamed. Quebec? Esquivel was not sure. He imagined Quebec to be lush and crisp and vividly beautiful, at least that is what it seemed like according to what he had read and heard about northeast Canada. In this vivid dream,

Esquivel sometimes trapped animals for a living. At other points in time, he worked in a large store. In his dreams, there was also a beautiful, light-brown-skinned woman. She always wore soft tanned leather dresses with exquisitely beaded handiwork on the sleeves and the tops of her boots. Clearly, she was the love of his life. Esquivel had not known such love and true devotion in his real life. Where was she? Who was she? He wanted this woman more than anyone he had ever met in his life. In these dreams, he felt no burden of duty or guilt, and Esquivel languished in the luxury of being free while he slept. He looked forward to his dream life each night and began to resent the interruption of the early morning songbirds announcing a new day.

Esquivel was disintegrating into a mere shell of a man, questioning life and its purpose. Then, finally, after almost ten years of marriage, Isabel became pregnant and Esquivel felt a stirring of passion within him once again. A baby! Yes! That is what he needed to give his life more meaning!

Isabel seemed mildly pleased about the situation, although she felt too ill to get out of bed throughout most of her pregnancy. The midwives were more than a little worried about Isabel. They were concerned because the baby was in a breech position and they knew all too well that a baby cannot turn on its own, no matter how skilled they might be.

In the middle of her seventh month, Isabel's labor began without warning and her agonizing screams were deafening. The midwives worked all through the night trying to save them both. But, in the end, their valiant efforts were of no avail.

In a single, horrifying, blood-soaked day, Esquivel's passions had been extinguished, along with his family, and he escaped into an even deeper depression. Sleep was his only refuge—he retreated into his dreams. While awake, he would open and close his watch constantly, so the music would play. The music! Each time, the sounds brought tears to his eyes.

"What is wrong with me?" he mumbled, catching his reflection in a mirror. For the first time in his life, Esquivel feared that perhaps he was losing his mind. He drifted through his days in a fog and hardly managed to attend to his affairs.

Almost exactly a year to the day after Isabel and their son had died, Esquivel received a letter from Ramone:
"My dear brother, Esquivel,

I write this letter with remorse in my heart for the many wrong things I have done in my life. You have been my faithful brother, and while I never thanked you enough for taking care of Palmas Ondeandos' financial problems, I certainly appreciated it. I feel I must get my priorities in order, as my life appears to be on yet another reckless path, which could well be my demise... I am in love, big brother. Her name is Pama and she is more beautiful than the most perfect rose... She consumes my soul... I want to make up to her for all my failings... especially for having our dark-skinned daughter sold into slavery. I cannot go into that subject in depth at this writing. Suffice to say that I am ashamed for doing such an abominable thing to my own flesh and blood. You have always been supportive of me and I want to ask your blessing in my desire to sign Palmas Ondeando over to Pama in the event of my death. Our family's holdings are vast and our parents have never cared about this estate enough even to come and see it. Pama's very essence is the heartbeat of this whole property. Of late, I have been little use to Palmas Ondeando since I am seldom there, and I want her to legally own the plantation, should I not return. Pirates attacked my ship twice in the past few days and I have lost over half my crew. I have incurred serious injuries and it is doubtful that I will make it back to Palmas Ondeando alive. I intend to have this letter delivered to the post on Dominica tomorrow morning and pray it reaches you swiftly. May God be with me and my ship as we sail home to Martinique, if it is His will."

"Please, brother. I beg you to handle this transaction should the situation arise. Consider it my dying wish..."

Esquivel waited many days before approaching his parents. Undoubtedly, he knew they would be alarmed that their youngest son was in harms way. With such delicate news to deliver,

Esquivel rehearsed how he would tell them several times before asking for their attention.

"Mother, Father—I received a letter from Ramone yesterday." His mother smiled and reached for the paper Esquivel held in his hand. "It is now two months old, so there is no way of knowing whether he is alive or not." His parents gasped and his mother stumbled as though she might faint. Esquivel lovingly assisted her to the nearest chair and handed her the letter. When she was finished reading, she clutched the front of her dress as if holding on to her heart. She struggled to breathe. When Esquivel's father finished reading, the three of them sat perfectly still while the news settled into their consciousness.

Within moments, there was a knock at their door. Esquivel's mother dabbed at her moist eyes and straightened herself in the chair, ever the gracious hostess. His father shrugged questioningly and went down the hallway to see who had arrived unannounced.

A servant escorted the visitor toward his employers and the man extended his hand to Esquivel's father. "Good evening, Senior Rodriquez. Please forgive my intrusion, but I have urgent news from Martinique that you must hear. My name is Franco Martina and I am a ship's captain. I have just returned to Spain after sailing the Caribbean waters for the past few years. I regret to inform you that your son, Ramone died on his ship off the coast of Dominica several weeks ago. He suffered serious injuries in a savage attack by pirates and he lost a lot of blood. His remaining crew buried him at sea. His battered ship is anchored off the coast of Roseau. I am sorry to be the bearer of such sad news, but I promised your son before he died that I would tell you myself when I reached Spain. Ramone was a long time friend of mine and I will truly miss him."

Esquivel's mother burst into tears and his father enveloped her in his arms. Ramone's letter had prepared Esquivel for this probability, yet still, the finality of this man's news pierced his soul.

"Are you Esquivel?" the visitor asked, but Esquivel barely moved. "If so, I am to remind you of your brother's request in his recent correspondence. He wants you to honor his dying wish." This reminder shook Esquivel from his darkened state. "I am only the messenger," the captain humbly added. "If you will excuse me, I must be going. I am sincerely sorry for your loss." With that, he bowed before walking down the marble hallway and out the massive double doors.

Ramone's family was mortified by the news of his death. His parents sobbed uncontrollably and they all shared a few sentimental stories about Ramone before they retired to their beds.

Three days later, Esquivel's parents were in a clearer state of mind, ready to address Ramone's request with Esquivel. "Father, Mother—we can attend to this matter after we have properly grieved. Nothing is urgent at this point. Ramone's slaves and overseer most likely do not even know of his passing, and all is as it should be for the time being."

"Nonsense, son," Esquivel's father replied. "We cannot wait. You will go to our solicitor in Madrid and secure whatever documents are needed to assure that *Palmas Ondeando* stays in our trust. God knows what Ramone might have promised this slave woman in his deteriorated state of mind! Thank heavens he had the sense to sell that Negro child before his death!" Esquivel was flabbergasted and he glared at his parents with utter disgust, seething at their comments. With all they owned, how is it that they suddenly cared about Ramone's plantation in a place they had never even bothered to visit?

"Your father is right, son. You need to take care of this legal documentation as soon as possible. Arrange to have it delivered to Martinique and recorded with the proper authorities. It is anyone's guess how valuable that property might be and we certainly do not want to have it taken over by some love-struck, slave woman!" His mother's voice was emphatic and her body language confirmed it.

He could no longer hold his tongue. "I am going to Martinique myself and will deal with the situation as my brother requested. SHAME ON YOU BOTH for rejecting your son's dying wish! Ramone was in love with a woman who bore you a grandchild and all you can do it pontificate about our holdings! Do not try to stop me! This is what my brother wanted. *Palmas Ondeando* was *his* plantation—not *yours!*"

Esquivel's parents were shocked at their son's manner, but they did not attempt to challenge him. They had already lost one son and they did not want to lose the love of their only remaining child.

In the fall of 1795, three months after receiving his brother's letter, Esquivel traveled to Martinique. His parents would either grow to understand, or not. In his mind, he had nothing to lose by going, and everything to sort out on behalf of his only blood brother.

Six weeks of stormy seas later, Esquivel finally set foot on Martinique soil. He was committed to seeing this mission through, even if his parents disapproved. If *Palmas Ondeando* was in more trouble than anticipated, he was confident he could deal with it. He needed this trip—his parents be damned!

Once in Fort Royal, Esquivel bought a sturdy horse, got directions to the plantation and headed northeast to the Atlantic side of the island. The balmy, tropical air and gentle scenery was an immediate elixir for his troubled soul and he found himself coming out of the emotional fog he had embraced for so long.

When Esquivel arrived at *Palmas Ondeando* the following day, the beauty of the property enchanted him and he could feel energy and passion returning to his life. As he turned down the plantation's long entry road, lined with the stately royal palms, he smiled. *Ramone always knew how to live,* he thought to himself. "What a paradise!" he exclaimed. Suddenly, a slave woman, who appeared directly in front of him, surprised him.

"Where might I find the barn?" Esquivel asked her in Spanish. She did not understand and she gestured absently. "Where can I put my horse?" he tried again, this time in French.

"Down beyond the mill," she replied, while pointing. She spoke in Patois, a dialect close enough to French for him to understand. He dismounted, nodded and headed where she had directed.

Esquivel found the barn and he stroked his horse lightly on the nose in gratitude for transporting him safely to his destination. He then handed the reins over to the stable boy. "Good day. Where might I find Pama?" he asked.

The boy nodded humbly, pointing in the distance. "That is her out there, sir. She is the one doing most of the work," he said with a chuckle. Pama was addressing an obvious irrigation problem. The foreman at her side appeared confused and was of little or no help to the situation.

Esquivel, dressed in an expensively tailored suit made of the finest silk and wool—was hardly dressed for the tropics. He was sweating profusely in the oppressive heat and longed to change into something more suitable.

He walked alongside the tool shack, so as not to be seen right away and watched Pama handle the man who seemed to be struggling to remain standing. He was arguing senselessly with her in his slurred, intoxicated speech. Pama was patiently trying to explain the reason the water in the ditch they were standing over was flowing off course.

Impressed by her manner, Esquivel could not help but feel a certain familiarity as he watched her manage the situation. There was something recognizable about her, although it was not her appearance. It was more her essence. Truth be told, he was confused by her appearance. Ramone had said in his letter that Pama was a Negro, but this woman was a gentle shade of beige. As he watched her, he became mesmerized by her beauty and energy.

I never considered it possible to fall in love at first sight, but it seems to be happening to me, he thought. Esquivel felt frozen in time. The longer he stood there, motionless, staring at Pama, the more he realized she was the same woman in his reoccurring dreams.

The tropical scenery began to fade away and he envisioned her in the light brown leather fringed dress with the beaded handiwork. Esquivel observed Pama undetected. He thought about what was happening to him once again. The fear of losing his grip on reality came over him but he shook it off. "Perhaps it is just the heat," he mumbled to himself, wiping the sweat from his brow.

Eventually, Esquivel snapped himself out of his reverie and walked over to the ditch. "Good day, madam. I am Esquivel Rodriguez, Ramone's elder brother. I have come from Madrid. Are you the Pama that Ramone described in his letter to me?"

Pama walked a few steps toward him, wiping her hands on her skirt, "Yes, sir, I am Pama." She glanced down her arm, making sure the mud was gone before extending her hand to him. "I am pleased to meet you, Senor Rodriquez," she said. Esquivel brought her hand to his lips and kissed it gently, not minding the bit of dirt that remained. Pama blushed and looked down at her feet, avoiding eye contact. She was not used to white men treating her with respect.

"Please, call me Esquivel. Now that I see you with my own eyes, I feel as though I have known you a long time. Perhaps it is due to Ramone's praise of you. He was quite smitten," he told her. "I can surely see why," he added. To his utter amazement, Esquivel felt completely at ease in Pama's presence.

"Yes, I know," she replied, not realizing Esquivel had referred to his brother's amorous attitude in the past tense. "Let's go up to the house, shall we?" Pama was eager to get cleaned up and she could see by his sweat stained clothing that Esquivel must be feeling the same.

Pama felt comforted somehow by Esquivel's presence. He had a familiar smile and a welcome spirit, which triggered a deep memory for Pama from another time. Esquivel's dark wavy hair, straight white teeth and sky blue eyes resonated in Pama's heart and she wondered if it were possible they could have met before.

Whenever Ramone spoke of his family, there was a vile bitterness in his voice on the subject of Esquivel. Based on Ramone's negative comments, Pama had assumed his brother was brash and calculating, someone deserving of Ramone's animosity. But Esquivel did not physically resemble Ramone at all. Neither did he have his younger brother's arrogance. No, this Rodriguez son seemed gentle and kind—not at all the dreadful man Ramone had portrayed him to be. There was no denying it. Pama had a powerful attraction to her new guest.

They walked to the great house, glancing at each other along the way and smiling when they caught each other's gaze. Esquivel's essence pulled strongly at Pama's emotions. She put her hand over her heart and felt how rapidly it was beating. When they reached the verandah at the top of the exterior staircase, she saw Soumana drying her hands on a tea towel.

"Esquivel, this is Soumana." Esquivel smiled warmly and shook her hand. Soumana blushed, looking down at her feet while she curtsied. She was also not used to polite treatment from white men. Pama added, "She is our house woman and will assist you with whatever you need." Esquivel nodded and Pama turned to face Soumana. "Please, take our guest to the room at the end of the hall and make sure he has plenty of clean towels," she added. Soumana smiled, curtsying once again.

Turning to address Esquivel, Pama said, "Please, make yourself comfortable and come downstairs whenever you wish. Be at home in this house—as well you should be. Your brother is off island but we expect him soon." Pama smiled warmly and left the room.

After Esquivel washed and changed into lighter weight clothing, he came down to the verandah. There, he and Pama spent time getting acquainted over several glasses of wine. He was feeling extraordinarily talkative and he found himself divulging intimate things about his life to her.

"I am afraid I have lived my life far too obediently. I have been a good son to my parents and a generous brother to Ramone but I now find myself without friends or the love of family. I have become quite a loner." Esquivel amazed himself with his own candidness. "I enjoy people, but I am somewhat shy, unsociable, you might say, although you could hardly tell by my behavior this evening," he said. "I think the wine is making me brave."

"Oh, do go on, please. I am thoroughly enjoying our visit. I too, have become somewhat of a loner over the years. I understand what you are saying," Pama said with a warm, genuine smile.

"When I turned twenty-one years old, I married a young woman named Isabel. I did not love her in the manner intimate couples should love one another. It had all been arranged by our parents when we were both quite young."

"My marriage was arranged, as well, but we did love each other," Pama told him with a touch of nostalgia in her voice. "I suppose we were lucky."

"Yes, you were. Is your husband still alive?" Esquivel asked.

Pama looked away, shaking her head. "His name was Yondua. He died several years ago. Your brother never knew he had purchased us both." As soon as she revealed the long held secret, she wished she hadn't. *Perhaps I am being too trusting of this man. After all, he is Ramone's brother,* she thought.

"Yondua lived in the slave village, and I was placed here, in the great house," she paused. "Ramone insists that I be available to him." *He must know I am Ramone's concubine,* she thought to herself. But Esquivel had nothing but admiration for her and it was evident. He appeared vitally interested in what she was saying, so she continued. "My husband got malaria shortly after we were captured in Africa. He never completely recovered and he died two years after we got here," she said sadly. She attempted to change the subject. "But, I want to hear about you, tonight. Please, continue with your story."

"I am sorry about your husband. It must have been very difficult for both of you to be separated from each other," he offered. Just then, out of habit, Esquivel reached into his pocket and took out his watch. He rubbed the cover on his pant leg to shine it up.

If he only knew, she thought. Pama watched Esquivel meticulously study the outside of his watch, inspecting it for smears before opening it to check the time. As he popped open the lid, his gestures reminded Pama of someone she once knew, although she could not recall who it was. It was the way Esquivel handled the timepiece, so gingerly and careful. She was searching her memory trying to find a connection when suddenly the music began to play. Pama stood up and stared at the watch as if it were a powerful idol luring her to a new religion. The music was so familiar to her, she found herself humming the tune between quiet tears.

Pama was immobilized. *Who is this man and where did he get that watch? How could I possibly know that tune? I have heard such little classical music in my life. Perhaps Ramone purchased it for Esquivel as a gift and he played it in my presence before sending it off to Spain. That could be it,* she thought.

"What is the matter, Pama? Did my watch make you sad? Clearly, you are upset. Here, sit down and calm yourself," he ushered her to a large, velvet covered wing-backed chair. Pama walked as if in a trance and sat down on the edge of the cushion. Now, even Esquivel's voice was unnerving to her. "I know my arrival has been very sudden. You must be overwhelmed by it all."

"Yes, perhaps that is it," Pama finally said in an uneven tone. "But, it was your watch that coaxed my tears to surface, not your sudden visit, Esquivel. May I have a closer look at it, please?" Pama took out her handkerchief and dabbed at the sweat on her brow as Esquivel handed her the heavy, gold watch. She looked at the image of the waterfall carved into the lid and was again, flabbergasted. "Did Ramone give this to you as some kind of present? He must have, because that is our waterfall! The music it plays is so very familiar to me. I cannot imagine where I might have heard it before, if not from this very watch."

"No, I am afraid that is not the case. Our parents gave it to me years ago on the occasion of my twenty-first birthday and I have kept it with me always. It is the only possession I own that I truly care about. My father had it custom made. It is one-of-a-kind. I love this music, it soothes me, which is the real reason I take it out and look at it so often." Esquivel was curious. "You say there is a waterfall on the plantation that looks like this one?"

"Yes, there is. It is exactly like the one designed on the golden lid."

"Are you all right, Pama? You look pale. Perhaps we have had enough socializing for one night."

"Yes. I am fine." Indeed, she was quite fine. Her heart was beating in its regular rhythm again as she listened to his calming, familiar voice. It had been a while since her intuition had jarred her consciousness this strongly. She was pleased to be reminded she had not lost the family "gift". Unconsciously, she gently rubbed the star-shaped birthmark on the index finger of her left hand. The intriguing design on her skin caught Esquivel's eye but he chose not to make mention of it.

"Please, let us go on with our conversation. I get so few visitors here and I am enjoying this opportunity to know you better." Pama smiled at Esquivel, looking him squarely in the eyes. He returned her steady gaze and felt duly comforted. "I would be pleased to show you the waterfall whenever you wish. It is one of my favorite places on earth."

Esquivel was honored that she trusted him with an invitation to a favored spot. He cleared his throat, continuing his story.

"Unfortunately, my life with Isabel was polite but oh, quite dull, indeed!" Pama laughed at his emphasis and could only imagine the situation. "After we had been married for ten years, Isabel finally became pregnant. Well, naturally, I was filled with joyful anticipation and hoped very much a child would bring us both the happiness we lacked. Unfortunately, my wife's pregnancy was very difficult and the doctor ordered her to bed as early as her second month. She was to remain there until after the baby was born."

Pama could feel the hurt reflecting in Esquivel's eyes as he continued.

"After five long months of bed rest, Isabel went into a grueling labor. Our baby was breech—completely upside down and despite the painstaking attempts of the skilled midwives, they could not remedy it. In the end, both Isabel and the child died." Esquivel paused and looked sadly at Pama. "As you can well imagine, I was heartbroken at the loss of my family. I very much hoped that being a father would give my life true meaning."

"Children do give meaning to life," Pama said without looking at him. "I am sorry you have had such a difficult time, Esquivel. Often life's lessons are painful to deal with." Pama got up and looked out the window. She thought she heard Ruby giggling outside, but of course, there was nothing. Pama turned to face him. "Believe me, I know." They were quiet for a few moments. "These ordeals are supposed to make us stronger. I must confess that my own circumstances have made me a bit cynical, which I am not proud to admit." They smiled in unison.

"I can tell you are a woman of great compassion, Pama. Cynicism does not come naturally for you."

"Hopefully, I will somehow outgrow it," she said, lightly.

"Nor does it become me." Esquivel took her hand to brace her for the main reason he had come to Martinique. "Pama—I must talk to you about another matter of importance." He gazed into her eyes and saw the pain in her soul for the briefest of moments. Clearing his throat, he continued. "Ramone is dead. He was killed eight months ago when pirates off the coast of Dominica attacked his ship. I deeply regret having to tell you everyone on board was killed before the ship was pillaged. It later sunk."

Somehow this news was not a shock to Pama. Ramone lived life dangerously on the edge. Each and every time he left the island, Pama was continually amazed when he would return in one piece. She could not pretend to be saddened or surprised by his demise, even in the presence of his brother.

Pama took her hand from Esquivel's grasp, stood up and went to look out the window again to consider what she should say. Slowly, she turned to face Esquivel.

"I hope you will not be too disappointed if I do not weep over this news. I am not aware what your brother wrote you about me, but I can only imagine." Pama paused to catch her breath. She could feel the floodgates of emotion opening and continued without hesitation.

"Your brother paid a handsome price for me years ago and I accepted my lot to serve as his obedient slave. But that was never enough for him." Pama started to pace. "Ramone wanted to own my very soul. When he realized it was impossible, a power struggle ensued between us, which never ceased. He was obsessed with me. There was a time when I had a measure of compassion toward him, although not to the degree he had wished. But, when he took our daughter away from me and sold her, I hated him from that moment."

"Up until the most recent letter I received from him, about ten months ago, I did not even know about you," Esquivel replied. "Ramone and I were not close. In fact, the letter I referred to was one of only three I ever received from him in all the years since he left home. The manner in which his letter was written was of a man attempting to get his affairs in order. When he mentioned you, he wrote with such admiration and respect, I had to come to this island and meet you for myself. He did mention your daughter and how ashamed he was at what he had done." Esquivel paused for a moment, expecting Pama to react to what he had just said, but she remained quiet.

"Poor Ramone..." Esquivel went on, "he was a tortured soul who never really knew his place in the world. He was continually on the prowl for the next experience. The only real things Ramone had in his life were this plantation and you—and he knew he did not have you willingly."

That's for damn sure, Pama thought to herself. She got up and poured herself another glass of wine as Esquivel continued.

"I believe you were Ramone's biggest challenge." He took a deep breath before continuing. "I need to tell you what his wishes were and how I have decided to carry them out, in spite of my parents' objections." Esquivel walked across the room and sat next to her. Pama patted him on the shoulder, pondering the ordeal he had been through in order to deliver this message to her.

"*Palmas Ondeando* is essentially penniless, Pama, but whatever is left—the land, the buildings, the slaves, and the crops in the ground, are all to be left in your charge." Although, he had not had time to draw up an official will, Ramone had indicated to his brother that he wanted Pama to own the plantation. "I am honored to finally meet the woman Ramone wanted to entrust with such a large enterprise," he exclaimed.

He explained his parents were livid that Ramone had been living with her and were shocked he wanted to leave her ownership of his property. "Our parents were eager to get this issue clarified quietly, so no one in Spain would get wind that Ramone had taken up with you." Pama cleared her throat, but did not speak. She nodded for Esquivel to continue.

"Even though it is accepted that slave owners have relations with their slave women, my parents are old fashioned and believe that their children should not *mix*." Esquivel went on to tell her that when his parents heard of Ruby, they were relieved Ramone had sense enough to sell her. Pama spun around and stared at Esquivel, her eyes blazing. His comments about her daughter pierced her heart and she fought the urge to cry.

"They insisted I hire a lawyer and have papers drawn up transferring the ownership of this plantation from Ramone's name to my own. They wanted to keep it a part of the family's holdings. But when I witnessed my parents' reaction to the news that their son was dead and he had a daughter, whom he sold into slavery; and he had you in his life—all my parents could do was insist that I clean it all up! My parents have always been remarkable snobs. I should not be so appalled, but I am!" Esquivel was too worked up to remain seated. He got up and began pacing around the room. "I had to defy them on this issue. I told them I was disgusted to be their son!" He was livid and he used his hands demonstratively as he spoke. "I told them I would hire a lawyer—but NOT to do what they asked, rather I was going to see to it you not only got put in charge of the plantation; but receive full and legal ownership as well." Esquivel could see the shock in Pama's eyes. "Ramone hoped that by giving you ownership of the plantation, it would somehow heal the resentment you held for his having sold Ruby."

Pama was flabbergasted at this news. How typical of Ramone to think that being a property owner would make up for what he did to their daughter.

Pama got up and put her hands on Esquivel's shoulders and looked him straight in the eyes, just as she used to do with Zenebu. "You are obviously a man of great integrity, Esquivel. You defied your parents and traveled all this way to give me this plantation," she said with deep admiration. "I honor you, and hold you in the highest regard for your actions."

"It is the only right and just thing to do, Pama." He said in earnest. "I would not have it any other way." Esquivel burned with sincere conviction. She was to be the plantation's owner. It was what his brother wanted.

They discussed the farm at length. Pama told him what had been happening on the plantation over the course of the past few years—what crops they had grown, which ones had done well and why. Esquivel knew nothing about farming, but he had a head for business and was ready to learn. He found Pama's hands-on knowledge of the property impressive.

"Since I am the first born, I inherited the family wealth. That was one of the many reasons Ramon resented me. Having to ask for money was rough on his pride, but clearly, it was not hard enough on him to stop his carousing. My brother was a stubborn man, yet I have always envied his passion for life. I suppose I have lived vicariously through him all these years," he confessed. Pama was never privy to financial matters concerning Ramone's life or that of his family.

"I have wanted to visit Martinique ever since Ramone won this plantation and I am glad I finally had a legitimate reason to come here. I desperately need to feel close to something in my life. Perhaps the magic of this island might just do it!"

They talked with the ease of old friends and Esquivel felt a deep comfort in Pama's presence. "I know it seems foolish, but I feel as though I have known you before. When I look into your eyes, there is a familiarity for me that goes deep into my memory. Even your voice is soothing in a familiar way. Perhaps I am exhausted and overly sentimental talking of my brother's death on top of the battle I had with my parents!"

Pama smiled, sympathizing with his desire to feel alive again. Ever since Ruby had been taken from her, Pama felt she lacked life's energy. She missed how spirited she used to feel.

"Please forgive me for staring at you, Pama. I do not mean to be rude or make you feel uncomfortable. It is just that I love to look at you. You are quite beautiful, you know?" Pama was not used to compliments and could not look at him while he spoke.

"You have a deep beauty which starts from the inside and blooms outwardly."

She was blushing. "Why, thank you, Senor Rodriguez. I also feel at ease in your presence and agree that you are familiar to me, as well. Our souls recognize each other because I believe that perhaps we have been together before, in another lifetime. I am sure these ideas do not sit well with your Catholic beliefs, but they are the beliefs of my people."

Esquivel was unfamiliar with the concept of reincarnation, but he nodded in agreement at her comment.

After Esquivel had been at *Palmas Ondeando* for a week or so, Pama was decidedly more settled in to his presence. "I want you to stay for as long as you wish," she said one morning after breakfast. She enjoyed having him there and found it increasingly difficult to keep her emotions in check. There was no denying she felt safe with Esquivel, much as she had with Yondua. She had built a wall around her heart as thick as a fortress and now she struggled with her new emotional vulnerabilities.

"Thank you, Pama. I appreciate your invitation and I accept. As I mentioned before, I have nothing to return to, particularly in light of the way I left."

Pama was challenged by Esquivel's attention and respect. It had been a long time since she had felt anything other than fear of being deeply hurt again.

For some inexplicable reason, she noticed Esquivel staring at the birthmark on her finger and it gave her great pleasure. "It is quite a strange design the gods bestowed on my body, is it not?" she said, smiling.

"Your body is perfect—every inch of it, including the art on your finger," he answered.

She blushed uncontrollably and smiled. "Thank you, sir," she mumbled shyly.

Chapter Fifteen

Esquivel had been on Martinique for more than a month, yet not once had he been off the plantation since his arrival. He was beginning to feel restless. "Pama, let me take you on an adventure. We can go all around this island and explore every corner of this amazing paradise! Please say you will come with me?"

"I would love to go!" She was beaming with delight. "Other than the beach below the great house, the surrounding mountains bordering the plantation and the town of Marigot, I have never seen the rest of the island. Can you believe that?"

"Well then. It is time you saw all of this island of yours."

They assigned the foreman a week's worth of simple projects and left early each morning, exploring what they could in a day. But by mid-week, they packed an assortment of clothing and headed north. First they traveled to Basse-Pointe, then southwest across the interior of the northern tip of the island, heading towards Saint-Pierre on the west coast. Pama had not seen the Caribbean Sea since she had first been brought to the West Indies and she delighted in the turquoise waves bouncing in the sunlight. *Palmas Ondeando* was on the northeast Atlantic coast and as much as Pama loved her beach below the great house, she seldom swam there. She soon found she preferred the calmer waters of the Caribbean.

The couple meandered south through Case-Pilote and into Fort Royal, where they loaded supplies for the plantation. Esquivel supervised the packing and Pama strolled down the street and sat on a bench, facing the harbor.

Pama watched the sturdy black woman at the fish stand across the street skillfully cut the heads off the morning's fresh catch and a wave of contentment flooded over her. These were the sights of her home now. She breathed in the salt air and gave thanks for her life, in spite of her pain. Africa was a dusty, precious memory of a time when she had been free. But now, she was free once again, and she was about to become quite powerful on this beautiful Caribbean island. The water sparkled and the laughing gulls dipped endlessly into the dancing waves feeding on the silvery needlefish that thrived on the insects just above the surface.

Pama watched a fisherman and a boy who appeared to be his son, folding their nets. She listened to them laugh as they rocked their skiff, almost tipping it over. "They must be free blacks," she said quietly to herself, "otherwise they would not have access to a boat!" Their nets folded, and lines secured, the father and son dove into the sea and swam ashore. She envied them their refreshing joy while she perspired in the afternoon sun. She hoped that she and Esquivel would have time for a swim before dark.

With one last vital chore to handle, Esquivel began scanning the street for a lawyer's shingle. Pama watched him, and in an instant, she saw a quick vision of the two of them long ago in a different type of setting. It was not a tropical setting—it was a place where the temperature was cold. The landscape offered endless hills of bushy trees with branches of sharp green needles rather than leaves. In this scant moment in time, Pama saw Esquivel as a powerful merchant and Pama saw herself waiting for him in front of his store. She was wearing intricately beaded buckskin clothing and a thick fur wrap. Her hair was in a long braid down her back and she did not look happy. There were people on the walkway by his store who were making fun of her and he came out and chastised them for being so rude. As quick as it came, the scene vanished but Pama felt dizzy from the clarity of it all. She wiped her brow, took a deep breath and looked up at Esquivel in the present, smiling and motioning for her to join him.

"Are you all right, my dear?" Esquivel inquired with obvious concern in his voice. "You looked a bit flushed. I think we need a swim the moment we have completed these errands." Making the point, Esquivel wiped the sweat from his own brow with his handsomely monogrammed linen handkerchief.

"Yes, I am fine. Thank you for asking, sir." Pama replied. "I think the heat is getting to me. A swim would be lovely. I was having that very thought just a few moments ago as I watched a man and his son playing in the water."

Esquivel smiled and nodded. "Let us get this tedious business over with so we can enjoy the rest of this fine day."

Locating a prominent solicitor's office he escorted Pama inside. There, he intended to have legal papers drawn up, transferring ownership *of Palmas Ondeando* to her.

Once he had explained what he needed to have done, Esquivel sat down across from the man's huge, mahogany desk, next to Pama. The lawyer got up and stood next to Esquivel's chair. "Sir," the lawyer whispered pulling him aside and lowering his voice to an evil growl. "I urge you to reconsider what you are about to do. It is a complete affront to our way of life, giving this Negro slave woman so much property and power. Surely, you can understand what slavery means to our society, and our fortunes." The lawyer leaned over, devouring Pama with his eyes. Suddenly, his voice took on a seductive tone. "Granted, she is a fine specimen of a woman, but there must be a less dramatic way to express your appreciation for her favors."

Without hesitation, Esquivel took his fist and shoved it in the barrister's face, squarely knocking him to the ground. "How DARE you speak so rudely of this lady. Apologize this instant, or I shall take my business elsewhere!" Esquivel commanded.

"Of course, certainly. Please forgive me. I sincerely apologize, Mademoiselle," he said while attempting to adjust battered specs on his crimson face. "I will have the papers ready for you this afternoon, Monsieur Rodriguez."

Pama had never felt as elated as she did at that moment. She knew that Yondua would have liked to defend his wife, but he never had the means. What an honorable moment! Esquivel went to Pama and offered her his hand and they walked out of the office, their heads held high. Once they were out on the street, Esquivel stopped and addressed Pama.

"Are you all right, my dear? I have got half a mind to march back in there and tell him I will find another more deserving professional to handle my business."

Overwhelmed with pride, Pama abandoned her reserve, jumped up and put her arms around Esquivel. "Thank you for your nobility on my behalf, sir. No one has ever done that for me."

He held her embrace as long as he dared. Pama did not pull away. "It was an honor," he whispered, his lips tickling the rim of her ear. "You deserve to be defended, Pama." His breath was warm on her skin, arousing her senses, awakening her heart. Esquivel was hesitant to let her go but felt the pressures of propriety. Yet, by the same token, this conservative society condoned the ownership of other humans. It was one of many double standards in life.

"It is indeed peculiar that slavery has been in place my entire life, yet until now, it happened outside my personal associations." He took her hand in his and looked deep into her eyes. "I have never befriended a slave before and it angers me to see you treated with disrespect. This experience is opening my mind to how horribly wrong the concept of slavery is." His voice was thoughtful and somber.

Pama felt alive with love for Esquivel at that moment, but all she could do was nod in awe. He had protected her before in another time, in a different place and now, he was doing it again.

The couple strolled along the waterfront. When they spoke, words flowed effortlessly. They sat down in the shade across the street from the water's edge and Esquivel attempted to answer her many questions about his childhood in Spain, his growing up with Ramone, and his journey to Martinique. She wanted to know all about the world beyond her childhood picture book and Esquivel delighted in her curiosity. He told her as much about himself as he dared as they shared a late afternoon lunch in a small seaside cafe.

Was time standing still? Esquivel pulled out his pocket watch. As he lifted the cover, the gentle tune began to play. Pama felt a hot sensation on the back of her neck. What was that enchanting tune? She knew she had heard it before.

Remembering her curiosity for his watch from her reaction the other night, Esquivel positioned the piece in her direction. "Unusual, is it not?" he offered.

Pama realized she had heard the music playing in her head countless times before. Perhaps it was from a distance whenever Esquivel had reached in his pocket to check the hour. Perhaps it was something else. Strange, she had never realized the source of the sound until now.

Her fascination with the watch delighted him. Not one to adorn himself in rings and baubles, his treasured timepiece was Esquivel's one concession to shiny accessories. For him, the watch was more than jewelry—its melody was medicine for his troubled psyche. He could see that it reached deep into Pama's soul as well.

Grasping the watch, Pama held it to her ear. She closed her eyes. For just a moment, she felt inexplicably peaceful. Not wishing to jolt her from her reverie, Esquivel cleared his throat. Smiling, Pama opened her eyes, placing the pocket watch in his open palm. Returning the watch to its nesting place, he continued their conversation.

"What about your life in Africa? Tell me about your childhood and your parents." He wanted to hear her stories, too. She told him about her mother who fell in love with her white employer's son. He was the father she never knew. Pama's eyes swam in tears as she spoke of her Mama and she sat tall and straight with pride. Pama told Esquivel about the book her Mama was able to get a hold of just before her employers threw her out, penniless and pregnant.

"She used to take that book out every night and tell me a story from the colorful pictures." Tears streamed down Pama's face. "We pretended we were royalty, traveling in grand carriages to the places on the pages." Pama spoke nostalgically and Esquivel listened. "Since I was a little girl, I always dreamed of exploring different places, but oddly enough, I am quite content here. Martinique is now my home."

Esquivel nodded knowingly and excused himself to pay the waiter for their lunch. "Let us cross the street and walk along the beach, shall we?" It was now too late to take a swim. Pama smiled and dried her tears with her napkin. They crossed the road and removed their shoes in order to feel the sand between their toes.

Esquivel felt as though he might explode with joy. Being with Pama on this beautiful island was like being in heaven. He realized then, as they walked slowly along the shore of the Caribbean, he was deeply in love with her, this amazing slave woman with the soulful eyes and searching heart. He wanted to tell her how he felt at that very moment, but he was not willing to risk the potential awkwardness of the situation. Before he knew it, Esquivel realized it was time to get their legal papers and find an inn for the night.

During dinner, they planned their next day's journey. After their itinerary was established, Esquivel paid the check and they strolled on to the nearby inn. Once settled in their rooms, he approached Pama's door with anxious anticipation, hoping she would invite him in. Instead, she leaned up and gently kissed his cheek.

Taking her hands in his own and pulling them to his heart, Esquivel stared deep into Pama's eyes. "I will see you in my dreams, as I do every night since I met you." He tenderly kissed each hand—then turned and walked slowly down the hall to his room, hoping she would call him back to her side.

Pama watched him walk away, thoroughly admiring his physique. She felt her heart beat deep within her chest. Quickly, she closed her door, hoping to dismiss her desire with the gesture. She paced about, finally calming herself down enough to put on her nightgown. Sitting at the dressing table, she let down her hair and began brushing it, thinking of Esquivel with every stroke. She could feel the moisture between her legs as she gazed out the window at the ocean waves crashing on the illuminated beach. The full moon painted a shimmering path on the water, creating a trail to the heavens. Esquivel's kiss had burned like fire on her hands and she could not get him out of her mind. Boldly, she put down her brush, grabbed her shawl and draped it over her nightgown. Taking a deep breath, she opened her door, walked down the hall to Esquivel's room and gently knocked.

"Just a minute," he called out. Esquivel had undressed and was about to get under the covers. He opened the door wearing only his trousers, his tanned chest glowing in the moonlight from an open window. His wavy hair was tousled; free from the slick controlled style he wore during the day. He looked delicious to Pama and she could no longer keep the wall around her heart. She pushed his door open and went inside, her eyes begging for gentleness. Pama had not made love since Yondua had taken ill. Yes, she had been forced to accommodate Ramone, but she was obedient, never the loving participant. Tonight was something new and exciting. He came over and kissed her passionately and within seconds they were in bed together. She felt immediately safe with him. His touch was familiar, resounding in her deepest memories. They had been lovers before, in another time and place—she knew it. Slowly and gently, he caressed every inch of her lean, light brown body, letting her know she was cherished and wanted. They spent that moonlit night in the throes of passion and did not awaken until high noon the following day.

From that point forward, their adventure was as wondrous and intricate as a youthful honeymoon.

From Fort Royal, they went east, toward the southern tip of the island. An accommodating waiter had told them that the most beautiful beach on the island was directly to the south, about a day's journey. When they arrived, Esquivel arranged adjoining rooms at an inn, although they used just one. Pleased with their surroundings, the couple remained in one place for almost a week, relaxing on the powder white sand of Grande Anse des Salines. Pama was delighted to discover how much Esquivel loved to swim. The water had always been her passion. Pama was well aware that she was letting down her guard. In spite of her silent vow to keep her heart sealed off and protected from danger, she was in love.

She got out of the water and lay down on the blanket next to Esquivel. All she felt was ecstasy.

"Pama. I like that name, 'P a m a'. What does it mean in your native language?" Esquivel asked.

"It means, *strong one.*" Pama replied, her voice going flat. "I have not felt deserving of my name for a very long time."

Esquivel took her chin in his hand and she looked into his gentle, blue eyes. In them, she envisioned all the love, acceptance, and respect the soul of Esquivel carried for her over many lifetimes. It was once again confirmed to her—they were old souls, who had known a deep love countless times over.

"Pama is not only a beautiful name, but one quite fitting for you. You are indeed a strong woman to have endured so much in your life." Esquivel took her hand and brushed a loose hair away from her flawless skin. "My sweet, strong, Pama." Esquivel cooed in her ear.

"I am delighted you appreciate my name, sir," she replied, rolling on top of him. They kissed passionately as the warm sunlight faded gently into the horizon.

Chapter Sixteen

Once the couple returned to *Palmas Ondeando,* they were inseparable. Pama moved her possessions out of the small downstairs room by the kitchen, and claimed Ramone's room as her own. It was the largest bedroom in the great house, well suited for the new owner of the plantation. Esquivel felt comfortable keeping his things in the guest room, but he spent every night in Pama's bed. Each day, they were consumed with their many chores, but somehow, they managed to slip away for a naked swim in the waterfall or a lovemaking romp in chambers.

Pama tried to remember back to a time before Esquivel was in her life but love had healed much of her pain and those days felt like a distant memory. His presence was comfortably familiar and now she felt as if he had always been with her.

A matter of grave importance had been stewing in Pama's mind for quite some time and she needed her lover's business advice. "Esquivel, do you remember the remark you made about slavery when we came out of the barrister's office that day in Fort Royal?" she inquired one morning after breakfast. "I vividly recall it because it was that very comment which made me realize I was in love with you." Esquivel smiled and nodded as she continued. "You said your mind was being opened to how wrong slavery is." Pama took hold of his hands.

"Yes. I do remember saying that. What's on your mind, my love?"

"Emancipation is coming to Martinique and eventually the rest of the world, but it will never be soon enough. I cannot keep my people captive and very much want to let our slaves go free if they wish to go; yet I also want to keep the farm running. The problem is we need their help to do it." The look on Pama's face showed her deep concern.

"My darling, the slaves belong to you and you can do with them as you wish. We need to come up with a plan to offer them freedom, or the option to stay on and work. If we can turn the plantation around financially, we can pay them proper wages." Esquivel offered as a possible solution.

"I want everyone who participates in the success of *Palmas Ondeando* to benefit. If the people continue to be fed and cared for—and if they feel truly appreciated, they might agree to stay on without wages for a while. Do you agree, Esquivel?" Pama asked. "I want them to have joy in their lives, they have suffered enough."

"All we can do is approach them with a plan and see how they respond." replied Esquivel.

Pama arranged to have some of the field hands build a bonfire on the beach below the great house the following week, and she assembled her people. When the group was quieted, Pama stood on an old weathered log that had washed up on the beach years ago, and cleared her throat.

"The master of this plantation is dead. He was attacked by pirates off the coast of Dominica." After such a bold, opening statement, she had their full attention. Other than the crashing waves of the powerful Atlantic, the moment grew silent and she waited a minute before continuing. "Due to the generosity of the master and his honorable brother, I now own this plantation and its contents, which includes all of you." The crowd grew noisy again and she held up her hand for quiet. "But—I REFUSE to own human beings for one more day, so I am setting you all FREE! YOU ARE NO LONGER OWNED PROPERTY!" Pama had to scream to be heard through the cries of joy. The slaves clapped their hands and broke into song.

Despite their initial merriment, most of the Africans were wise enough to realize there would be few places to go on the island as free blacks. As that reality settled in, the crowd grew quiet again and Pama continued.

"I have every intention of keeping this plantation operating but I need you to accomplish this task. The plantation is in financial trouble, which means I cannot afford to pay you wages now. But, it is my sincere hope that we will all benefit from the success of this property and I want to draw up a plan which gives everyone a stake in this plantation." That statement got the crowd humming again and Pama waited for them to settle down before continuing. "Go to your beds tonight and sleep on what you have heard. You are free to do whatever you please after a day's work. There will be no overseers to watch you. I believe prosperity, along with this new freedom, is in all our futures. Good night. May the Great Spirits bless each and every one of you." Pama stepped down from her driftwood podium to resounding cheers and applause.

Most of the slaves were immediately agreeable to Pama's new arrangement and they returned to their shacks as free Negroes.

To no one's surprise, Esquivel decided to stay and help turn *Palmas Ondeando* around, as did most of the slaves. The few who did depart the plantation permanently wished Pama well as they made their way off the farm for the first time since they had been forced onto the island.

Within a few short years, the plantation was growing enormous yields, more than it had ever before produced. They planted coffee, as Yondua had suggested long ago and it was a huge success. Pama ran the plantation with leadership and motivation, giving the workers a sense of ownership and pride for their unified efforts.

Esquivel fell more deeply in love with Pama with each passing day. She loved him as well, but over time she had gradually slipped back to the safety of her protective, sealed-off spirit. Esquivel had proven he could be trusted with her heart, but her survival patterns were too deeply rooted.

Esquivel felt her increasing distance, but hoped it would melt away as it had on their island vacation. Truth be told, he wanted to marry Pama, and eventually, take her back to Spain with him. He loved Martinique but had been feeling more and more guilty about the manner in which he left Spain. His parents had written him several letters in an effort to make amends for their behavior. They even went so far as to agree that Esquivel had done the right thing in giving *Palmas Ondeando* to *that woman* if it pleased him to do so.

His father was getting on in years and could no longer manage the family business without his help. Esquivel pondered their recent letter for days before finally speaking to Pama about it. He knew her response would alter the course of his life, forever and he was careful to pick just the right moment to bring it up.

Chapter Seventeen

The cool morning rain kissed the rising sun, creating a complete rainbow. It arched over the sugar mill like a colorful bridge. Up in the mountains, toward the waterfall, lay a dreamy mist draping over the canyons like a damp, nurturing blanket. The humidity was thick and the air lingered through layers of diffused light. Esquivel inhaled deeply as he sipped their homegrown coffee with a sense of satisfaction, tempered by a dose of regret. Being an active participant in the yields of *Palmas Ondeando* these past few years had given him an overwhelming sense of pride. He had enjoyed his time there and it was obvious the tropics agreed with him. His skin was tanned and his hair, which he no longer wore slicked back, had lightened in the sun. Best of all, Esquivel's passion had surfaced and his heart had truly learned to love again. But, on this particular morning, he wore a serious face and Pama could see the stress on his brow. Sadly, family duty involuntarily overtook Esquivel's thoughts now, much as Pama's own armor of independence enveloped her.

After he and Pama had finished their breakfast, a stable boy appeared on the verandah. "Your horses are ready, sir." The boy bowed shyly and left as quickly as he had come.

"And where are you going this fine day, Senior Rodriquez?" Pama asked like a coquette—hands placed flirtatiously on her hips.

"Come, my love. We are riding to the waterfall. I have something important to discuss with you and I want to do it in the heart of this plantation."

Nodding in agreement, she mounted her horse and adjusted her skirt. "Are you all right, Esquivel?" Pama was genuinely concerned. "You seem upset about something."

"Yes, I am fine and hopefully, I am about to be better!" By this point, Esquivel felt he might explode with anxiety and he was eager to get his business over with and done. "Let us go," he cried out.

Esquivel took off in a gallop and maintained that pace all the way to the waterfall. Pama sensed his urgency and wondered what could be on her lover's mind. Once they had arrived, Esquivel took her by the hand and sat down on the large, flat rock. He was sweating profusely; his hands were clammy and damp; his hair was sticking to his brow. He nervously pushed it away and cleared his throat. Pama could see he was struggling so she waited patiently, smiling at him with a heart filled with love and a bit of fear.

Fidgeting, Esquivel cleared his throat, again before starting. "Pama, I love you with all of my heart." He put both his hands over his chest in an effort to contain his emotions. "You must know this is true. Am I correct?" Pama nodded and smiled. "I want us to be married and I want us to have children. Children born in Spain." Pama was stunned and could not reply. "I need to return there, and I desperately want you to come with me, as my wife." Esquivel looked at her with such a deep sense of love, it brought tears to her eyes.

She was unnerved by his proposal. They had lived so peacefully without the bounds of a proper marriage, and she had not given the idea of matrimony a moment of concern. She loved Esquivel, but at that moment, all she felt was fear at the idea of leaving her home. She took his hand in hers. "I want to accept your offer, Esquivel. I do know you love me." Pama paused to take a breath. "I love you too, so very much, but I need time to think about what you have asked of me. I must admit that I am a bit startled by your idea."

Esquivel was hoping for a resounding *yes* but settled for her explanation and nodded his understanding. "Well, then," he said. "You take your time and think it over. As for now, why not take a swim with me? I need to cool off and the water will do us both good." Hoping a swim would lighten the mood; he had already taken off his boots and was unbuttoning his shirt. Pama slipped out of her garment and into the cool, fresh water of the pool, and prayed it would wash away the protectiveness that bound her spirit.

Whenever possible, Pama spent the next several days walking on the beach and hiking in the mountains. She swam in the waterfall, observing her island as if she were seeing it for the first time. While she breathed in the intoxicating smells of frangipani, jasmine and gardenia, she had a new appreciation for the wonders of Martinique. She watched the green parrots as they swooped into the flamboyant tree above the falls and she listened to their chatter as if it were a symphony. The humidity in the air was luscious and she remembered how dry and cracked her skin had been while growing up in Africa. She realized how much she appreciated this natural moisture on her body. Was the air in Spain moist like this? Were there parrots there—and delicate orchids? And what about Esquivel's parents? How could she possibly go to their country and live amongst their prejudices? They might have expressed civility in a recent letter, but Pama vividly remembered Esquivel's account of their bigotry. She knew it was a belief that resided deep in their core.

Oh, but Pama did love Esquivel so, and she would adore having children she could actually keep at her side and raise until they were grown. But she could not go to Spain. Nor could she open her heart and truly love Esquivel like he deserved to be loved.

After several days of soul searching, Pama lead Esquivel out on the verandah. He sat with legs crossed, his arms resting on the smooth, wide teak supports of the planter's chair. He eagerly awaited Pama's answer, watching her pace to and fro. Whenever she went out on her walks, Pama practiced what she was going to say—but now, with Esquivel looking at her with his heart so exposed, she hesitated.

"I wish things were different, Esquivel, but they are not." Pama paused, went to the railing and looked out towards the sugar mill. "I love you so much, it fills my heart with pain to refuse your proposal." She had her back to him but she could hear his labored, disappointed exhale. After what seemed like hours of silence, Pama went to him with her eyes filled with tears. She took his hands and put them to her lips, kissing them lightly. "I am sorry for both of us."

"I am devastated, Pama. I do not know what to say except that I will honor your decision and pray for you to change your mind while I am away. I must go to Fort Royal to get my transport in order for the trip. Can we talk about this more when I return?" His deep blue eyes were so desperate; she could barely glance up at him.

"Of course we can." She smiled at his hopeful suggestion, but knew she would not change her mind. "Be safe on your journey, my love." Pama's cheeks were wet with tears as she gave Esquivel a hug. He clung to her and began to sob. They eventually let go of one another, each one forever changed. He stopped short a moment, took out his pocket watch and opened it. Checking the hour, the music of his watch caught her ear, piercing her soul to its depths. Esquivel kissed Pama on her forehead before going to his room to pack his belongings.

Pama struggled with her decision, playing the scene over and over in her mind. She tried to imagine her life in Spain as Esquivel's wife. Adventures and new experiences were all she ever used to dream of, yet now, with another exciting possibility before her,

Pama could not accept it. When Esquivel returned to *Palmas Ondeando,* she was waiting in his room, seated at the edge of his bed.

"Esquivel, I love you but I am afraid I cannot allow myself to let go of my protectiveness to freely love you as you deserve to be loved. But it is not that alone, which keeps me from your offer. I cannot move to Spain. My people and I need each other. We have been ripped from our homes and crossed the oceans together. We have been through years of slavery and freedom together. We have delivered one another's babies and buried our dead. These people are who I am and I could not live the rest of my days far away from the only family I have. We are Africans, living on a French island which accepts our skin color." She paused a moment and watched Esquivel's expression turn sheepish at the mention of race. "You know as well as I do that as light skinned as I may be, I am not white enough for Spain—or your parents. Our children could well be born as dark as the night sky. What kind of life could they have on a Spanish manor? And where would they fit in, once grown? No, this is where I belong, running this plantation with my people." Esquivel understood all too well her need to be with her people. He shared that very same need.

"The pain I feel in realizing what my decision means for us goes to the far corners of my memory. I feel we have journeyed together before, my love. This decision has been a familiar struggle for me, yet my dream-life has been dormant and uninformative these past years. I have little intuitive sense what lies beneath the surface of our situation."

"Familiar in what way, Pama?" Esquivel wondered. Her mystic nature was not something to which he was accustomed. She had not been flowing with that energy since he had gotten to know her.

"It is difficult to explain," she paused nostalgically. "In earlier times, I often received intuitive messages from the spirit world—before fear and daily business matters invaded my senses.

Now, it seems I mostly fill my head with day-to-day matters of this plantation. I am far too focused on protecting myself, and my workers to find the time to commune with that world. It used to be that certain people or situations had a familiarity to me, or I would dream about a situation and its significance would be far beyond a regular dream. When I first met you, my soul recognized your presence and I felt I already knew you. But the familiarity was not from this lifetime."

Esquivel was enchanted to hear his own inner thoughts brought to life. "Oh, my beautiful, mysterious Pama. Believe it or not, I also recognized you from a recurring dream I used to have." Esquivel proudly confessed.

"Really? You have not shared that with me before. Will you tell me about the dream?" Pama was anxious to learn of his experiences.

"I have never shared these thoughts with anyone," he said in almost a whisper. "I used to dream it often. I would look forward to going to sleep each night, hoping my subconscious would go there while I slept. In my dream, you were dressed in buckskin clothing with beautiful beaded handiwork—like an indigenous woman and I was clad like a rugged mountain man. We were very much in love—as we are now. Your people loved me and welcomed me into their fold and it was a warm and loving experience. Before we met, my life was quite empty. I had been alone and sad. But you, the woman of my dreams, changed everything."

Pama smiled at her lover, nodding as he told his story. "As you speak of this, it seems familiar to me but not because I dreamed it myself. The day I heard the music from your watch, I knew we had been together before. It is as though I remember being that woman in your life. Perhaps the music was special to us then, as it is now. You know how I love to hear it when you check the time." Pama smiled at Esquivel and he patted the pocket where he kept the watch. "There was another time during our venture around the island when I had a brief vision of us together dressed in the clothing you described. I did not mention it at the time because I was still getting to know you. I did not wish to frighten you away from me." With a concerned look in her eyes, she added, "I feel a sadness about our outcome in that lifetime. Did your dream have a finale? Whatever became of us?"

"I do not know. I only dreamed the part I told you. The joy I had with you in that dream is what kept me alive when I could not find myself. It is as though the universe was preparing me to finally meet you in this life. Now that I have, I no longer experience the dream. We have been living it—save for our surroundings.

"Yes, we have, my darling and I have enjoyed every minute with you." Pama said, gently taking his hand and placing it on her lips for a kiss.

"I want you to be with me Pama. I love you so much, I cannot bear my life without you." Esquivel paused, looking into her eyes. His own were swimming in tears, his words flowed with honesty. "I understand why you feel you cannot come with me. You are correct about my parents. I detest their bigotry, but my bond with them goes beyond it and I am needed back home. I am filled with despair at the thought of returning there without you, my love. I admit I feel regret about my decision, yet I know that not going would grieve me even more over time. My duty to family is strong and I cannot change who I am."

"Well, then, be safe and go home with my love and my deepest respect for all you have done for me." Pama kissed him lightly on the lips before leaving him to his packing. She understood what it was to have family ties that bind.

The couple spent the next few days struggling not to dwell on their upcoming separation, yet they were already grieving the loss of one another. Pama honored Esquivel's duty to his family, as he honored hers. They were tribal beings. Their lives were laced with obligations to others, as much as to themselves.

Pama packed a picnic lunch and they hiked to the waterfall each day for an afternoon meal and swim. They made love as they had on their island jaunt. Pama languished in those precious, blissful moments when she lay in his arms and the world felt safe and perfect. Periodically, she saw glimpses of the two of them by a frosty lake high in the mountains. The lush woods were thick with the same type of green needle trees she had seen in her mind. The love between them was as strong then as it was now. All she could surmise from these images was they had been lovers before, in another lifetime, in a different place, much as in Esquivel's dream.

During his few remaining days, Esquivel found himself more and more observant of Martinique's natural wonders. He knew he would miss this paradise the moment his ship untied from the dock. He had been focused on Spain since receiving his parent's letter, but as he breathed in the delicate wafts of gardenia and jasmine, he was filled with a deep sadness.

Three days later, Esquivel's ship left Fort Royal, bound for Spain—his heart lay in broken pieces on the pier. He knew his duty would be the prison it had been before, but he could not turn his back on his family. As he watched the ocean roll and tumble during the long passage home, Esquivel wished he could have been more like his brother. Ramone never once struggled with choosing to live his own life. He had been as free of guilt and duty as Esquivel was consumed by it.

With each passing year, the ache in Esquivel's heart for Pama grew in intensity and he fought the urge to return to Martinique. His parents were getting on in years and he was getting set in his ways. Once they were gone, Esquivel hoped to return to the island. Perhaps they could resume their life together, if only Pama would have him.

Pama received numerous letters from Esquivel and she always responded immediately. The two of them remained the best of friends—their love for one another remained constant. But, over time, Esquivel's passion for daily life was all but extinguished. The only reason he felt alive at all was the steady pain he felt in his heart for his lover—his sweet, amazing Pama.

Chapter Eighteen

Pama had several suitors during the years following Esquivel's departure. Initially, these men were attracted by her inner strength, but much like Ramone, they eventually became resentful.

With the emancipation of slavery on Martinique, Pama had become a powerful woman on the island. *Palmas Ondeando* was fast becoming the top sugar and coffee producer in the West Indies and other plantation owners admired her success. A few even tried to win her over, with the intention of combining her holdings with their own, but Pama was not at all interested. Her heart remained alone, untouched by any local man. She had become a fierce businesswoman through managing the plantation and her ever-growing knowledge of economics added to her quiver of survival skills.

She established a reading program for the parents and children on the farm and eventually invited neighboring residents to participate. Soon thereafter, she added swimming lessons to the curriculum. Because of her effort, Pama experienced the joy of having children around her, which helped soothe the empty mother-space in her heart. No longer scorned by the white community when she went to town, Pama eventually enjoyed social appreciation for her dedication to the island youth.

Letters from Esquivel and thoughts of him kept her going—but they grew fewer as time wore on. Walking along the beach one day, Pama pondered the past, present and future of her life. *I miss the untamed, free-spirited woman I used to be—where did that dancing, spiritual soul of mine go? I was once able to transcend my enslavement and be that wild, vibrant person. I have not done that in so long.*

"YONDUA? WHERE DID I GO?" Pama yelled to hear herself above the crashing ocean waves. "AM I WITH YOU?" she paused, waiting for the reply, which did not come. "I CAN NOT FIND MYSELF ANYMORE," she called out again above the crashing surf.

Out of nowhere, she experienced an intricately detailed vision. In it, she saw herself mourning the loss of someone. She laid in a strange, primitive lodge, made of huge, thick logs from tall trees, not at all like the huts in Africa. She wore tanned, beaded clothing, the very type that Esquivel described from his dream. There was a caring man, evidently a brother who was attempting to comfort her but she could not be calmed. Her face was pale, her brow wet with perspiration. She shook with fever and seemed enveloped by some kind of disease as well as a heavy sadness. But feebly, she sat up and propped herself against the wall and stared straight through Pama's soul before she spoke. "Staying true to ourselves seems to cost us the companionship for which we ache. Can we not have both? We need to work on this." She then lay back down and continued to gaze into Pama's eyes. Curling up like an infant, she took one final shallow breath and died. At last, the pain had stopped.

Suddenly, the finger bearing her birthmark became excruciating and it catapulted her into the present moment. It was on fire! Pama put it to her mouth, hoping to cool the skin.

She was startled by the return of her *gift* and the message it delivered. "Why can we not have ourselves and our lovers? Why, Mama? Why do we have to choose one or the other? It is not fair! I am tired of life's unfairness!!" She demanded answers from the crashing waves on the beach, but, or course, there was no response.

Over the years, Pama's health had been slowly and silently suffering from her bound up spirit. Herbal elixirs helped ease her troubled digestive system for a time, but she understood full well the source of her discomfort. It was pain that came from a deeper place. She had let it continue unchecked for much too long and the damage to her physical body had been done.

The large log she had stood on long ago to make her freedom speech to the slaves was forever on that beach. Now, she sat down on it to catch her breath.

That night seems so long ago, Pama thought. *Yondua knew it, too . . . he told me I would free our people.* Breathing in the heavy salt air fused with a faint odor of fish, her thoughts shifted to Ramone. Amazingly, she found herself missing his passion. He had such a desperate need for adventure, a quality she admired. But his obsession for her was unbearable. While Pama deeply loved many of the people in her life, she had learned to be self-reliant. Yondua had been her companion and her best friend as well as her husband and she had loved him. But, she was not consumed with him. They had a strong, healthy relationship, a solid connection. Pama knew she had an even stronger connection with Esquivel but she was too fearful from the pain of her life to grab hold of it. And now, in her sixty-sixth year, Pama hungered once again for that level of connection with another person. She now realized the emptiness in her soul could only be filled by one person alone—*Esquivel!*

As she walked in ankle deep surf along the shore, Pama remembered the moments of abandon in her youth; how she would take off her clothes running naked along the water's edge with the wind whipping through her hair. She missed that Pama as she tried to recall when and how she had let go of that wildness. How had she become the person she was today?

Pama felt robbed of her mystical essence—her life had grown spiritually bankrupt. Long ago, Pama had been the gifted one. The Tulu chief had sought her advice on countless occasions. How could this outcome be her fate? She wanted to reunite with her inner soul—to what was pure—to what she already knew. Pama held up her left hand and gazed at the star on her index finger. She did not feel deserving of such a symbol. Would there be enough time to accomplish this reunion of spirit? Her intestinal cancer was ravaging her body. Fate had spoken. This destiny would have to unfold in another life and time.

The morning after her day of soul searching on the beach, Pama took her last breath. She passed peacefully in her sleep. People of the plantation and throughout the entire Caribbean mourned her passing for weeks. Neighboring plantations hung their flags at half-mast. A light had gone out on the island of Martinique and the impact was felt throughout the West Indies. Little did she realize how famous she had become, being the only black woman to own a thriving plantation.

Once Esquivel received word of Pama's death, he arranged to travel back to the plantation to tend to a host of business affairs. He had endured the lonely years since leaving Martinique as one would tolerate an incurable disease, convincing himself family duty had kept him away so long. But over time, he developed doubts that he would have been able to share his own, fiercely independent life with Pama. He, too, had learned to insulate his heart with protective self-reliance. Now, he felt completely grief-stricken, knowing they gave up the opportunity to spend their lives together.

As the ship got ever closer to Martinique, Esquivel was filled with sweet memories. The distinct fragrance of frangipani flowers, the sweet mist around the waterfall. He was anxious to see Pama's beautiful island paradise again. Realizing he would not have her there to share it filled him with a familiar emptiness he had grown to accept. Regret enveloped Esquivel like a smothering blanket and he felt a deep sadness for his life's choices. Family duty paled next to the brilliance of life long love. Why was this realization finally clear to him for the first time?

As the ship pulled into Fort Royal, Esquivel noticed how much the port had grown into a bustling harbor town. He was amazed at how sophisticated it had become. It took but a moment to hire a horse and buggy to take him to the plantation and he mused at having to buy a horse years ago because there was no livery business on the island back then. As the coach traveled along the north shore to the plantation, Esquivel sobbed softly to himself as familiar sights and sounds filled his senses. He observed the neighboring plantations with their impressive entrances. He missed the natural beauty of the island more than he realized. His memories of Martinique over the years had been consumed solely with thoughts of Pama.

By the time the coach turned down the royal palm lined road *to Palmas Ondeando,* Esquivel was weeping steadily. Attempting to have his wits about him, he turned his thoughts to the business decisions that lay ahead. What would happen to the plantation now?

Once they were in front of the welcoming arms staircase, a gray-haired Soumana appeared in the upstairs doorway. She had received notice of his arrival and heard the buggy's approach over the loose gravel in front of the great house. Esquivel was immediately comforted at seeing her face. He took his handkerchief, blew his nose then smoothed back his salt and pepper hair before getting out of the carriage to accept her greeting.

She welcomed him with loving arms and soft comforting eyes. Esquivel held onto her tightly and they both cried for their beloved Pama. "You look well, Senor Rodriquez. The years have been kind to you," she commented while escorting him to his old bedroom.

"I was thinking that very same thing of you, Soumana." He patted her lovingly on the shoulder. "It feels as though I have finally come home, having you greet me in this manner. I have missed being here and have longed to be on this plantation." Soumana knew he meant every word he said. She could see it in his eyes.

The stable boys were now adults but they remembered Esquivel and expressed a sense of joy at his return. All the former slaves were now proud co-owners of the plantation and the revenues continued to grow as heartily as the cane. But without its mistress, it was clear the spark had gone out on *Palmas Ondeando.*

Esquivel remained on the plantation for three months, wallowing in grief and regret. Perching himself on Pama's freedom log on the beach below the great house, he realized he and Pama had missed their chance for a life of love. "Why is it that I had never returned to Martinique?" he asked himself. For that question he had no answer.

"HOW DARE WE TAKE SO MUCH FOR GRANTED IN OUR LIVES!" he called to the brown pelicans diving for their supper. As he watched them dance about, he envied their freedom.

The ocean waves crashed on the shore. It sounded like enchanted music to his aching heart. The repetition caused him to slip into a trance. He remembered Pama telling him they had been together before, in another time. He saw her face clearly, as though she were sitting on the log next to him. He reached out to touch her. He knew she was there, in spirit.

"PAMA, I KNOW YOU CAN HEAR ME, LOVE." He yelled above the noise of the surf. "YOU ARE THIS BEACH... YOU ARE THIS PLANTATION ...YOU ARE IN MY HEART RIGHT NOW, MY DARLING, AS YOU HAVE

ALWAYS BEEN...I CANNOT BEAR THE THOUGHT OF THIS BEING OUR FINAL FAREWELL."

His energies spent, Esquivel sat back and was quiet for a long while. Tears flowed freely down his cheeks and he reached for his same embroidered, linen handkerchief from his back pocket. He removed his watch from his vest and opened the lid. As the music played he remembered Pama said it was their special tune from another lifetime.

"You say we have been together before, then let us be together again, my love. We cannot leave each other this way—both of us empty and dying alone. I will look for you, my *strong one,* and I will find you again," he promised aloud to his soul. "I will find you Pama...I will. I have to. I must."

Esquivel stayed on the beach long into the night, basking in the glow of the full moon on the water and the love he had once experienced. Martinique was the only place he had felt true love in this lifetime. It was, for Esquivel, the most special place in the entire world.

Returning to Spain broken hearted, emptiness soon played host to illness. In his perpetual state of despair, he had no desire to continue living. In less than a year, Esquivel gladly left the earth to join his precious Pama in the spirit world.

Part Two

1985 – 2005

"There is no doubt in my mind concerning the eternal quality of the soul and its journey through human existence. It is my belief that we have worn many 'costumes' in our soul journey. We have been different genders, races and nationalities in many time zones and zip codes. The common thread is that we have been a soul having a human experience."

— Susan Barry

Chapter Nineteen

Hungrily, he breathed down her neck leaving a moist film of desire on her skin. She had dreamed this before! Was she dreaming it now? With one aggressive swipe of his hand, he ripped off her clothes, forcing himself on her.

Numbness, draped over her like a protective shield. The man was attempting to overpower her, yet again. The sting of his hand striking her face caused Mariah to flinch in her sleep. Pulling the covers up over her shoulders, she drifted back to the place where she knew her deepest wisdom resided—walled within her dreams, the place of deep memories.

There were two children within her family circle referring to that same man as father. Clearly, she was, Mommy. It seemed the youngsters were the only reason she remained in this painful place. There were pine-tree covered, snow-capped mountains surrounding them and she was resolved to be in that frosty environment. Her children were her deepest loves and she smiled in her sleep at their vision. Mariah repeatedly experienced the nightmare of the youngsters being ripped from her arms. But tonight, this was not that dream.

Suddenly, it was an earlier century. She was still in the north woods, but this time she was in an Indian village by the side of a river. A tall, slim woman arose out from the water and dried herself in the afternoon sun. Tears formed in her deep brown eyes and Mariah instantly recognized the woman as herself. She bore the same strange star-shaped birthmark ring on the index finger of her left hand.

"Listen to me, child," she said. "Hold on to your identity. Love yourself so you can better love others." The exotic looking Indian maiden nodded and smiled at Mariah before slipping back into the river

Again, her dream shifted and this time Mariah was no longer in the north. She was on a sugar plantation by the edge of the ocean on a tropical island with hundreds of other slaves. Once again, there was a male figure dominating the scene and he seemed to be someone of stern authority. He whipped the weaker ones and ridiculed her in front of the others. Despite his powerful status, she found him foolish.

Then, out of nowhere, a handsome blond man arrived onto the scene and took her to the great house. The dream continued where it had begun, although in a following scene, the blond male also attempted to overpower her.

Mariah wondered what this reoccurring dream signified. At times, she even wrote about it in her journal. But after a while, she gave it less and less thought—that is until her life began to unfold in an eerily similar way.

Chapter Twenty

1985

As Mariah sat at the intersection listening to the monotonous cacophony of her windshield wipers, she looked out the window, nearly overcome by a wave of despair. "Where the hell am I?" she mumbled to herself. Intellectually, she knew she needed to turn right and get on the freeway, but on a soul level, Mariah was at quite a different crossroads. As was the daily norm, her children were at the daycare center and she silently berated herself for allowing them to spend so much of their youth there, rather than at home with her.

Since moving from Idaho to Puget Sound, Mariah's life seemed divided equally between her mediocre, middle-management job at the local newspaper and living in their four-bedroom, two-and-a-half-bath home in the suburbs. Her life had become neatly packaged like a detergent commercial and Mariah was numb to it all.

Her oldest sister, Olivia, had been living the island life on St. Thomas in the U.S. Virgin Islands for the past twelve years and she continually urged Mariah and Bill to take a vacation and visit. Sitting in the rain drenched traffic, Mariah thought back to last night's phone conversation with her island sister and that morning's confrontation with her husband.

"Come on, Bill, let's get away for a few days. This damn rain is driving me crazy!"

"Mariah, consider our finances, for God's sake." Bill snipped. "Just when we start to get a little ahead, you want to do something frivolous." He paused to catch his breath and Mariah seized the opportunity to respond.

"What's frivolous about wanting to visit my sister?" she asked. His snide attitude was losing its hold over her and once again, she wondered how she had endured life with such an intolerant man. If not for their children, she would have left him long before.

"Your timing is off, as usual. Have you seen the price of gas lately? We can't afford to go anywhere except back and forth to work." That was hardly true, but it delighted Bill to make Mariah seem extravagant. He walked to the window, looked outside and sighed. "I suppose these grey skies are starting to get to me, too," he remarked as rain streaked across the window. "The bad weather rumors about this place are all true!"

He snapped up the remote control from the table and turned on the TV. It usually infuriated her when he watched television while they were talking, but this time, Mariah let it go.

"Well," Bill said reluctantly, "if we do find some way to squeak a vacation out of the budget, we'll leave the kids in Florida with the folks. You and I haven't been away together since they were born."

"Sure, that sounds great!" Mariah exclaimed, although she would rather have brought their children with them. Thoughts of leaving her darlings behind ripped at her heart but she opted not to protest. After all, Bill was actually open to the trip. She fought back the panic squeezing her chest at thoughts of being separated from her babies.

CNN Daybreak was roaring in the background. I can't believe he is agreeing to go, she thought to herself, in amazement.

"I'll call the travel agent as soon as I get to work and see if there are any good deals on airfare. My work schedule is lightening up and I'm sure I could take a few days off by the end of the month. How does that sound?"

"It sounds expensive," Bill snapped. Turning his attention back to the steel gray skies, he softened his delivery ever so slightly. "The sound of that pounding rain is wearing me down almost as much as you do. Go ahead. Book the flights for the end of the month—whatever."

Now, hours after their conversation, she was feeling anxious, but it wasn't because of the heavy traffic. "Changes in latitude, changes in attitude," she sang out loud to the freeway, attempting to entertain herself. *God knows, I need something to help me feel alive again,* she thought. The concept of a life less structured filled her thoughts as she tried to concentrate on the vehicles crowding all around her.

The rest of the month dragged on but, at long last, they were headed to the airport.

They landed in Tampa, Florida, leaving their six-year-old son, Jason and four year old daughter, Emily, with Bill's mom. The plan was to split up the time with each grandmother equally. With the children well on their way to being spoiled rotten, Mariah and Bill were headed for St. Thomas without a worry.

As their plane approached the island, Mariah's eyes were glued to the small porthole window. "Look how beautiful it is, honey!" she exclaimed as they made their decent to St. Thomas

"Uh, huh. Yeah. It's pretty," Bill replied without glancing up from his newspaper. Once again, he was in one of his sullen moods. Bill's natural pessimism was constant sandpaper to Mariah's enthusiasm.

She made up her mind to ignore it. The lush tropical scenery was a welcome distraction and she kept glued to the window until they were firmly on the ground.

"Hey, look. There's Olivia! I see her!" Mariah said. "Oh God, she cut her hair! Can you see her, babe?" She turned around to face her husband. His expression was blank. Mariah took a deep breath and silently prayed for patience. She had never adjusted to his changeable moods, even after living with him for more than ten years. More than ever, she struggled to not let him bother her. She ran ahead to meet up with her older sister, leaving Bill behind to pout and deal with the bags.

"Olivia! You look 'mahvelous dahling', you really do," Mariah said, attempting an imitation of Billy Crystal. Laughing, Olivia turned sideways to accentuate her protruding profile. She was three-and-a-half-months pregnant and already showing. Mariah put her hand on her sister's belly and they each glowed with maternal love.

Bill caught up to them, watching the reunion with dark curiosity. His only sibling was a distant younger brother—gushing sisters was something he never understood. "Hello, Olivia. Nice to see you," he mumbled, giving her a dutiful, impersonal hug. "Thanks for having us."

"Sure Bill, my pleasure." Olivia noticed his cool demeanor and glanced over at her sister. Mariah shrugged, her eyes wide open. *Classic Bill.* "Well, Sweetie," she said, switching her attention to her sister, "what do you think of my island so far?"

"I had no idea it was going to be this beautiful," Mariah said as they drove away from the airport. "I imagined it more level like our good old' Sunshine State. You mentioned there were mountains here, but I didn't expect this! I guess I thought there might be a single range in the middle and the rest would be flat," she added.

"I always meant to send you some postcards or a Caribbean coffee table book," Olivia replied. "Oh, well. Now you can take your own photos. Can you believe the color of the water?"

"So many gorgeous shades of blue!" Mariah exclaimed. "I can't wait to dive into it. What are those big, orange flowering trees on the mountainside? Didn't we have one of them in our front yard when we were small?"

"Yes, we did. We call them, *Flamboyants*." Olivia was thoroughly enjoying showing off her island. "Isn't that the perfect name for them? In Florida, they're called Royal Poinsettias."

"That's right. I remember now!" Mariah said. "There are so many big coconut palms everywhere. I would love to drink some fresh coconut milk. It's been years since I've had any," Mariah said as they passed exquisite residences with impressive palm-lined driveways. "I've always loved the Royal Palms. They look so grand."

"Do you remember when we were growing up in Florida and the coconut palms got that strange 'lethal yellow' disease?" Olivia asked Mariah while glancing back at Bill who was still sporting his sour face. "Wasn't it sad when all the palm fronds fell off and we were left with tall, naked trunks with no tops?" Her sister nodded, remembering.

"I like this lush look better," said Mariah who drank in the view out the tinted windows of Olivia's silver Land Rover. She was elated to be surrounded by so much natural beauty. Olivia followed the north coast on their way to the east end. They pulled over at an overhang known as Drakes Seat for a photo opportunity. Olivia explained the site was where Sir Francis Drake long ago surveyed his fleet and watched for incoming pirate ships as they sailed through Pillsbury Sound. Mariah was awe struck by the spectacular vistas of Magens Bay, Hans Lollick, St. John and the many nearby islands in the British Virgins. Bill made a stab at small talk, but it was obvious he was not enthralled by any of it.

Olivia left them at the beachfront condo she had rented for them and Mariah changed into her bathing suit. She tied a colorful sarong around her waist, picked a pink hibiscus from the potted plant and put it in her hair, and smiled at her reflection in the mirror. *I've missed wearing tropical clothes,* she thought to herself. The air smelled of flowers and saltwater and the tropical temperatures were warm; not hot and sticky like her childhood home in Florida. Soft trade winds blew cooling thoughts through the sunlight.

"Don't you think it's fantastic here, Bill?" She started to put her arms around his neck to kiss him, but sensed he was still in a funk. He ignored her, stepping outside on the deck. Mariah followed him. He hadn't said but a few brief words since they arrived, so she tried again to lift his spirits.

"It's nice to feel this clean, fresh air." She paused and took a deep, salty breath. She struggled to not let his gloomy disposition drag her down. "Olivia told me these gentle trade winds blow year round and they rarely turn on their air conditioning at home." Bill remained silent. *God, he is such a trial for my patience,* she thought.

"To me, it's like coming back to a place I've known before. It's familiar somehow," she paused. "I can't really explain it." The view from the condo faced northeast and she gazed over at St. John and several of the British islands, transfixed by her surroundings.

Bill looked around and shrugged, then went inside and turned on the air-conditioner.

Chapter Twenty-one

Mariah's dream life had been particularly active since deciding to take this trip. Seemingly out of nowhere, she remembered a scene from one she'd had just the day before. She saw Bill wearing a hat with a wide brim. He was standing at the edge of a newly plowed field. He had on black riding boots with muddy spurs and he wielded a whip in his right hand. Draped across his chest was an elaborate gun holster. Clearly, he was overseer of the many slaves who were working the fields behind him. She recognized herself standing on the verandah of the plantation's great house.

"Pay attention, child," whispered the woman. "You need not succumb to him again." As quick as a blink, Mariah was back in the present.

A bit shaken from the event, she sat down on the chaise lounge to regain her composure. *Dreams are so strange sometimes,* she thought. *But, it's not much of a stretch imagining Bill as an overseer. He's certainly controlling enough!* Mariah looked at her husband who had just reclaimed a position on the deck. He was standing firm, arms folded across his chest, his face in a frown.

"You've been quiet since we arrived." She coaxed, "what's on your mind?"

"Well, of course it's beautiful here! I'd have to be an idiot to not think these islands are beautiful, Mariah." His voice was bitter as he stormed back inside. "You're so damn manipulative." He yelled to be heard above the air-conditioner and the surf outside. "I know you're going to try and talk me into moving here. You probably have some kind of wild, long-range ideas about this place!"

"What's manipulative about making conversation? I happen to love it here" Mariah replied. "I've never been anything but honest with you about not liking Seattle, Bill. Quit projecting your fears on me." Mariah held her head high as she spoke to him, then turned away. "Perfect! We've been here three hours and we're already fighting," she mumbled to herself.

"Oh, that's right." Bill jabbed. "You're the mystic in the family, I forgot. There's probably some weird reason we're supposed to be here."

Mariah refused to engage in their familiar power struggle. "I'm going for a swim. Stay, or come with me and cool off. It's your choice!" She grabbed a plush, colorful towel from the basket and let the screen door slam behind her. Bill did not follow.

Tension washed away as she swam the length of the beach in slow, even strokes. Mariah loved to swim in natural water. Floating on her back, she bobbed on the small, gentle waves, thinking back to when she first met Bill.

He didn't used to be such a moody jerk, she mused. Touching the soft sandy bottom with her toes, Mariah began to walk waist deep in the water. "Or maybe he was and I just didn't see it!" She let out a deep sigh, whispering to the sea before going underwater. "What in the world do I do now?"

Surfacing from her swim, Mariah considered the message in her dream. *There was something oddly familiar about Bill when we first met,* she thought back. *I was strangely drawn to him, even though I knew deep in my soul he wasn't my type.* She never would have married him if she hadn't gotten pregnant.

"I've succumbed to him long before this," she said to the seagulls that were dancing next to her towel, "but I don't have to do it again." The birds squawked in agreement, flew into the air and circled three times before disappearing from sight. "He'd better lighten up or I will go and stay at Olivia's!" Mariah rubbed her wet hair with the towel, then strolled back toward the condo. She was not going to let Bill ruin her much needed vacation.

Chapter Twenty-two

Mariah spent her first night on the island tossing and turning, in spite of the soothing sound of ocean waves outside her door. The long hours were interspersed with fitful dreams, none of them clear enough to write about the next morning. At first, she made an attempt, then finally gave up, placed her journal back in her suitcase and took a shower. Bill was drinking coffee on the deck, reading the local paper when Mariah stepped into his vision wearing a tight yellow dress, straw hat and pink sandals. He looked up and smiled, admiring her outfit.

"How do you feel this morning, Sweetheart?" Mariah asked, pouring herself a cup of coffee. "Did you sleep well?"

"Yes. As a matter of fact, I feel almost as great as you look! Olivia called while you were in the shower and she's coming to get us. You'll be glad to know we're going sightseeing." Mariah nodded. He was so much more agreeable this morning and she wondered how long his upbeat mood would last.

Within an hour, they found themselves on the waterfront, standing on a sidewalk looking back at the town of Charlotte Amalie. Bill was busy taking pictures and making conversation with some locals. Suddenly, out of nowhere, Mariah saw a quick vision. She saw the town long ago. The commercial area looked essentially the same; except for the modern signs on the old stonewall rum storage buildings, which were now shops and restaurants. She remembered how Water and Hassel Islands stood out just to the right of the harbor. The image flashed across her mind, then instantly dissolved.

"Olivia, do you know if the cruise ship docks were always across the harbor, or did they used to be along this waterfront?" Mariah asked. That morning, there were three massive white cruise ships at the West Indies Dock in Havensight. As she looked at them, Mariah saw another instantaneous scene of an old-fashioned wooden ship anchored in the harbor. She felt seasick as she saw herself on the vessel, shackled and chained.

"Don't choose imprisonment of the heart, child," the bound woman said to her own reflection, her hands raised as high as the chains would allow. "Be true to yourself." Mariah heard the words, as if they had been spoken aloud. She felt queasy and weak in the knees, so she leaned against a street sign and took deep breaths to calm herself. Slowly the wooden ship faded away with Mariah's nausea. All that remained were the sleek, modern cruise ships. It had been a long while since Mariah's intuition was this active.

"You know, I'm not really sure," Olivia replied, looking at the cruise ships. She was unaware of her sister's physical discomfort.

Mariah contemplated her vision as she watched a red sailboat pass in front of her. The name *Camrita* was decoratively painted across the bow of the boat. Olivia and Bill walked ahead, not noticing that Mariah had stopped to watch *Camrita* put up her sails. Just then, she was startled by a soul-piercing scream.

"No, no Mama, pleeeeze!"A small child and his mother were walking on the sidewalk next to her. The little boy was jerking his mother's hand so violently; it looked like her arm might come loose from its socket. Trembling, Mariah put her hand over her heart and felt it pounding. Her eyes filled with tears, panic rose in her chest.

"You know, Bill, the economy and the weather are so agreeable here, you can work in your shorts all year long," Olivia bragged. She looked over to wink at her sister and saw that Mariah was lagging behind. It was only then, that Olivia noticed her misty eyes. "What's the matter with you, little sister? I know you aren't crazy about living in Seattle, but you don't have to cry about it."

"I don't know," said Mariah, rubbing the birthmark on her index finger, trying hard to compose herself. "I just felt something sad as I watched that boat sail away." She pointed out to the now disappearing *Camrita.*

"Something from another lifetime, no doubt. God, once a witch, always a witch," Olivia quipped, holding up Mariah's finger with the star shaped symbol. She put her arms around her sister, hugging her tightly. "I thought you might have outgrown that stuff by now. Although—you do have that incredible magic mark!" Olivia was trying to be funny, but it seemed to annoy her sister rather than humor her.

"I'm not a *witch,* Olivia," Mariah said, clutching her left hand with her right one. "And you know damn well this is just a birthmark, not some kind of *magic* symbol," she declared holding up her index finger. "I have keen intuition and I sense things sometimes. It's not something I'm going to outgrow." Mariah's family had always made light of her visions. "A few minutes ago, I saw a name on a sailboat and heard a screaming child and it triggered something in my subconscious." She put her hands over her heart. "That's what made me cry."

"You are so fucking weird, Mariah, for God's sake!" Bill said in disgust. "Give it a rest, will you?"

"I'm not *weird.* You're just incredibly shallow," Mariah fired back at him with rare self-confidence. "Don't start with me, Bill. We're on vacation. If you can't be civil, then stay away from me." Bill stood with his mouth open, mentally preparing a verbal attack but changed his mind. It was best left alone, at least for now.

Olivia tightened her hug around her sister and brushed away her tears. "You know Mariah, we don't have a weekly classified newspaper on this island and it's sooooo needed." Olivia tried changing the subject to something Mariah was interested in. "There aren't any decent secondhand stores on the island either and people need a way to buy good used items for a fair price." Olivia saw she had Mariah's full attention. "It's not as though someone can load up a U-Haul with their household possessions and drive here."

"That's for sure," Bill mumbled. Olivia went on describing her community's need for a niche 'penny-saver' style newspaper.

Mariah had worked at a small community paper in Idaho before moving to Seattle and she admired everything about the business—its owner, the lean way it was run, the profits, the effectiveness and it's consistent popularity. "You've always wanted to start your own publication, Mariah, and you would actually have the only classified one on the island." Olivia added, ignoring Bill. "Hell, our power-boat rental business is booming, like everything else on the island. It's fantastic living in a place that's warm and profitable year 'round!"

For Mariah, this tropical world held endless opportunities and she realized she hadn't felt creative and energized in a long while. She let her sister ramble on with her island sales pitch. She knew Bill would be a hard sell. Who knew? Perhaps Olivia could win him over.

When they returned to their condo, Mariah wasted no time at all getting back on the beach. Already, her skin was turning a rich, dark brown. "Hey, Blackie!" Olivia called as she walked the white sandy beach at Secret Harbor. "Remember when we used to call you that, Mariah?" She took the sunscreen and spread some on her sister's back. "I would lay in the sun for days but never get as tan as you."

Bill was sick of listening to their sister-banter and made every effort not to listen. He already knew about their father's grandmother being Afro-American, as well as psychic and Mariah was the only one in the family who inherited the dark skin and the insightful gift. *Who cares? I can turn dark too,* he thought, rolling over on his back.

"Wow, Olivia. I can't believe how much I'm enjoying the ocean again. I've been a northwest mountain woman this past decade, but it's so soothing to hear the wind in the palm trees and watch the pelicans dive for their dinner." Mariah paused and took a deep breath. Several brown pelicans were swooping in front of them. "When I left Florida, I swore I would never live in the tropics again because I couldn't take the severe heat, but this island is a true paradise. Who'd have ever thought you could actually travel further south, and the temperature would be cooler?" Indeed, soft trade winds continually cooled the fragrant air. Mariah loved beautiful scenery and a pleasing climate and St. Thomas had it all.

"I also enjoy the off-beat rhythm of this place—it's something I've missed since we moved to the 'burbs. That's one thing I loved about Idaho, its lack of structure. But, I sure got tired of those winters!" Bill only grunted and rolled over again on his towel.

"We really should consider moving here, honey!" Mariah blurted. "Western Washington is so dreary and we've both said more than once that our jobs bore us to death." She looked her husband in the eyes. "I'm serious Bill. It fills me with despair that we have settled for that life—there's no magic in any of it!"

Bill was stunned. *Hell, I didn't think she'd go in for the kill so soon—we've only been here a few days.* He hated it whenever she went off on tangents about *magic* and *vibrations.* He had no patience for her 'woo woo' philosophy but he decided to feign amusement at the suggestion while they were in Olivia's presence. "Oh sure, Mariah. I'll call my boss and tell him I'm not coming back!" His dripping sarcasm was not lost on Mariah. Later on, when they returned to their condo, he unloaded on his wife.

"Why aren't you ever satisfied, Mariah? We just moved to Redmond three years ago, and now you want to move again! Maybe it isn't good enough for you, but I think we have a nice life there and I won't let you fuck it all up." Bill was pacing back and forth on their deck. The palm trees danced and swayed in the moonlight, attempting to seduce him, but Bill was unflappable. Mariah saw how contrary she was to her husband. He was motivated by fear and she was motivated by adventure.

Why did I marry this man? she wondered. *He would rather work in the rain than come here and make money in the sunshine.* Mariah hadn't noticed their blatant differences when they first started out because everyone is on their best behavior in the beginning of a relationship. Her husband was becoming more rigid the older he got and his best behavior was long gone.

In spite of Bill's attitude, the remainder of their vacation was relaxed and fun. They went on Olivia and Steve's boat and explored nearby islands with some of their friends. "I just love the people we've met. They have great stories!" Mariah gave her sister a thumbs-up. Bill rolled his eyes and grunted. "They're my kind of people—daring and interesting!"

As the days passed, she dreaded their return to Seattle even though she was anxious to pick up her children at the Miami airport. Her eyes were riveted to the car's open window the morning they drove to catch their flight and she soaked up the last bit of scenery. She stamped it on her memory knowing that in twelve hours, they would land in the damp Seattle rain. The anticipation of it felt unfamiliar and odd, even though she had called the Pacific Northwest home for the past three years.

Chapter Twenty-three

St. Thomas became an obsession with Mariah. It was hard to concentrate at work between daydreaming about moving and starting her own publication in the Caribbean. She came up with the name*: The Trade Winds Trading Post and* designed a logo along with laying out a mock issue. She had paintings from the Virgin Islands hanging on her walls and she tucked her children into bed each night with her tropical tales. She imagined her children swimming every day, their skin tanned from the sun. She had grown up that way and wanted the same healthy lifestyle for her kids. When the opportunity presented itself, Mariah carefully broached the subject to her ever-reluctant husband.

"The real estate market is strong now, Bill. I'll bet we could make a healthy profit on our house. Then we could trade our foul weather gear for tanning lotion!" Bill was disinterested, but Mariah pressed on. "Jason and Emily hardly know our families. Now, with Olivia expecting a baby, our kids could actually grow up with one of their cousins." Still, there was no reaction. *I hate it when he ignores me,* Mariah thought. "I want to live around family, Bill."

"Damn it, woman! Why can't you ever be satisfied with what we have? Why do you need to stir things up when our lives are going so well?"

"I am satisfied, Bill, but I'm not thrilled and I think we deserve to be thrilled with our lives. Besides, I don't feel things are going well here. We're mortgaged to the hilt and we both work constantly to make our payments. Our children practically live at the daycare center—which we swore we would not let happen—and neither one of us has formed a real, meaningful friendship since we moved here." Bill couldn't have gotten a word in if he tried. Mariah was just getting warmed up. "We have acquaintances from work but they're not like the friends we had in Idaho." She paused to take a breath before continuing. "We don't fit here, Bill—not really. We didn't move here because it touched our souls." Mariah got up and walked to the window and watched their neighbor's BMW disappear into their Bat-Cave garage. "This affluent suburb is all about material wealth and ever since we moved here, we've been caught up in making money. I feel out-of-balance." Mariah's eyes searched her husband's soul. "None of it matters to me." *Please God. He so seldom hears me. Let him hear me now,* she silently prayed.

"Life is too short to remain in boring situations just because they seem secure. I am not afraid of change if we can live a better life," Mariah urged. "Come on, Bill. We both have nieces and nephews we hardly know because we've lived so far away. I want to be closer to family and live in a place that is not only beautiful and warm, but full of opportunities!"

It was a long, tedious conversation but Mariah was determined and she stayed focused on her dreams. It helped that the company Bill worked for had a huge restructuring and his job was not real stable. Outside their mortgaged house, the rain continued to fall.

"There's a construction boom in St. Thomas, honey and sparse competition. It's foolish to stay here working in this rain when we could be making steady money in paradise."

The storm was subsiding and Bill joined his wife by the picture window. "I don't know, Mariah. Maybe you've got a point."

His voice revealed his reluctance but he seemed to be coming around. "I suppose we could put our things in storage and if we don't like living in the islands, we can move to Florida instead." Bill had talked about moving to Florida ever since his mother settled there, but Mariah was well beyond that place. All the same, he seemed to be softening, so she nodded as if Florida was an alternative. She knew they would like it on St. Thomas. *What's not to like?*

Her dreams were coming true! Within ten months of their vacation, Bill and Mariah had sold their house for a decent price and were on their way to island living. Their parents thought they were being impulsive and Bill made sure to tell them it was all Mariah's idea.

"If this doesn't work out, Mariah, you'll be getting *three* jobs to put us back together again." He got agitated while they were packing. "This is your idea, so don't be surprised if it sucks!" Bill felt powerful when he belittled his wife.

"Don't go through with this if you're against it!" Mariah fired back. "No one has a gun to your head." She was tired of his negativity and had made up her mind she would go, whether he went or not. "Stay here in the rain, if you must. This can be a wonderful experience or a miserable one. It's a choice, and I choose to make it wonderful." Bill's choice was misery.

Chapter Twenty-four

1986

Since their arrival on the island, Bill's construction talent was in demand because of the healthy island economy. Mariah was also busy doing freelance graphic work for various advertising agencies and she was determined to eventually start her own publication.

"I've been thinking about trying to get an SBA loan to start my business, honey. What do you think?" Mariah asked while putting the finishing touches on dinner.

"Oh, sure. That's perfect. More debt! What a great idea."

Why do I try to get support from him, she thought as she set the table. *I'll talk to Steve about it. He's a good businessman and he'll believe in me.*

The next morning, she called her brother-in-law and invited him to lunch. "Bring Olivia and the baby if you like," she told him.

"Actually, Olivia is taking him to the doctor this afternoon. He has an ear infection."

"That's got to be rough. Poor baby."

"Yeah, it's rough on all of us. Sleep is a thing of the past these days." He yawned. "I'll meet you at Horsefeathers, say around noon? They have the best pizza on the island and I'm in the mood for anchovies." Steve knew Mariah was an anchovy fan, too.

"Sounds perfect. I'll be there."

Mariah got there first and ordered a couple of beers while she watched some fishermen clean their morning catch. The air was an interesting mix of saltwater, diesel, fish and garlic. When Steve arrived and settled in, Mariah explained her dilemma.

"Your idea is great, Mariah and I know your *Trade Winds Trading Post* will take off like a house on fire! I'm pretty sure I can get my hands on about ten thousand dollars. It's all yours, if you think it's enough to get you on your way."

"Are you kidding? That would be great! Are you sure it won't pose any hardship on you and Olivia?" she asked. "I could sure use the cash to open my doors."

"No hardships on our end, sweetheart—except for our lack of sleep since Jeffrey was born." He yawned again and stretched his arms over his head. "You take the money and make us proud. I believe in you, sis," he added with a warm smile.

What a difference from my own husband, Mariah reflected as she drove to her next appointment. She knew she could do all the administrative tasks, the graphics and the distribution for her new business. She just needed to find a top-notch salesperson to sell the advertising.

Jason and Emily had recently become friendly with a man who managed the video rental store at American Yacht Harbor, which was where they gathered after school. They jabbered about him almost every night at the dinner table. "Mom, his name is Karl and he's really cool. He lets us do chores for money and sometimes he gives us free drinks! Come and meet him when you pick us up. He said he wanted to meet our parents."

"Yeah, well, I want to meet him, too. He sounds like a nice man." After living in the Seattle area where there were missing children's faces on the sides of milk cartons, Mariah definitely wanted to meet anyone who interacted with her kids.

When she got to Red Hook after work, she went into the video store in hopes of finding her children, but they weren't there. As she walked down the aisle, she saw Karl waiting on some customers. Instantly, Mariah had a psychic attraction to him and in a quick flash, she saw the two them on a verandah covered with flowers. It overlooked fields of sugar cane blowing in the breeze. The image vanished as fast as it came and Mariah vaguely remembered it from her recent dreams. When Karl looked over and saw her, she flinched under his penetrating stare. She rubbed the star on her index finger, as was her nervous habit whenever she experienced such moments. He smiled, raised his eyebrows and motioned that he'd be right with her. Blankly, she read the back of one of the videos and waited.

Just then, she had another quick vision from a different dream. Karl was dressed in a white shirt with billowy sleeves, holding firm to her arm as he coaxed her up some dark wooden stairs. She obediently followed as he led her to his large mahogany, four-poster bed. *"You know this man, child,"* she heard herself whisper quietly in warning as she took off her clothes and surrendered her body. In a blur, the vision was gone. Standing in the aisle, Mariah blushed and glanced over at Karl. Her index finger burned and she rubbed it once again.

While he did seem somewhat familiar, she couldn't imagine where she might have met him before. She felt uneasy and a bit shy but quickly regained her composure as Karl came over to her. Mariah hadn't realized the couple he was waiting on had left.

"Hi, I'm Karl Vonschmidt. You must be Jason and Emily's mom. They told me you were the prettiest mom on St. Thomas."

What a charmer!

"I'm supposed to tell you they went to their friend Paul's boat. They should be back soon. They left over an hour ago."

"Thanks. I'm Mariah Patterson," she extended her hand and Karl put it to his lips for a kiss. *He's really too much.* "You look familiar, Karl. Have you ever lived in Seattle?" Mariah asked.

"No, I'm originally from Spain, but I did spend some time in California before I came here." In reality, he had spent much of his time bouncing from college to college partying up and down the coast of California. If it hadn't been for a job offer in the exotic Virgin Islands, Karl might still be in L.A. mooching off rich women.

"Spain, huh? That's an interesting place to be from. What brought you to St. Thomas?"

"I came to help get a new ad agency off the ground. Unfortunately, it never made it so I decided to stay for a while and work a stress-free job," he said as he looked around the store. "I'm thinking of doing some traveling around the Caribbean before returning to Spain." In reality, Karl's reckless lifestyle had taken a toll on his parents and they had cut off his trust fund. He wasn't welcome under their roof in Spain until he cleaned up his life.

"I do freelance graphic work for several ad agencies on the island and I remember when that one failed." Mariah guessed it was no fault of his. Karl seemed to be the kind of guy who could sell anything. "I think this island may be too small to support another agency," she added.

"Well, I guess it wasn't meant to be. I'm glad, actually, because the owner was a jerk to work for."

"True enough," Mariah laughed in agreement. She had unpaid invoices from that failed agency and did not like dealing with them at all. Karl seemed to have enough panache to be just the salesman she needed. He was well dressed, well spoken, bilingual and charming enough to sell anything.

"How would you like to work for me selling advertising?" she asked point blank. "I'm starting a publication, and I know it is going to take off like a house on fire! The ads should be pretty easy to sell because we need a classified alternative to the Island

Daily. They're expensive and I know we can undersell them by more than half," Mariah eyes lit up like fireworks as she talked about her new business.

"Well, this video store job would be hard to give up with all the numerous opportunities for advancement," he said sarcastically. "But hey, why not? It would be a challenge to help you get your new venture going. It's a great idea and the timing is right. When do I start?" Already attracted to Mariah's energy, Karl was intrigued by the idea of working with her. Her spark and ambition was just what he needed to help him get his life on track.

Four months earlier, Karl had hit bottom and finally realized his lifestyle was going to be the death of him if he didn't get help. He had almost been arrested at a bar for disorderly conduct. After boozing long into the night, he provoked a fight with a Puerto Rican man who had been flirting with his then-girlfriend, Manuella. She was an incredibly sexy, trust-fund girl from Argentina who he had enjoyed a hot, dysfunctional relationship with. After that incident, Karl broke up with Manuella and made an appointment with a therapist on the neighboring island of St. John.

Partying and avoiding responsibility had been Karl's continual life pattern. He was finally growing up and had begun to change his ways. With this new job offer before him, Karl could live clean, save money and gain favor with his family. One day, he would return to Spain and live the privileged life he sorely missed.

Chapter Twenty-five

"Go for it! Start the publication! Hire that Karl person! DO IT ALL!" Bill proclaimed his lip service in front of other people, but deep in his insecure soul, he felt nothing short of contempt for the whole idea. He was amazed by his wife's gumption, but he wrestled with the green dragon of jealousy. Bill couldn't handle Mariah becoming a success, not really. He was a man who let fear rule his life.

He resented Mariah's entrepreneurial spirit and grew to despise the idea of her operating a business. Bill also resented her gregarious, good-looking sales rep, although he did find one thing fascinating about Karl—his choice of women. Bill considered Manuella the sexiest woman on the island, and thought Karl an idiot to break off a relationship with such a gorgeous female. He noticed her at various social events around the island and he lusted after her, as did many men. Bill fantasized about Manuella constantly—he even began writing poetry about her! He found himself daydreaming about the satisfaction he would feel if he ever had the opportunity to take up with her.

Mariah never suspected the depth of his passion for her. All men drooled over Manuella and Mariah teased Bill about her being his *eye candy*. Perhaps she was a bit naive, but she had never been the jealous type.

Over time, Karl became more and more helpful when it came to her children as well as the business. In fact, he was overly accommodating when it came to Jason and Emily. She knew Karl enjoyed kids but she marveled at how he worked himself into the role of *uncle*. It was almost as though he owed it to her somehow. Since Jason and Emily already trusted him, Karl started picking them up after school. He did the marketing for Mariah in between appointments and kept the kids occupied in the office so Mariah could meet their deadlines week after week.

Bill seethed whenever Karl came around. He could see Karl was more than picking up the slack in his family and he was not about to look at his behavior to see why there was fatherly slack in the first place. "What is going on with you and that gigolo, Mariah?" he demanded. "You two seem to be playing house, as well as office these days." He delighted in accusing his wife. It made him feel powerful to project his own thoughts of infidelity on her.

"There is not a damn thing going on with Karl and me! If you were around more often, you would see that for yourself," she fired back.

"It's too bad Mommy is so busy since she started her own business," he would tell the kids. "It seems she can't find time to tuck you guys in, or read to you anymore."

"Why can't you read to us, Daddy? Mommy has always read to us." Emily responded, sticking up for her mom.

"Because Daddy has an important show to watch tonight, Sweetheart. Maybe I will tomorrow." He tucked them in and turned off their light before going to the living room to watch football.

Bill began going on long weekend boating trips with his friends to St. Maarten. Coincidentally, the exotic half-French, half-Dutch island had become Manuella's most recent haunt.

Tension was growing between Bill and Mariah. "Why are you going away now, Bill? Thanksgiving is less than a week away and my family is coming. I could really use some help getting things prepared."

"A friend of mine needs me to be part of his crew for a race. I'll be back before turkey time, I promise."

Mariah knew he was lying about a race. She covered the racing circuit in her publication and there was no sailing event in St. Maarten that weekend. She said nothing, giving him enough rope to hang himself. With their marriage at odds, Mariah dreaded the upcoming holidays.

The night before Thanksgiving, Mariah and her family had dinner at an open-air restaurant overlooking the Caribbean Sea. "I didn't realize Bill was so into sailing," her father said. "He is going to be back in time for Thanksgiving dinner tomorrow, isn't he?"

"I really don't know what to tell you, Dad. He's been in his own orbit for weeks now." Thankfully, her Father did not pursue the matter any further.

The next afternoon, Bill arrived home an hour before the family feast was served. He needed a shave and his attitude was smug and cool.

"Where have you been, Bill?" Mariah asked. A friend of hers thought she had spotted Bill at a nightclub on St. Thomas, and mentioned it in passing to her the previous day. Now Mariah was sure the story about going to St. Maarten was a complete fabrication.

"Well, if you must know, I've been with Manuella. We've been getting to know each other in ways I've only fantasized about until now," his voice was confident and bold. "While you and Karl were busy being business buddies, Manuella and I have been consoling each other. How does that saying go? While the cat is too damn busy, the mice will play with each other—or something like that...." Bill let out a sarcastic laugh.

How does that other saying go? Mariah thought to herself, *Pride cometh before the fall.*

Mariah wanted to lash out at him and give him a piece of her mind but instead, she struggled to hold back tears and remain strong. She wasn't about to give him the satisfaction of showing him how hurt she was. Thanksgiving dinner was in two hours and she was determined to not ruin it for their whole family with their sordid marital drama.

Truly smitten with his conquest, Bill was oblivious to the fact that Manuella was only using him to get back at Karl. For months, she had seethed with jealously over his professional relationship with Mariah and hoped her little tryst with Bill would hurt them both.

When Karl heard what she had done, he was more relieved than ever to be rid of her. He knew more than anyone that that woman was poison.

Bill however, was in for a rude awakening.

Chapter Twenty six

"We've had fun together Bill, but I can't see you anymore." Manuella didn't even look at him while she spoke because she was busy packing her bag to go back to St. Maarten. They had been together for the better part of a week and Bill was still in blissful lust.

"I have a whole life that has nothing to do with you, nor do I want it to," she hissed.

"Are you joking?!! I just risked my *family* for you!" Bill shrieked. "Was this just a game to you, or what?"

"No, not a game! Just some fun times, that's all." Her tone was flip and she refused to look him in the eyes. "I'm not the settling down type. You need to realize this about me." Manuella had little regard for the men she left in her wake. "Please try to be glad it's ending this way—quick and clean." On St. Maarten, she already had another man who eagerly awaited her return.

Bill was horrified he had put his twelve-year marriage in jeopardy over a woman so flimsy. That night, he attempted some damage control. "Come on, Mariah—Please! You have to forgive me. I swear I'll never do anything like that again," he begged. "It's this island lifestyle. I knew it was going to be hard to adjust to, but you're the one who insisted on moving here." Guilt trips had always been Bill's specialty, but Mariah was surprised he would resort to such tactics while he was very much in the hot seat. "You've got to give me another chance."

"We've got to get through these holidays with all the family company that's coming." Mariah's parents had just gone back to Florida, but within ten days, Bill's relatives were arriving to celebrate Christmas. "I need some time." She spoke in a monotone. "Right now, it's all I can do to look at you."

"Come on, babe—we've been together for so long. You can't just throw it all away because of one little mistake," he pleaded.

"Little mistake! You threw away our lifelong commitment for a week of sex with the town slut." Mariah glared at her husband with disgust. "Don't talk to me unless it's absolutely necessary." She felt a familiar numbness draping over her and she knew she was shutting down.

A few days after Christmas, while at the beach with Bill's mother, sister and her children, Mariah broke down and began to cry. She tried to hide her emotions while she watched an adoring couple frolic in the water, but she couldn't pretend anymore.

"Mariah, what's wrong with you? Why in the world are you crying, for God's sake?" Bill's mom asked.

"Because I'm upset that your son cheated on me when I needed him most," Mariah blurted. "You might as well know that Bill has a sexy new girlfriend!"

Except for Mariah's sobs, there was complete silence for several minutes while her mother-in-law loaded her verbal gun. "Well, it is your duty to hold your family together, young lady, and overlook this minor indiscretion. Wives have done this for centuries. I'm sure it didn't mean a thing. Men will be men, after all." She spoke as if her son had used her car and returned it with an empty gas tank. "After all," she continued, "what was Bill to do with you devoting all your time and energy to your new business? He told me you hardly cook dinner anymore and that he has to do all the household chores, take care of the children and make a living. It's no wonder he found solace in someone else's arms." Bill had obviously learned his guilt trips from a real pro.

"Your son is a liar!" Mariah snapped. "He barely lifts a finger in our house." She shook her head and tried to calm down but her mother-in-law was poised and ready for a fight.

Suddenly, Mariah heard the far off voice of that mysterious woman shackled at sea on a wooden ship. *Never choose imprisonment of the heart, child.* An inner strength empowered her deflated spirit. Rubbing her birth-marked index finger, Mariah looked her staunch mother-in-law straight in the eyes. Her expression was stern and she looked like an evil warden.

"Bill is a self-centered, unsupportive control freak and I don't want him in my life anymore." Mariah said calmly. "You can be in denial all you want, but the truth is your son is a cheat and a liar. How dare you lecture me about duty." The conversation was over and her mother-in-law knew it by the tone in Mariah's voice. Both of them were glad their vacation was over the following day

That evening, Mariah watched as Bill brushed his teeth. It wasn't anything he did exactly—he just stood there gargling and rinsing, but at that very instant, she decided her marriage was over. Whatever feelings she had for Bill were gone. Now, all she felt was contempt. When she needed her husband to be her best friend, he had found another woman and Mariah wanted him gone.

She walked into the bathroom as he was wiping his mouth. "I'm filing for divorce and you need to look for another place to live. I want you out of my bed starting tonight. Sleep on the couch."

Bill was mortified. "Come on, Mariah!" He sounded like a whining child. "I thought we were working it out. We can't throw it all away. Things have been going so well!"

"Maybe in your mind, but not mine. I mean it Bill—we're through. I will never trust you again. Your choice to have an affair has shown me who you really are and I see you as a shallow, self-centered man whom I no longer want in my life. It's over." Mariah turned and went in their room and closed the door.

Bill didn't want a divorce and he tried everything he could think of to prevent it from happening. After his mother and sister left, he called their children in the living room for a family meeting.

"Mommy wants to break up our family and she wants me to move away. You guys don't want Daddy to move away, do you?"

The children stared at their mother in shock. "Mom! Why would you do such a thing! Please, don't make Daddy leave!" they cried in unison. Mariah was horrified he stooped so low, using their children that way.

"Kids, this is between your Dad and me and . . ."

"It's about *all* of us Mariah, and you know it! Try to get your eyes off yourself and think of your children." Both kids were crying and clinging to their father. Mariah had lost that round and she did her best to comfort the children and change the subject. A trip to the beach quelled the tension—if only for the moment.

Within the next week, Bill had found religion! He began going to church and bible studies, hoping it might save his family. He was also becoming 'Mr. Helpful' around the house. He picked up the kids, prepared dinner, and even went grocery shopping, but Mariah wasn't the least bit impressed.

Meanwhile, Karl took every opportunity to encourage their break-up. "Bill's religious pandering is pathetic, Mariah. You deserve better. Press on with your divorce and don't give in to any of his tricks."

Throughout the struggles of their drawn-out divorce, Karl was there for Mariah—spending time with her and the kids, listening to her complaints, praising her and telling her how special she was. He was her champion in the office, and she found herself leaning on him more than usual. Still, she held tight to her independence, refusing to rely on Karl or anyone. Mariah did need the support; she longed for it, but her survival instincts were in overdrive and there was something suspicious about Karl she didn't fully trust.

Her new creed was to not get used to a man being there for her. Her dissolving marriage was living proof.

After weeks of excuses, Bill still had not made any effort to move out so Mariah finally took action. She noticed a rental advertisement in the classifieds of her own publication and came home with it circled in red. She had already spoken to the landlord by phone.

"It's one big room with an alcove kitchen. The electricity and water is included and the view over Magens Bay is magnificent. Not bad for six hundred and fifty dollars a month," he explained.

"It sounds perfect. We'll take it. My soon-to-be-ex-husband will be over tonight to get moved in and settle up with you." Mariah smiled as she hung up the phone. Bill would have no more reasons to stall. When she and the children arrived home that afternoon, he was still at work.

"Kids, Aunt Olivia wants you to go over and play with Jeffrey for a while. Why don't you show her your artwork from school? She'll love it! She was just saying the other day how much she needed new pictures for her fridge." Mariah escorted Jason and Emily out the back door to her sister's house. She had called Olivia earlier with her plan.

While her children were busy next door, Mariah packed Bill's things and put it out on the front porch. The circled ad and directions to the apartment were taped to the top of the pile. Then she called a nearby locksmith to change the locks. By the time Bill got home, the message was as clear and the Caribbean sea. He loaded his truck with his scant belongings and realized this was the end.

Mariah sat quietly on the edge of her bed. She knew he would try to manipulate her if she allowed him inside the house but her mind was made up. He peered in through the louvers and called out to her, but she did not reply. There was nothing left to say. As she watched Bill pack his truck, she was tangled in mixed emotions. It was the end of their family unit and she grieved the loss of that. She felt sad for her children, but relief for herself. It was time to move on.

As he drove away, Mariah saw a glimpse of herself wearing a long skirt and an apron. Bill wore a wide brimmed hat and riding boots. He was ridiculing her in front of a group of slaves. She held up her left hand with her star-marked index finger pointed upwards. Looking into the eyes of the slaves, she winked. They smiled at her and nodded their support.

Not only was what just happened in terms of her marriage a lot to take in, her intuitive visions always left her a bit dazed. She was emotionally drained and she curled up on her bed and stared up at the slow moving ceiling fan. She dreaded the talk she would have to have with her children in a short while. But for now, she rested with an inner peace knowing she had done the right thing.

Chapter Twenty-seven

Bill declared war! The scorned husband instructed his lawyer to go after Mariah's business and do whatever it took to make things as difficult as possible for her. Included in the drama was Bill's mother who strongly urged him to go after custody of the children. She was wealthy enough to help him fight the issue in court and vindictive enough to hurt her daughter-in-law for not taking her advice.

Mariah was beside herself at the thought of losing custody. She was at her sister's house when she got the call from her lawyer. "Olivia, I can't BREATHE! OH, MY GOD!! They can't take my children from me!" She felt as though someone had taken a spear and stabbed her in the back. "This pain goes deep. You don't understand!" Mariah shrieked.

"Of course I understand, Mariah. I just know it's going to work out. Please, try to relax." Olivia held her sister's hand, hoping to settle her but Mariah jerked her arm away and started pacing through the house.

"I CAN'T LET THEM TAKE MY BABIES FROM ME. NOT AGAIN! I CAN'T BEAR IT! I KNOW I CAN'T! !" Mariah was flailing her arms in the air. "OH MY GOD!! PLEASE, OLIVIA, DON'T LET IT HAPPEN. PLEASE! YOU HAVE TO HELP ME." Olivia tried to put her hand on her sister's shoulder and lead her to the couch, but she pushed her away.

Mariah rushed down to the beach below Olivia's house and began hurling rocks in the sea, but in her mind, she was throwing them at a horse-drawn carriage. She started screaming for attention from the driver. "God Damn it, Ramone!" she yelled. "I hate you! I hate you!" Once she caught her breath, she realized she was flailing between lifetimes.

Olivia heard her yelling out the name *Ramone* and was convinced her sister was having a nervous breakdown. She looked at Mariah and saw her body heaving as she sobbed. Her feet were bleeding from the rough coral and rock but she didn't seem to care.

"Who are you screaming at, Mariah?" Olivia called out from the deck railing. "Are you having a vision? You're scaring me, for God's sake! Who is *Ramone*?" She was familiar with her sister's intuition, but never had she seen her so out of control.

"These palm trees ... this place! ... A MAN TAKING MY CHILDREN AWAY FROM ME! It's all happening again, Olivia, don't you understand?" Mariah rubbed her index finger nervously while she paced back and forth over the rocks at the waters edge.

Olivia did NOT understand, although being a new mother, she could relate to the panic her sister was feeling. "Mariah, please try to calm yourself. Steve already told me he will help you pay for the legal defense so it WON'T happen—*again* ...please, come up here and sit down. Let me get you an ice pack and some aspirin. We need to tend to those cuts on your feet!"

Mariah ignored her sister. Instead, she dove into the water and swam the length of the beach, which helped her to settle down. After her swim, she sat at the waters edge and tried to focus on what was happening now. Having her mind flip back in time with such clarity left her with a feeling of vertigo. Eventually, she came up into the bathroom and splashed water on her face and neck. "I'll be OK," she said flatly as she dried herself with a towel.

She then went and laid by the edge of the hot tub. And still, yet another vision was brought on. In it, she was laying naked by the edge of a magnificent waterfall, feeling the same fear and exhaustion as she had just experienced. Suddenly, in the vision, she sat up and looked right at Mariah and whispered: *"It is all right. It was not he who had your children sold, but he did applaud the act. In this life, he is powerless over you."*

In an instant, the image was gone and she saw Olivia on her couch, holding Jeffrey close to her breast. Mariah breathed in the salt-scented air and gradually her heart rate began to slow down. Tears of relief streamed down her cheeks. She continued to take deep breaths until she felt strong enough to walk next door. Olivia put her baby to bed and then attended to her distraught sister.

Fortunately for Mariah, Bill's mother was much like her son in regard to follow through. He couldn't handle the children anyway and the issue disappeared a few months after it had begun. Thousands of dollars later, the couple was finally legally free of one another and Mariah was granted full custody of their children.

Chapter Twenty-eight

Matthew Baxter, Mariah's circulation man, often stopped in the office to bolster her spirits and Mariah was pleased that she'd had the sense to hire him. Ever since she met him, he periodically appeared in Mariah's dreams. In them, he was usually her loving father, which explained his natural protectiveness over her.

Matthew suspected Karl had ulterior motives and his dubious thoughts were confirmed when he met, quite by coincidence, some people who knew Karl in Spain. They were hardly reserved when telling their *Karl* stories and Matthew silently vowed to keep an eye on that good-looking, smooth-talking Spaniard.

"You're a big girl, Mariah, but I want you to watch yourself with him. He's a snake in the grass, that one," he warned. She listened to the words but her judgment was clouded. She assumed Matthew's dislike of Karl was merely a personality clash between the two.

"You watch my back, and I'll keep this machine going so we can all get paid," Mariah said to him one afternoon after he had made his deliveries. "Like him or not, we can't afford to lose him."

Matthew couldn't argue that fact—Karl was an outstanding salesman.

The next week, after a family dinner, the two sisters were chatting about various things. Olivia could see Mariah had a lot on her mind. "I've been thinking about selling the *Trading Post* and moving back to the mainland. I don't really want to, but this island is so expensive and I'm drowning in lawyer bills from the divorce. I'm feeling panicky and selling my business seems to be a solution. What do you think?"

"Well, it's certainly one idea but not necessarily the right one." Olivia loved having her family on the island and didn't want them to leave. "You have a good business going Mariah, but at this stage of its growth, what could you possibly get for it? You would have to start all over someplace else and go back to working for *the man* again! I know you don't want to do that! You've become too damn bossy to work for anyone," Olivia said with a laugh. "Plus, Jeffrey needs to grow up with his cousins and his Auntie Mariah around to spoil him."

"I know, you're right. I'm just scared and don't know what else to do. I think I'll put an ad in the classified section of the Wall Street Journal and see what happens."

A few weeks later, Karl was catching up on stateside news in the office with his feet on his desk, and the ad in the Journal popped out at him like a slap in the face. "What the hell are you doing Mariah?" he shrieked, pointing to the page. "Were you going to consult with me about this, or were you just going to do whatever you wanted?"

Unbeknown to Mariah, Karl had been telling people he was the owner of the publication and Mariah was his partner. Many clients assumed that spin to be true, mostly because in Karl's mind, they *were* partners. He was becoming more obsessed with her and their business association every day and he couldn't allow her to sell the publication and move away. He needed them to stay a team. Inspite of having his own agenda, Karl genuinely loved her and her kids and wanted the best for them all.

"I can sell even more ads now that the *Trading Post* has such island-wide popularity. There'll be plenty of money to keep us supported," Karl assured her. He needed her energy to keep him motivated and he loved being part of her family. He was counting on his parents to be impressed by Mariah's intelligence, ambition and accomplishments enough to overlook her dark skin. Karl had long-range plans for them—plans Mariah knew nothing about. In a few years, when the business was worth more money, he wanted her to make him a full partner and then sell. With a business success under his belt and a happy family in tow, Karl was confident that when she was out of her divorce mess, she would realize how much she needed him. He would make her see things his way. After all, he was a master at working situations to his advantage—or so he thought.

"What I do is my decision, Karl and you are just going to have to accept that, even if you don't like it."

He didn't like and it and he slammed the copy of the Wall Street Journal on his desk, grabbed his sunglasses and headed for the door. "Fine! Since you don't care about the business anymore, I guess I don't either. I'm going to the beach."

It was three days before Karl came back to work.

Chapter Twenty-nine

Ron James was a young, successful businessman from Chicago who loved the tropics. He often daydreamed of having a small business on an island in the Caribbean—nothing too stressful, just something he could build and watch grow. Whenever he found himself with a free moment, he would close the door to his office and take his tropical magazines and travel brochures out of his desk and look at the pictures of sandy beaches with relaxed people lying in hammocks, drinking cocktails, and enjoying life. When it came to *Islands* magazine, he especially enjoyed the classifieds. Often, he would take his highlighter and circle houses and businesses that interested him that were for sale. The truth be known, he had never actually contacted any of them—at least, not yet.

At the age of twenty-three, Ron started a one-hour photo developing business and his concept took off like a forest fire. Before long, he was the owner of the Photo Block Corporation. His popular operation had forty-five drive-thru locations all over the country and more on the way. By the time he was thirty-five, he was wealthier than he could have ever imagined.

Although his business grew each year, he was continually looking into side ventures to invest in—start-ups he could help develop. He needed constant stimulation to keep him happy and business gave him that. The more stress his work-pace added to his life, the better he operated, and his empire did nothing but flourish.

His marriage, on the other hand, was mediocre at best. If not for his two beautiful daughters, he may well have abandoned the concept of wedded bliss. His wife had long ago chosen the joys of country clubs, social engagements and over indulgence in the material world over loving communication, sex and a happy relationship. The void he felt from the lack of intimacy was nothing short of a deep cavity in his heart. The only antidote to ward off his loneliness was more work. Business was his only diversion from the cold emptiness in his life.

Mariah's classified ad contract was about to run out with a zero result, to date. Oh, there had been a few calls from dreamers with empty wallets, but not a single serious businessperson. Meanwhile, Karl had almost convinced her they could continue to build the business. If no one inquired by week's end, Mariah decided she would take it off the market and stay on island, at least, for now.

Ron was completely taken off guard by the tiny ad in the Wall Street Journal. *Stop talking about it—do it! Move to the Caribbean and run your own popular, publication. Growing, exciting, well established weekly. Call today for details.* Ron read the ad several times, circled it and started to put the paper down, but stopped himself.

"Publishing. That would be something different," he said to himself, staring at the ad. He stared at the page so long, his eyes nearly glazed over. He could almost smell the salt air and feel the breeze on his face. Impulsively, he dialed the number and when Mariah answered, Ron felt her energy charging through the receiver like electrical current. He almost hung up, but his curiosity took over and he had to see it through.

"Hello. I am Ron James, and I saw your ad in the Wall Street Journal about a publishing business for sale."

"Good morning Mr. James. You are a brave soul to inquire about a business in this potential disaster area. You've probably seen our hurricane weather forecast on the news these past few days." Mariah replied with candid honesty.

They chatted for a few minutes and in spite of the threatening weather forecast, Ron told her he'd be there in a week to meet her and check out the operation. He hung up the phone with renewed excitement. "Rose, get my travel agent on the line, please," he told his secretary. "I'm going to be out of the office for a few days."

He had no idea that waiting to go to St. Thomas was going to be such torture. It wasn't as if he didn't have enough to keep him occupied. His desk was a nightmare and everyone needed him to make decisions and put out fires. Three more states were opening Photoblocks and his schedule was more than full. But all he could think of was going to St. Thomas. Ron knew nothing about publishing, but he knew a lot about business. And, he was inexplicably drawn to the enthusiasm in Mariah's voice. He found himself looking forward to meeting her and seeing her thriving publishing operation.

Historically, September is the highest risk month for hurricanes in the Caribbean and Hurricane Hugo was already big news on the weather channels. It was a direct hit to St. Croix and St. Thomas got hit with the outer bands just three days before Ron was due to arrive. Hugo did the worst of its damage to St. Croix, but St. Thomas had close to forty-five percent devastation when it had done it's worst.

Ron watched the news channels the day before he was to leave and he tried calling Mariah for a damage report but the phone lines were down. He thought about canceling his trip but felt strangely curious about the condition of the island. The ticket was bought, and the airport was open. Hurricanes were a freak of nature and Ron figured if there were a lot of damage, it would be a temporary setback. Economies often thrived after a disaster from all the rebuilding. In fact, the publication could well be in for some good months ahead if much of the competition was out of commission.

Once he arrived on the island, he drove his rental car to the east end of the island. Along the way, he marveled at Mother Nature's raw strength. Palm trees were either stripped bare, or the fronds hung limp. Roofs were ripped off many of the houses and roads were buckled in several places.

As Ron approached Mariah's office, the many noisy generators in the parking lot greeted him. There was still no electricity in the area and Mariah felt embarrassed at their *Hooterville* set-up. She thought his interest was some sort of morbid curiosity at this point. *Maybe he needs an excuse for a tax-free getaway,* she thought.

When he walked into her office, Mariah looked right at him and was startled to her core. Ron was instantly familiar to her and she gave him a warm smile. "Hi, I'm Mariah," she said while extending her hand. He took it and smiled. "Why don't we close up the office and go across the street. I could use a cold beer right about now. Business has been slow with the phones and the electricity down."

He glanced at his watch and saw that it was three-thirty in the afternoon. "Sure, why not? This is one of the many reasons I love the Caribbean—no hang-ups about locking up and taking a beer break in the middle of the day! If we did this in Illinois, we'd be seriously gossiped about!"

Mariah put a note on the door before locking her office. "Slowing down is the general way of life in the West Indies, which is one of the many reasons I live here." He smiled in agreement and they walked across the street to Rummy's, which overlooked the small marina. At first, their conversation was about the hurricane, but they quickly found a comfort level with each other.

"I feel as though I've met you before. You seem very familiar to me, somehow," Mariah finally said, once they had ordered their beers.

"It's strange you would say that. I felt that same way when I heard your voice over the phone before I got here. But then, when I saw you, I wasn't so sure." Ron said. They went through the typical list of their past associations, but could not find a single connection. Still, Mariah felt sure she had known him from somewhere.

Later that night, they had dinner together and Ron listened to Mariah go on and on about her business. He saw how animated she became with the telling, and he sensed her passion for her creation.

"You don't really want to sell, do you?" Ron asked when she was through. Reluctantly, Mariah shook her head 'no'. "Why am I here, then? Your publication is barely off the ground and it seems to still need your leadership." Mariah shrugged and realized he had made this trip for naught. Truth be known, she wanted the money from selling, but she wasn't really ready to part with it.

As he spoke, his voice faded to a mumble and Mariah saw a split-second image of him talking to her about business matters in another time and place. Again, she was wearing a long skirt and apron. He was frail and sick, yet anxious to explain to her how to manage things after he passed on. *"This is your friend,"* said the voice of her spirit woman. Her vision followed gently. Her eyes looked straight into Mariah's soul. *"We are safe with him."* The scene passed as quickly as it came and because of it, Mariah felt instant trust in Ron.

"Are you OK, Mariah?" Ron asked. "You look a little pale. Should we go outside for some more air?"

"No, it's OK. I'm fine," she took a deep breath and let it out, slowly. "Sometimes I get images, like a flash of information—sort of like a déja-vu thing." Mariah stopped herself realizing she was being too candid and personal for a business meeting.

"What do you mean? Did it just happen to you?" Ron looked puzzled and a bit concerned.

"Yes, actually, it did." Mariah gulped. *God! How I wish I could shove those words back in my mouth!* Now, she was in too deep to let it be, so she continued on. "I believe in the possibility of reincarnation, Ron and I feel as though you and I might have known each other before. That's why we couldn't figure out where we knew each other this afternoon. Perhaps the recognition is on a soul level rather than the conscious." Mariah hoped he would leave it at that. She rubbed her burning index finger nervously and hoped he wouldn't think she was some *new-age* mental case.

"I do agree you are familiar to me, as well. Was your image of us specific?" he was not at all put off by her comments.

Sensing his genuine interest, she immediately felt more at ease. "Somewhat. We were dressed in attire from another time period and you were showing me something important about business." Mariah replied. "You looked quite ill, but what you were showing me seemed urgent. That's all I saw. Weird, eh?" Ron nodded. "My sisters call me a witch—mostly to piss me off! I just have really strong intuition, that's the long and the short of it. My great grandmother had it, too."

"It seems a lot of women do." Ron smiled and exhaled. "I suppose it explains why we feel so comfortable with each other." Ron took a sip from his beer and smiled. "So, what's that strange mark on your finger," he asked, taking her hand for a closer look. "Is it a tattoo?"

"No. It's actually a birthmark? My sister's say it's my magic mark."

"It's unique, alright. Kind of mystic in a way."

"I suppose so." Mariah held her finger up and showed him how the star-like design went all the way around her finger like a ring. Ron smiled and nodded, but added nothing more.

She then told him about her divorce and why she felt the need to relocate to somewhere less expensive to raise her children.

Ron was impressed with her feisty nature, her honesty and her keen sense of survival. They sat in the ocean-side restaurant as the water flowed in a soothing rhythm through the mangroves. The island was magical in spite of the effects of the storm. The breezes were balm to Ron's frazzled nerves and unsettled emotions and Mariah's voice was like an old, favorite song. As he continued to watch and listen to her, he felt a deep, familiar peace. *Maybe she's right about us knowing each other in another time,* he thought. *I can't ever remember feeling this comfortable with a stranger before.*

They talked into the early evening as the restaurant began closing up around them. With no power, the island-wide curfew was eight pm. The friendly but law-abiding staff chased them out, and Mariah gave Ron a ride to his hotel. "Why don't we have breakfast and discuss an alternative to me actually buying your business outright?" Ron offered. He wanted the excuse to come to the islands frequently on business.

"Sure. I'll meet you here at nine o'clock. Thank you for a lovely time. I had fun getting to know you—*again!*" They both laughed. "You're a nice man, Ron." Mariah smiled and shook his hand before heading for her car.

That night, he lay awake thinking of a clever deal to offer her. It needed to appeal to her financial needs and give him the involvement he desired. Ron thought it would be fun to help build her thriving business. He listened to the ocean waves outside his window and felt free from anything that might hold him back.

To Ron's delight, Mariah was keen on the idea of a partnership, as long as she was the majority shareholder!

"I've been remembering my life in Seattle and how my kids spent so much time at the day care center." Mariah reminisced over coffee. "That's never been the way I wanted to raise my children. I want them with me and having my own business gives me that. If I sold it and moved to the states, I'd probably end up with some stuffy job that would sentence my kids back to daycare."

"You're right about that. I don't think you're the cubicle type! Let's close at my attorney's office in Chicago." Ron suggested. "That way, you can go to that big publishing trade show in October I recently read about. See, I did do some industry homework!"

Mariah laughed. "Sounds like a good plan. I could use a trip off-island!"

Chapter Thirty

Karl was relieved that Mariah had decided to keep her business. Together, he knew they were an unstoppable team and he continued to plan for a long relationship between them. He didn't know Ron James had called on the ad, much less that he was on island because Mariah chose to not tell him.

The day after Ron's offer, he stopped in the office to see Mariah. "I was hoping I could kidnap you for a few hours so you could join me and some great people I met at my hotel yesterday. We're going out on a powerboat." Ron said excitedly. "I hope you're not too busy."

"Hmm. Is that a trick question?" She smiled up at him, adding, "We're always *very* busy here."

Karl had been talking on the recently repaired telephone with his back to the door, when Ron came in. He turned around slowly to get a look of this strange man who was inviting Mariah to go boating. Karl mumbled something into the receiver about calling the person back. He glared at Ron and Mariah and wondered what the hell was going on.

Mariah glanced over at Karl and a glimpse of a scene of them flashed through her mind. Karl was beating Ron with a whip as he backhanded her across the face but she didn't flinch. She looked straight ahead with anguished eyes and said, *"See him for who he is, child."* As always, in an instant the image was gone. Mariah pushed her hair from her face in an effort to gain composure.

"Ron, this is my sales rep, Karl Vonschmidt," Mariah stated. Ron extended his hand and Karl reached for it. "Karl, this is my new partner, Ron James." Speechless, Karl limply shook Ron's hand.

"New partner, huh? Well, is that *so*?" Karl quickly gathered his things. "I think I'm done here for the day. I bid you both adieu." He felt as though he might explode at any minute so he got up and left the office, slamming the door behind him.

Ron was shocked at his attitude but Mariah excused it. "He has a lot of personal errands to run today. I'm sorry, but I need to *man* the office this afternoon. I'll have to pass on that boat invitation."

"No problem, some other time." Ron answered. He waved good-bye and left for the marina, leaving Mariah to her work.

Karl drove around the island trying to cool off. He couldn't believe Mariah had taken on a partner other than himself, even though he didn't have any money to buy in. He didn't care how rich or powerful Ron James was. He wasn't about to let him ruin his future plans.

Although he had no direct access to his family's money, Karl knew he had plenty of charisma. Once he calmed down, he began to feel confident he could still sell Mariah on himself, especially once Ron James got the hell off the island and went back to wherever he came from.

Chapter Thirty-one

Between dealing with her business, being a single mom and the drama of her divorce, Mariah felt much like a lone, tired sled dog. The last thing she was in the mood for was a romantic relationship, but now Karl seemed to have little else on his mind.

He started to seduce Mariah in his own, alluring way, knowing the best road to her heart was through her children. He continued to be the 'step-dad' she so desperately needed, which was easy since he genuinely loved her kids. Under his calm exterior, Karl still seethed about her selling part of her business to Ron, but it was necessary he put it to rest for the time being. Ron was in Chicago, and he and Mariah were together. Karl had lots of time to sweep her off her feet.

Her demeanor had changed and she seemed much more relaxed now that she had sufficient funds to pay her attorney. With her divorce well behind her, she could give her business and the rest of her life the attention it needed.

Conflicts with Bill about the children arose periodically, but overall, Mariah found them manageable. The absence of any support from Bill became the norm, and after seeing he had no intention of living up to his legal obligations, it wasn't worth the time and effort to pursue in court. Mariah was getting used to raising her children without help from Bill, but Karl was constantly urging her to take her ex-husband to task.

"You need to leave a paper trail, Mariah. You never know when Bill will rear his ugly head." Even though she knew it was good legal advise, she didn't have the energy or money for more lawyers.

Karl was pouring attention on Mariah in the form of sentimental cards, floral bouquets and continual flattery, more determined than ever to have his way.

Ron called the office periodically but Karl failed to give Mariah the messages. Ron could see that Karl was trying to undermine their partnership, although he said nothing directly to Mariah. In fact, she continually bragged about Karl's sales ability, stating what an asset he was to the business. Ron couldn't put his finger on anything specific, but he sensed Karl was less than above board in his professional life.

What he couldn't see was how obsessed Karl was with Mariah. Truth be told, Karl was reeling with possessiveness and consumed with feelings for Mariah and the lifestyle he so desperately wanted. The prodigal son dreamed of going home with a new family and money in his pocket. He envisioned this scenario often and it motivated him to stay on track and work diligently. Never having worked hard at anything in his life before, he rather enjoyed the feeling of accomplishment, which was a new sensation, to be sure.

At last, Karl had his way. Mariah couldn't resist the pull and welcomed him into her bed. Karl was extremely attentive and he stroked her bruised emotions. They operated a thriving business while attempting to establish a relationship. However, despite her initial delight, there was a general lack of true emotional availability on Karl's part, and that left Mariah feeling empty. The situation confused her because her basic domestic and professional needs were all being met and she found Karl surprisingly easy to live with. *Why am I not happy with this relationship? The kids like him and it all seems fine on the surface, but I feel lonely when I'm with him.* She questioned herself often, and hoped she could sort it all out.

They had been having a bumpy time at the office and decided they would retreat to the safety of home for some time to recoup. They closed the office early, vowing to leave their squabbles behind and spend time with the kids as a family. Mariah was exhausted from overwork and looked forward to a peaceful evening in paradise.

The temporarily reconciled couple stopped off at Marina Market to gather ingredients for a sumptuous dinner. They held hands as they entered the store and seemed to enjoy selecting everything from the Mahi Mahi to the French wine and candles for the table. When they moved to the checkout line, Karl impulsively kissed Mariah on the top of her head sending a ripple of warm relief down her spine.

"OOOOOO, meh son," said Kishma, their favorite checkout person, "Looks like you got limin' or some kind of romancin' on your mind." Her melodious West Indian voice and chest deep chuckle made Mariah smile as she absorbed the simple earthiness of the statement.

Why do I always have to over-think everything? Mariah mused as they walked toward the car. *I spend all this time sparring with Karl and look at him. He's gorgeous, he's good to the kids, he's a great roommate, he picks up the dry cleaning—why am I so critical and wary? Why am I scared to just let myself go in this relationship? OK! I'm going to give it up...right now and just have fun!* She punctuated her new conviction by giving the door of the car a good slam.

Arriving home, they parked the car and began ferrying the groceries up the long wooden boardwalk to *Crow's Nest,* their cozy home overlooking Magens Bay and the island of Hans Lollick. Mariah had found the place the previous year. She had fallen in love with the eccentricity of the multi-leveled wooden structure and the wildness of the location out on a windy point. Karl hated the place and longed to live in an expensive gated complex.

Emily and Jason were already both home and everyone was looking forward to being together and playing *Twister* after dinner. The kids had pre-set the table in anticipation of the special meal. Karl and Mariah shared a glass of wine and the dinner preparations. *This is the perfect family picture,* thought Mariah.

"You can go ahead and call the kids, Babe," suggested Mariah. She was suffused with good feeling and the deliciousness of the scene. Karl went to the head of the stairs. "OK you two...haul it in here, but wash your hands first," he offered good-naturedly.

Everyone sat down at the table to the beautifully prepared meal of fresh Mahi Mahi, coleslaw and rosemary potatoes. Mariah felt whole, yes, that was it. At that moment she felt more at home and whole than she had in months. When was the last time they had all been together, sitting down to a dinner she had thoroughly enjoyed making? Her heart smiled as she looked around the table.

"Karl," said Emily, "I've been meaning to ask you . . . who is that red-haired lady I see you pick up every day when I go outside in the school yard at lunchtime?" Karl's fork stopped midway between his plate and his mouth. In that nanosecond, all the energy in the room shifted. It was like the severe drop in barometric pressure before a hurricane. Mariah's heart was racing, her limbs immobile. The air went out of her lungs as though she had been slugged in the solar plexus by a sandbag. The whooshing sound escaped her involuntarily. And then she knew.

"I don't know what you mean, Sweetpea," answered Karl, as smoothly as if he might be telling the truth. "I don't know any red-haired ladies."

"Oh, I know it's you," persisted Emily. "One day, I even went over near the car and tried to get your attention. I saw the mocko-jumbie I gave you for your birthday hanging from the rear view mirror, but you didn't notice me. Almost every day, I look out and see you. The red-haired lady waits for you under a shade tree. She gets into the car and you both drive away. I even saw her kiss you," said Emily nonchalantly as she sucked a slice of mango into her mouth like a string of spaghetti.

Mariah was living a re-run. "Who's the red-head, Karl? Do I know her?"

"No, Sweetie, you don't." Karl was cool and smug and avoided looking in her eyes. "She is an old friend of mine from college who was here on vacation. I didn't mention her because she is not important—hardly worth the conversation."

"She's not important to you?" Mariah asked in a voice laced with suspicion. His explanation was hardly plausible, especially after he had just lied to Emily. His body language was dismissive and his lack of eye contact made him even more suspect. She knew he was lying, but she could not prove it.

"No, she isn't," he responded flatly.

"If you all will excuse me, I have a headache and need to lie down," Mariah said. "I want you two to clear the table and put the dishes in the dishwasher."

"OK, Mom, we will. Take some aspirin so you feel better." Jason said in a caring voice. He sensed his mother's discomfort and felt protective over her. Jason avoided speaking to Karl for the rest of the evening, even though he had originally planned on having Karl help him with his math homework. The *Twister* game never made it out of the hall closet and Karl got absorbed in a TV show once the dishes were done. Their cozy family evening came to an abrupt end.

Mariah went into their bedroom and had a good, hard cry. She was devastated that once again, the man in her life had betrayed her. The pain stung her heart like a swarm of angry wasps. She hoped Karl would come into the bedroom and attempt to console her, but he didn't. He was sticking to his story and had no intention of digging himself an even deeper hole.

Later that week, Mariah opened the *Island Daily* newspaper and saw a photo of Karl and a glamorous red-haired woman on the social page with a caption that read: "Look Who's an Item!" The story revealed that Karl's redhead was the new general manager at the Limetree Hotel, hardly some old college friend visiting on vacation. But when Mariah confronted Karl about the photo in the paper, he dismissed it.

"She came here on vacation and liked it so much she got a job and moved here. For God's sake Mariah, quit being so paranoid! We're old friends, that's all!" He scolded her with the arrogance of a corrupt politician.

With no proof to the contrary, Mariah struggled with forgiveness and tried to move past the red flags waving in her mind. But deep down, she knew she was right not to trust him. Alone in her bed one evening while Karl was at a business meeting, Mariah mumbled into her pillow, "Why can't I have a loving, supportive family life? All I want is some assurance that I am safe and loved. Instead, I feel betrayed and, I'm frightened for my children's welfare. God, help me to relax!"

Her little prayer was futile. Mariah knew she had sold out to false security, by ignoring her inner red flags. She felt enslaved by her responsibilities. If being with Karl kept food on their table, her kids well educated and her business afloat, then so be it. The price for keeping it all together was this emotional loneliness and she'd just have to pay it—at least for now. Her situation was hardly unique.

Chapter Thirty-two

For six years, Karl and Mariah maintained a rocky personal relationship. During that time, Karl had become increasingly disgruntled, which took a toll on them as a couple. After his years of service, he expected Mariah to give him a percentage of her business. Even though he had been paid handsomely over the years as the business continued to grow and he received invaluable benefits and perks, it wasn't enough for Karl. He felt entitled to partial ownership, and he assumed his loyalty and sales talent was enough to grant him automatic partnership.

Over the years, her partner, Ron James kept quiet about this issue. He and Mariah talked about other things but they avoided conversations about Karl's attitude and Mariah appreciated his sensitivity on the matter. She wondered if he thought her unprofessional to have entered into an intimate relationship with their top salesman, but he never let on that he did.

Over time, Mariah began loosing respect for Karl. He had behaved like a spoiled child, and he wore his entitlement like a monogram. She couldn't relate to his smug attitude. They were from completely different upbringings and did not see eye-to-eye on this matter.

Ron knew Karl was an asset to the business because their advertising numbers were steadily growing. But on a personal level, it confused him that Mariah would choose to be with someone as slick as Karl. He guessed Mariah was feeling somewhat trapped. She was juggling a lot, with supporting her children on her own and Ron knew what she paid herself. He wondered about people's choices and why they entered in and stayed with mates that didn't seem to suit them. He was hardly an expert on the subject, considering his own unfulfilling marriage. Mariah had issues to work through and apparently Karl was one of the many instrumental people in her life path. Whatever the reason, Ron was determined to watch her back. He had high regard for her and considered her a good friend as well as a business partner.

Chapter Thirty-three

"I can't imagine why, but ever since I've lived in the Caribbean, I've been drawn to the island of Martinique," Mariah admitted one afternoon after work while she and Karl were discussing vacation options. "For some reason, that place holds a mysterious fascination for me and I've always wanted to hike in the mountains and swim in the beautiful waterfalls." Mariah turned on her computer so she could look up Martinique on the web. "There are incredible flowers there, too. It's actually nicknamed the *flower island.* I could wear a different kind in my hair everyday!" For years, she had worn a fresh hibiscus behind her left ear on occasion.

"I know very little about that island, Sweetheart, but if that's where you want to go, that's the place." Karl tried to sound sincere but he couldn't have cared less about Martinique. He would have rather gone to St. Barths, a more chic, French isle full of wealthy, fashionable people—just the type of place Karl adored. But he knew his relationship needed some finesse so he decided to go wherever she wanted.

"My French is obviously not as good as my Spanish, but it should come back to me once I'm around it," said Karl. "I don't know if I ever mentioned it, but we had a maid when I was growing up who was from Paris and we had to speak to her in

French. Mother insisted on hiring an international staff because she wanted us speaking as many languages as we could." Matilda Vonschmidt worked as an interpreter at the embassy in Spain and she spoke German, Spanish, French, Italian, and Russian, all fluently.

On the second day of their vacation, Karl put on his bathing suit and began assembling a poolside deployment bag: his novel, tanning lotion, sunscreen, lip salve, the crossword puzzle from the daily paper and his cell phone. "Even *you* are looking a bit pale, Sweetie. We ought to turn a few shades darker today by the pool."

"I'm not sunbathing today, Karl. You can stay here and relax it you want, but I'm going to explore the countryside. I'm tan enough, thank you."

"Oh, sure, Honey. Yeah, right," he added compliantly. "Let's rent a car and drive around. I remember you said there are ruins here from the slave days and I know how much you love all that historic stuff." Karl lit a cigarette and put on his expensive Italian leather shoes. "Let's go exploring. I'll still bring this bag along," he said, stuffing towels into it. "And if we see a pretty beach somewhere, we'll take a swim. How does that sound?" Mariah nodded, smiling. Karl hoped they would find a beach sooner rather than later.

He couldn't have cared less about ruins from the slave days, as he had no particular objection to that way of life. Neither did he have any interest in hearing Mariah preach about oppression and the violation of human rights—again! Karl was a child of the seventies, but he had been raised a 'blue-blood' with old world values. His parents were wealthy Germans and his father had been high in the ranks of government. When it came time to flee Europe after the war, they went first to Brazil before settling in Spain, where they set their lives up even more lavishly than they had enjoyed in Germany. Numerous household servants waited on their every need.

"This sounds more like the kind of day I imagined," Mariah was a little surprised at how thoughtful Karl was being. His usual behavior was more self-centered. "Are you sure you want to come?"

"Sure, of course I do. I want to be with you every second of this vacation," he answered flatly, without a look in her direction.

He's got the lines. It's sincerity he lacks.

They rented a car and drove around the island and were confronted by bumpy, pot-holed roads that were much worse than St. Thomas' most remote by ways. Mariah spoke very little as she drove. The scenery was lush and the road leading to Marigot was becoming familiar to her in an odd sort of way. She imagined being in a horse drawn coach. There were thick forests of Mahogany trees stretching all the way to the tops of the mountains.

"I'll bet they get a lot of rain on this side of the island. Look how lush it is on the north facing slopes. That mango tree is loaded and so are those papaya trees over there," she said pointing to the sagging fruit trees. Karl was working on his crossword puzzle, totally removed from the moment. *Physically here, but emotionally absent. That's Karl.* She slowed down almost to a crawl when they came along the northeast coast, past Marigot, before Saint Marie. Her intuition was very keen and she paid close attention to her gut feelings.

"Why are you going so slowly, Babe?" Karl asked, looking up from his puzzle. Mariah said nothing and continued to creep along. "Hey! Mariah. Didn't you hear me? Why are you driving so slow?"

"SSSHHHHH. Be quiet, Karl. Please! I feel a strange sensation and I need you to let me be."

"Where the hell are you going now?" he asked, as she confidently turned right down an unmarked dirt road.

She glared at him but said nothing and continued driving for half a mile before instinctively turning left at the mouth of an overgrown driveway that was lined with grand, Royal Palms. It had been quite some time since her intuition had felt this strong and she didn't want distractions. "Please, Karl, pay attention. This area feels extremely familiar to me and I need to see what's down here. Doesn't it feel familiar to you?"

"No, it doesn't... well, maybe it reminds me of where you used to live next door to Olivia."

That wasn't it at all, but Mariah remained quiet. They had come upon the remains of an old plantation. "I love this long entrance with the palms," she said with a far-off tone to her voice. The trees were huge, many over eighty feet tall. In between them lived every color of bougainvillea, so overgrown; it was choking the Bird of Paradise struggling to survive along the base of the trees.

I know this place, she realized while getting out of the car. Her heart was racing and she began to perspire, despite the cooling trade winds. The great house was partially standing and all that appeared to be missing was half of two walls and the roof. When Mariah approached the front of the house with it's traditionally elegant, welcoming arms staircase, she was overcome by emotion. She looked to the left where the cone-shaped sugar mill stood behind the big tamarind tree. She was amazed to find it completely intact. A chill went down her spine when she noticed the broken grinding wheel leaning up against the outside wall of the mill. She stood there, staring at it and found it hard to breathe. "Have I seen this scene in a painting before? It's all so familiar," she asked out loud.

Mariah walked about an eighth of a mile against the hillside and stared out at what remained of the slave village. A few shacks still had a partial wall or two, but most of them had scant remains of their original foundations. Mariah stood in the middle of one of the shacks and felt heavy with grief. Someone she cared about had been sick in the shack where she stood and that person had passed away in her presence. Mariah felt sadness deep in her memory and she knew what she was experiencing was real.

Karl was more than bored with this situation and wondered why Mariah would waste their precious afternoon in such a deserted old place. He trailed a good distance behind her, being careful to not get mud on his Italian shoes.

Mariah wandered up to the great house and walked through what remained, as though she had entered the Twilight Zone. The banister, which led upstairs felt familiar in her grasp and she continued upward to look at the bedrooms. Karl was many yards behind her, debating whether to keep up or go back to the car. Curiosity caused him to follow.

When they were inside what had been the master bedroom, she stared at Karl, her eyes penetrating his exterior.

"You're giving me the creeps, Mariah. What's the matter with you?" He hadn't noticed her tears. "Come on, Babe, let's go back to the hotel, and lay by the pool. I could use some sun." As was his way, his voice was like a whiny child. Karl presented his arm, attempting to dramatize his fading tan line.

Mariah ignored his gesture, and continued to wander around, in spite of his protests. "Go back to the car if you don't find this interesting," she snapped, looking at him with much clearer vision.

"Actually, it's NOT interesting to me. It's downright miserable. This place is probably haunted with disgruntled old slaves!" Not realizing that his comment wasn't far from the truth, Karl went back to the car and struggled to find a radio station to entertain him while he waited for Mariah. She spent another twenty minutes wandering around the ruins. Periodically, she heard African voices singing along with a drumbeat, but the sounds faded as quickly as they came into her consciousness.

She then walked down to the beach on the well-worn path behind the house and breathed in the thick, humid, salt air. A large, weathered log seemed to beckon her to sit down. The wood felt smooth and familiar to her touch as she rubbed her hands across it. She felt certain she had been on that beach before. The log could well have served as her special thinking place, which was what she was doing now—thinking—not only about this plantation, but also about Karl and his suffocating obsession for her. Being in that place drove the dynamic between them to the front of her conscious mind. Life was more about the lessons than the details and she knew she needed to stay alert.

Mariah went back to the car and got in, but did not start the engine. "I'm going to hike up into the mountains and take a swim in the waterfall. Do you want to come with me?"

"What waterfall?" he asked. He got a guidebook out of the glove box and tried to find waterfalls located in that area.

"I didn't read about it in that pamphlet, I just know it's there," she said, pointing to the left of the mountain behind the slave shacks. "It's up there, about a quarter of a mile."

"Actually, I didn't wear the right shoes for a hike. I wish you had told me we were going off-road. I would have worn my Nikes," he said, looking down at his sleek imported loafers.

"I don't know why you insist on being so dressed up all the time. We headed out on an exploration. That kind of activity doesn't usually call for wearing expensive, slick bottomed dress shoes, Mr. G.Q." She smiled at him and he returned the expression, half-heartedly. "It doesn't matter. Stay here if you like, but I'm going. It's a gorgeous waterfall and the pool is easily accessible," she said with a strange confidence.

"How in the world could you possibly know this? You're freaking me out, Mariah. Did someone tell you about this place, or what?"

Her left index finger with the star birthmark began to itch and she rubbed it vigorously. "I just know about it, that's all. Turns out, I've been here before," she replied.

"I thought you said you had never been to Martinique,"

"I haven't been here, this time. It was in another life." Mariah was tying her shoe as she spoke. When she stood up, she saw Karl's shocked expression and it made her laugh. "Don't be so shortsighted, Karl," she said taking a towel from the beach bag before starting down the path. "Things are usually deeper than they seem." She added. "I'll be back in a little while. Come find me if you dare," she teased.

The trail curved around, out of Karl's view. He was somewhat curious about the waterfall, but not enough to soil his expensive shoes. Instead, he returned to his struggle with the radio tuner.

The breeze carried the familiar scent of local flowers. She knew exactly where the bends in the path were and was amazed at how well the trail had held up over the years. *Maybe the local kids come up here and swim,* she thought to herself. There was no sign on the main road indicating a waterfall, so likely no tourists ever ventured here. Mariah was delighted the area remained a private treasure. "It's MY special place," she said out loud to no one. She went down into a gut, still muddy from the rain. Once she was up the other side and around a bend, she heard the waterfall. The air had a heavy mist and the vegetation was thick with giant philodendron leaves climbing up every tree trunk. Hundreds of ferns exploded from cliffs along the edge of the sixty-foot falls and the air was filled with the symphony of green parrots. To the right of the pool was a huge flat boulder that protruded over the water like a natural diving board. She stood on it, relishing the moment.

"How many times have I come here to find some sense in my life?" she asked the heavens. She slipped off her clothes and dove into the water. Gliding through the cold, clear liquid, she released years of angst brought on by relationships with Karl and Bill. "Both unsuitable partners for me, yet for some reason, I chose them," she stated out loud. "Please," she prayed, climbing to the flat rock, "teach me what I need to learn so I can finally eliminate this sordid re-run. PLEASE!"

Mariah stayed by the waterfall for nearly an hour before heading back to the plantation. She wished Karl had joined her so they could both stay there all day, but he hadn't. She found it difficult to enjoy herself, knowing he was waiting for her in their small rental car. While she dressed, a flock of green parrots flew overhead and landed in the big tamarind tree at the far edge of the pool. "That's where they always nest," she remembered, listening to their squawking as they took residence in the tree. As Mariah walked back down the trail to Karl, she felt a pain in the pit of her stomach, a feeling she was sure she had felt many times walking that same path.

"So, how was the waterfall?" Karl asked. He accepted Mariah's non-committal response. For some reason, he began chatting incessantly on their way around the island back to the hotel. "What do you want to do for the rest of the afternoon? We could go shopping in Fort-de-France, perhaps, or maybe we can sign up for a sunset cruise. This brochure features a sail from Fort-de-France to Les Anses-d'Arlet and back again. It takes about two hours, and they serve cocktails and light fare."

"You can't be quiet for any length of time, can you, Karl?" Mariah stated, smiling at him. "Didn't you feel anything unusual back at that ruin? Are glamorous surroundings all you can think about?" Karl started to answer, but Mariah pressed on. "Does it occur to you that perhaps you and I have been down this road before? I don't know—maybe there are some issues together that we need to work out this time around?" Karl seemed utterly clueless but Mariah wasn't about to let his attitude stop her.

"Do you believe in karma? How about reincarnation?" Karl stared at her but said nothing. "I don't know that much about it, but often, I know I have been in a place before. I felt it back there. Don't you ever feel that déjà vu feeling?" She waited for him to answer but he didn't respond. This topic was not the least bit interesting to Karl. "Never mind," Mariah said.

When they got back to their hotel, Mariah went to their room to take a nap and Karl went to the pool and flirted with a woman he noticed when they first checked in. Mariah sat at the edge of the bed and thought of all the red flags she had felt since she got involved with him. Their perceptions of life were worlds apart. When she went downstairs to the pool and caught him making his moves on the slinky blonde—that was it! Her decision to leave him was as profound as the night she broke apart from Bill.

Chapter Thirty-four

It worried Mariah to break up with Karl. From the beginning, he had been a vital part of her business and she knew it would be difficult to find a replacement. He had indicated that he would be quitting soon. She began interviewing salespeople on the island and was delighted that there were several qualified candidates who wanted to work for her. *Perhaps things will be all right after all,* she thought to herself. *No one is irreplaceable!*

When Karl caught wind of Mariah's interview activities, he went ballistic. He had been traveling off-island and interviewing for various positions—very much planning to leave the publication—but on his terms, not hers. Their romantic relationship was over but he wasn't prepared for replacement at the business level—not until he had something substantial to go to. The mood in the office shifted dramatically and Mariah now understood why big companies had policies about inter-office relationships.

Karl's long-awaited dream of returning to Spain a successful businessman with a new family had been destroyed. Why did he do it?

Mariah's life was a struggle but she did not consider herself a victim. She had chosen both Karl and Bill of her own free will. *I'd better pay attention and maybe, I won't have to repeat this little drama again,* Mariah vowed to herself.

Within six months, Karl left the island and went back to Spain. Mariah promised herself she would try to make better choices and select men who would compliment her strengths. Someday she hoped to find someone who would embrace her strong character and not be threatened by it.

Chapter Thirty-five

It was a Mother's Day tradition for Mariah and her friend, Katie Barry to go on a trip together. Katie was a freelance writer who wrote feature articles for the *Trading Post.* From the first day they met, they became fast friends. Over time, they both felt there was some sort of soul connection to each other because their interaction had a familiarity right away, almost like reuniting with a long lost, special relative. Katie had gone to a therapist a while back who used hypnosis in his practice. She had experienced a few past life regressions during the sessions. In one lifetime, she had been a Huron Indian woman, and in the other, an African woman. Both times she had a child and she recognized them both as being Mariah.

"You and I are such awesome single parents, I think we deserve to go somewhere outrageous! How about Hawaii?" Katie asked over lunch. "What do you think?"

"I think it's a great idea! I've wanted to check out those islands for a possible relocation. They don't seem to get as many hurricanes as we do and since it's a state, they probably recover more efficiently when they do have one." After enduring many storms in the Caribbean over the years, she was tired of being braced for disaster.

Ron James had family reasons for not wanting to exercise his right to buy Mariah out so she was actively trying to sell her business. Several potential buyers surfaced but none with courage enough to buy it. Mariah was confident someone would take it off her hands when the time was right.

On Mother's Day, Mariah and Katie found themselves sipping cocktails at the beach bar of the Royal Hawaiian Hotel, on Waikiki beach.

"We've been single for a long time, Kate," said Mariah as she watched youthful honeymooners playing in the water. It had been several years since Karl had been in her life. "Sometimes, I long for a true partner—someone to share my life with. I'm tired of doing everything alone." Mariah sighed and took another sip of her fruity drink.

"I want a healthy relationship. All we've both had are men who thrive on power struggles. What we deserve is someone to respect us and not spar with us all the time."

"True! All three of my husbands sparred with me constantly and it was exhausting." Katie agreed. "Hey, WOW! Look at that sky!" They watched the sunset streak shades of red and pink across the vast Pacific sky.

"Let's put out a declaration to the universe, to God and all our spirit guides. We'll describe this partner out loud and concentrate on what we want." Katie suggested. "Be careful what you wish for," she added with a wink.

Katie went first. They were more concerned with virtue and character attributes then physical requirements. They each wanted partners who could soothe their souls, not someone to look good on their arm. They even made up names for these *dream-guys* so it would be easier to refer to them during the rest of their vacation. They pretended these men were real and already in their lives. Katie's future man was named *Dan,* and Mariah's was named *Sam.*

"Katie, *Dan* called while you were in the shower and said he'd meet you at the sushi bar in a half an hour," Mariah joked the next afternoon after their 'practical magic' at the Royal Hawaiian. "He wants you to wear something sexy."

"That *Dan* is always kidding around. Can I borrow your pink dress? He just loves me in that dress!" Katie jumped in and played along and throughout the evening, they continued with their boy-friend banter.

"What about you, Sweetie? Has *Sam* called? You two are probably doing something fabulous tonight, aren't you, Darlin'?"

"Of course we are. His helicopter is taking us over to Maui for dinner. Don't wait up."

"Yeah, right, uh huh. Pass me that TV Guide and let's see if there are any good movies on the tube tonight." Katie poured herself another glass of Merlot and they both had a good laugh.

Part Three

"If you wait for me, then I'll come to you.
Although I've traveled far,
I always hold a place for you in my heart.
If you think of me...
If you miss me once in a while...
then I'll return to you.
I'll return and fill that space in your heart..."

— Tracy Chapman

Chapter Thirty-six

1640

As Samuel began clearing the snow from his walkway, he thought back to how much he had loved winter when he was young. As a child, he used to make snow caves and pretend he was a whale fisherman with a large family living by the edge of the big waters. But over the years, Samuel dreaded winter's approach. It seemed to come earlier every year in this French Canadian province. The snow was already a foot deep and it was only late October.

It was Samuel de Fontaine's twenty-first birthday and his family was coming to see him. He brought in more wood and stoked the fire, wanting his house especially warm for his uncle, Jean Pierre. Nothing was too much trouble when it came to pleasing his uncle and in fact, Samuel often felt guilty for caring about him more than his own parents.

"Uncle Jean is so different from father," he said out loud to himself while stacking the wood. "Hell, father rarely ever stays long enough to take his coat off when he comes here." It was true. Henri de Fontaine was not comfortable in his own skin much less in his only son's oversized house.

Samuel took his rugs out earlier that morning and beat them to create a fresh smell. Suddenly, there was a single loud thud on the door and Samuel's father, Henri, bounded into the living room, without the courtesy of knocking snow and mud from his boots. At once, dark wet puddles formed on Samuel's clean floors.

"Where the hell are you, boy?" his father grumbled. "This house of yours is so damn big you did not even hear us coming in. How much *house* does one person need?"

"Hello, father. I heard you just fine. I was in the kitchen stoking the stove." Samuel reached out to shake his father's hand but as usual, Henri ignored the gesture. Samuel turned to his other parent. "Hello, mother. The oven is hot and ready for whatever you needed it for."

"Hello, son." Marie kissed him lightly on the cheek. "Thank you. I thought it would be nice to have the aroma of food cooking in your house, so I brought your birthday cake over here to warm up." His mother placed the cake carefully in the oven and came over and took Samuel's hand in hers looking him in the eyes. "I pray every night that you find a wife, son. This place needs a feminine touch."

It annoyed him when his mother urged him to marry, even though he also wanted that for his life. Samuel glanced around the inside of his house and shrugged. It was sparsely furnished and somewhat plain. There were gun racks on two walls and traps piled in the far corner of the kitchen. However, he did have a few personal touches. The star design he made himself from seashells was imbedded in his mantle over the kitchen fireplace. He was also pleased with the display of blue-and-white enameled dishes he had gotten from his trading post. But overall, the house lacked hominess. Samuel shrugged, "Thank you for your prayers, mother. I appreciate you thinking of me." So far, neither parent had officially wished him a happy birthday.

Samuel heard the front door open again and this time, it was his uncle, Jean Pierre standing in the hallway with a brightly wrapped box in his hand.

"Where is my grown-up nephew?" he laughed, crossing the room to hug Samuel. "Here," he said, handing Samuel a gift. "This is your birthday present, son." Obviously, Jean Pierre's heart was filled with the deepest love and affection for his nephew. "Let me get out of these heavy clothes. It feels nice and cozy in here Samuel. You know how I appreciate a warm house." Jean Pierre gave his sister-in-law his garments and she hung them in the hall closet. "Thank you, Marie. Where is my charming brother, this evening?"

"I'm right here, Jean. How are you these days?" Jean turned to face his older brother. He offered his hand for a shake, but Henri ignored the gesture just as he had done earlier to his son. "I suppose we should be honored to have a big, important man such as yourself find the time to spend with us little people. If it wasn't for the boy's birthday, would we see you at all?" In addition to owning a lucrative shipping business, Jean Pierre was now the Prime Minister of Quebec, or *New France* as it was called in that day.

"Actually, I come over here quite a bit, but I seldom see you here. I can always find time for my favorite nephew." Jean said, smiling at Samuel. He had no children of his own and thought of Samuel as the son he never had. He patted him on his back and sat down on the striped Hudson Bay blanket that covered the cushioned bench closest to the fire.

"So, let's see what extravagance your uncle has bought you." Henri said, sarcastically. He picked up the small box from the table and began to shake it, vigorously. "Catch!" he said suddenly, throwing it at his son.

"Careful, Henri! It's a good thing Samuel has a quick arm and a good eye. That gift is breakable. Have some respect for your son on his birthday."

"Don't tell me how to be with my own children," Henri blurted. The hostility between them had grown more powerful in recent years and a family birthday was no exception for his curt displays.

Samuel sat down and gingerly opened the package. Inside was a dome-shaped, dark blue velvet, hinged box, bordered with a thin strip of fine embroidery. He picked it up and studied the craftsmanship before opening the lid. "It's such a lovely, tiny thing," Samuel said, smiling at his uncle who nodded in agreement. Inside, was a shiny gold pocket watch lying on a bed of light blue silk. Samuel picked it up and gazed at the carvings of a spectacular waterfall etched on either side of the cover. As the lid opened, lilting music began to play. "It's so beautiful. I'm at a loss for words." Samuel, deeply moved by emotion, paused to compose himself before continuing. "This is the most precious gift I have ever received. Thank you, Uncle Jean."

"My pleasure, son," Jean Pierre replied. "You don't turn twenty-one every day."

"He's not *your* son, brother, and he's not responsible enough to own a fine watch like that, either. I don't care if he is twenty-one years old. That boy has been forgetful his whole life. He'll probably leave it in the woods while he's out trapping." Henri's emotional discomfort had given his stern weathered face a permanent look of disgust. The frown on his brow stretched like a deep ravine.

Samuel was used to his father's cruelty but he didn't expect it on his birthday.

"He is the most responsible, young man I know," Jean Pierre said turning to face his nephew. "I believe in you, Samuel and I wish you many more happy birthdays in the years to come." Jean got up and gave his nephew another generous hug.

"When is that cake going to be ready, Marie? I want to go home." Henri barked and his wife scurried to the kitchen to check. Social settings were hard to endure with someone as rude as Henri.

"Go ahead and leave, father. I can put it together from here" Samuel offered. "Really, mother, it's all right. I know how to frost a cake. Thank you for bringing it over." His mother looked crushed but her obedience to her husband came first. Birthday or not, she knew it was time to go.

"Goodnight, Henri. . .Marie," Jean Pierre said as they walked Samuel's parents to the door. "It's not a crime to not like your family members, you know, Henri. I love you, but I don't always like you."

Henri grunted and Marie pulled her mink collar up around her neck. "The feeling is mutual, I assure you." Henri switched his attention to his son. "Samuel, don't lose that watch. It's probably worth something," he blurted. "Good night." His parents turned and walked down the shoveled walkway and were gone within fifteen minutes of their arrival. Samuel watched dully as they vanished from sight before closing the door. Then he joined his uncle by the fire.

"Uncle Jean, YOU are my real family. I appreciate this gift more than you could know and I shall treasure it always. Despite my father's rash prediction, I will NOT lose this watch." Samuel put the watch in his vest pocket and gave it a little pat. "It will be with me wherever I go and whatever I do."

Jean put his arm around Samuel's shoulder and looked him in the eye. "I'm glad you like it, son. It is a very special timepiece—quite unique. I had it made for you in Paris." Jean Pierre got up and stoked the fire, clearing his throat. "You know, Samuel, I pray that you will find a woman to share your life with. While I did not have my own children, I did have the blessing of sharing my life with your aunt Antoinette before she died," Jean Pierre said. "She gave my life more meaning and not a day goes by that I don't miss her."

Samuel took his new watch out of his pocket, admiring its beauty and mystical music before putting it back. Somehow, when his uncle urged him to find himself a woman, it was less irritating than when his mother did it. The watch was such a beautiful, unique gift, considerably more interesting than discussing his lack of a love life.

"I want to share my life with someone, Uncle Jean, but the women in this town are too preoccupied with mimicking the social lives of Paris. I have nothing in common with them." Samuel got up and poured them both a glass of brandy. His uncle held his snifter toward Samuel as a toast and they each took a sip. "I know this may sound strange, but often, when I am out in the woods trapping, I call to my future woman and speak aloud to her. I believe she is out there somewhere, listening. I trust that one day, she will respond to my call," Samuel said with conviction.

"I'm sure you're right, son." Again, Jean Pierre tipped his glass. "Happy birthday, Samuel, and may this be the last one you spend in your bed alone."

"Amen! I'll drink to that!" Samuel laughed, finishing the remainder of his brandy in one, hearty gulp.

Chapter Thirty-seven

1976 – 1987

Chris Patolino had two older sisters and was the fraternal twin of his only brother, Robert. Chris was athletic, talented, and ambitious and by sharp contrast, his twin was the quiet, inward type. From his earliest recollections, Chris and his siblings were frightened of their father, Marcello. The youngsters did whatever they could to stay out of his angry path. Indeed, Marcello Patolino was a hotheaded Italian who ruled his family with the accumulated rage of his own dysfunctional childhood.

Chris' grandparents were Italian immigrants. His mother's parents immigrated to Quebec, Canada, eventually settling in the small town of Coteau-du-Lac, twenty-five miles due west of Montreal. Marcello's parents put down roots farther south in the United States in New Haven, Connecticut, which is exactly where Chris' mother, Lucia and her older sister, Silvia moved to when the girls were old enough to travel to America by themselves. There, Lucia met Marcello, and married him after a brief courtship and raised their family.

Chris remembered visiting his Canadian relatives as a young child. There were countless cousins and he felt close to several boys who were around his same age. Of all the children in their family, Chris enjoyed traveling to Canada the most. He especially enjoyed his jaunts down by the river. His cousins took him downstream in their canoes and they called each other Indian names. Whenever it was time to return to Connecticut after these visits, Chris was unquestionably the saddest one to leave.

At the age of fourteen, Chris' favorite Canadian uncle gave him a small, Super Eight movie camera. Chris never forgot the card that came along with the spectacular gift, which read: *To my dear nephew—I hope this will allow you to keep the beauty of Canada with you wherever you may be. Love, Uncle Ernesto.*

Chris soon discovered he had a knack for capturing images on film. Over the next few years, he nearly drove his sisters and brother mad, shooting movies of their daily lives. When it came time for college, Chris chose a technical school where he majored in filmmaking and television production. He worked like a demon doing extra credit projects whenever they were offered. Chris had grand financial plans for his future and he was confident that by staying focused, it was guaranteed. A few weeks before graduation, recruiters from several major networks came to his school to interview a few of the better students for positions with their companies. Chris was one of the prized chosen ones and at the ripe age of twenty-two, his life was on a fast track for success.

'Eye Of The Nation' was a TV news magazine show that was just being launched, and Chris found himself an integral part of the crew. It wasn't long before he was director of photography for the entire production. Although home base was Manhattan, he traveled all over the world, interacting with movie stars and politicians for the next decade of his life. With the continuing popularity of the show and the overtime he worked, his bank account swelled. Before he knew it, his dream to own property and build a big house in the country was possible. Whenever he could,

Chris went out with realtors, scouring every area of Westchester County, New York. Ultimately, he found three quiet, wooded acres in Bedford, right above a large reservoir loaded with small-mouthed bass. In a strange way, the acreage reminded him of his youthful ventures in the woods of Canada. For years, he lived in a small, studio apartment, saving his money. Between deadlines, Chris went to his land to clear trees where his house would one day be built. He could see the stately structure perfectly in his mind and he was determined to see his dream through.

In his early-thirties, Chris met, fell in love and married a California girl named Janine. It was beginning to look as though he was establishing a somewhat normal life in the midst of all the show-business glitz.

With a new wife, construction underway on his house, and constant travel, Chris was one busy guy. Janine on the other hand, had time to spare. Her life was not nearly as glamorous as she had first thought it would be. With Chris filming programs that spotlighted celebrities around the globe, Janine assumed she would become part of that scene. But 'round-the-clock pressures to create intriguing productions for the network left no time for Chris to indulge his wife's fantasies. In three years time, she decided that a life in New York with an absent husband was no life for her. She found a more available man and went back to Santa Rosa, leaving Chris with a dull and constant ache in his heart.

He was devastated, not only for the loss of his wife, but the death of a dream—the big house in the country, family, kids, soccer games, the two of them working in the garden. Just as he had done for so long, Chris had been focused on his overall life plan—getting the whole picture in place. He had done his best but somehow it wasn't enough and now, Chris considered himself a failure.

The loss of his beautiful Janine burned in his heart like a slow burning fire for months after their divorce. The only way he could endure the pain was to get lost in his work. Rather than sell his land, Chris proceeded with the construction of his house. The effort called for considerable financial gymnastics, but he didn't care. He hoped his building project would take his mind off his sadness. Once built, the dramatic post and beam house became his fortress, a refuge against the hurtful world.

Chris had sporadic, guarded relationships from that point on, but nothing too serious. Overtime, he became fiercely independent the more time he spent alone. No longer would he allow himself to dream of true romance, children and a family life. That dream was dead.

Chapter Thirty-eight

1641

When Samuel de Fontaine was twenty-two years old, he befriended a young Huron warrior one day while trapping along the St. Lawrence River. They often trapped in the same area and over time, they became good friends. The warrior's name was Giawiio, which meant *Good Word* in his language. Samuel found his friend's words were not only good, but also humorous and lighthearted.

"Some of my people are too serious and it is my self-appointed job to bring laughter to my village," he exclaimed to Samuel one day as they shared a joke. As was his habit, Samuel pulled his watch from his vest pocket to check the time and the haunting music began to play. "Do you have an obsession with clocks?" Giawiio teased. "Why do you always need to know the time?

"I don't. It's just something I do. This watch is special to me and I carry it with me everywhere," Samuel said, slowly putting the watch back in his vest pocket.

"I know you do, brother. It has become special to me, as well. The music it plays is a part of my life now. I would love for my sister to hear it someday. She is always singing around our lodge."

Giawiio had invited Samuel to come to his village many times, but Samuel always had an excuse.

"I promise your sister will hear it soon, my friend." Samuel replied.

There was actually nothing pressing in Samuel's life, but he had been living like a recluse for so long, he felt awkward accepting his friend's invitation. He questioned his own social manners and wondered if he could contend with introductions and dinner conversation.

On a particularly frosty, early autumn morning while checking his traps, Samuel found himself considering his life's direction. The realization of how far he had slipped into himself made him feel sad and lonely.

Later that same day, the two of them were paddling up river in Giawiio's canoe when the typically calm weather instantly switched to violent winds and beating hail. The sky grew ominous in every direction, and it was apparent to the men this was no ordinary storm.

"Come, brother, we must head for my village! It is not far from here. This looks like a big one," Giawiio yelled to be heard in the wind. Samuel nodded as they pulled the canoe out of the river, turned it upside down and shoved it into the low, thick underbrush before making a run for Giawiio's lodge.

Despite the unfortunate circumstance, Giawiio was pleased Samuel had accepted his invitation. *Finally, he will meet my people.* He particularly wanted Samuel to meet his sister, who was not only beautiful, but also unattached.

Soaked to the bone with his teeth chattering, Samuel shivered next to the fire while Giawiio sought out some dry clothes for them both. They quickly got out of their wet things and hung them on the pegs by the fire to dry. Giawiio's mother, Haywathna, came into the lodge just as they were finished dressing. She surprised Samuel with her ageless beauty and her command of the French language.

"I am glad to see you both safe, my son. This must be your brother, Samuel de Fontaine," his mother offered her hand and Samuel gave it a light kiss. "Our son has spoken of you so often, I feel as though I already know you," she added with a warm, trusting smile. "Come, sit by our fire and warm yourself. You will stay and eat, will you not?"

"Yes, thank you. That would be nice." Samuel answered as he relaxed on the buffalo pelt. "Does everyone in your family speak French, Giawiio?"

"Yes. I taught them myself," Giawiio said, puffing out his chest. "The study of French gives us something to do over the long winter. It is good for us to speak it with you so we do not forget."

"We have heard much about you these past months since you and my son have become brothers. I have wanted to meet you for quite some time," Haywathna told him.

"Giawiio has invited me many times but I was not able to come until now. I have a trading post in Quebec and cannot leave it without supervision for long periods of time." Haywathna nodded sympathetically. She honored his attitude toward his responsibilities.

"I, too, have wanted to meet your family and I appreciate the refuge from this sudden storm," he added. Samuel was touched that she referred to her son as his brother.

Haywathna was also interested in introducing Samuel to her twenty-year-old daughter, Jigonsassee. To date, the attractive Indian girl had no apparent interest in any of the village's eligible braves. Like all mothers, she wanted her daughter to have a family and a lodge of her own. Jigonsassee knew exactly what she wanted in a mate and vowed she would rather remain single than settle for just any man. Jigonsassee told both her parents that her soul partner had visited her in her dream state quite regularly since she was fifteen years old. She was patiently waiting for his arrival in her life.

"My man has eyes that twinkle like the north-star when he smiles and his teeth are as white as freshly fallen snow. He has dark, wavy hair, and his skin is light brown. He has a strong, slender build with a height equal to my own." Jigonsassee was confident she would recognize him when the time came for him to appear.

As Haywathna spoke with Samuel, she couldn't help but wonder if he was the man in her daughter's dreams. He was strong and slender with pure white teeth and dark wavy hair.

"Your daughter has an interesting name—*Jigonsassee.* Where does it come from? What does it mean?" Samuel asked.

"It means: *New Mind* or *New Face.* Her father and I named her after a woman her great, great grandfather had come across in his travels. His name was: Deganawidah. He was a prophet of his time, but was rejected by his own Wendot people, who were much more interested in war than in peace." Haywathna shifted on her buffalo pelt. She could see Samuel was genuinely interested in her discourse.

"We used to be called the *Wendots,* before the French changed our name. The early Wendots were not ready to embrace Deganawidah's profound message of peace back then, so he set out to spread his enlightened word to anyone who would embrace what he had to say. As he traveled, he came across a woman who fed him. She not only listened to his message, but also she embraced it. He called her *Jigonsassee,* and appointed her *Mother of Nations* or the *Great Peace Woman.* Our people have told this story for generations and when our daughter was born, we named her Jigonsassee because we felt she would also have deep insight. Did you know that my daughter is in our Medicine Council?"

"Yes, Giawiio told me. You must be proud of her." Samuel said.

"Both of our children make us proud. They have each given us immeasurable joy in their own ways." Haywathna said in earnest. "My husband will be here any moment," she added. "I know he will also be glad to finally meet you."

Tekakwida had been out securing the horses and was soaking wet when he burst inside. "It is violent out there!" he exclaimed. "Stoke that fire, son and get me something dry to put on," he barked his orders before noticing they had company. Tekakwida then smiled at Samuel. "You must be my son's white brother. We were beginning to wonder if you were his imaginary friend," he said with a chuckle, hanging his wet things on a remaining peg.

Samuel laughed. "I can see where Giawiio gets his sense of humor. Yes, I am Samuel."

As soon as Tekakwida had changed his clothes, he positioned himself next to Samuel by the fire and began loading his pipe. He had heard his daughter's description of her soul mate many times and as Tekakwida looked at Samuel, he couldn't help but notice the similarities.

"I apologize that it has taken me this long to finally get here." Samuel now felt foolish for dodging Giawiio's many invitations. It was easy to spend time with this family. "I am afraid I have allowed my life to get too busy," he added.

"It is not good to be so busy. You must learn quietness, my son. Now, tell me about the white men and their busy plans for our world," Tekakwida asked with a wink. "And after we discuss that, I want to hear about your beliefs." He lit the pipe and took a long drag, exhaling slowly before passing it on to Samuel. "What is your relationship to mankind and nature?"

Samuel took a minute to enjoy the smoke before answering. He reflected on the level of conversation and was instantly comfortable skipping small talk and diving right in to topics that truly mattered. "My relationship to nature is easier to talk about than my relationship with mankind. Besides your son, I have no one close to me other than my uncle."

"Why is this?" Tekakwida took another long, slow drag before handing the pipe to Giawiio. "Where is the rest of your family?"

"They live close to my house, but we do not get on very well. My father is an angry man and quite difficult to be around."

"And what about your mother?"

"She trails behind my father with no real mind of her own. I have never felt a close connection to either one of my parents. Luckily, I have an uncle who is more a father to me than my own." Samuel's words held deep affection as he reflected on Jean Pierre's kindness throughout his life.

"As we grow older, we can pick our families," Tekakwida said with a smile, handing Samuel the pipe. "You are part of our family now."

Samuel nodded as he inhaled the pungent smoke. He was safe from the storm and relaxed from the effects of the pipe. Gratitude flooded over him as he visited with his new family.

As Samuel talked, Tekakwida's respect for him grew. Samuel felt the same way the Huron felt about the Earth Mother and her abundance, and how she should be protected and valued. They were also in agreement about the white man's vanity and materialism and how it will eventually be their demise.

"It is good to have communication with someone outside our village. I am glad you are here. Whenever you are trapping in this area, you must come and share our fire," Tekakwida said with a nod. "Where is our daughter, woman?" he asked Haywathna, after they had finished their smoke. "She should be out of this storm and home by now," he said.

"She is with the council, meeting about the recent plague." His wife had a worried tone in her voice. "It ravaged the Iroquois village down river and they are concerned it might come this way."

"We are much stronger than the Iroquois. Giawiio, go to the medicine lodge and see if they are finished. If so, tell your sister to come home and greet our guest." Tekakwida hoped Samuel would spark his daughter's interest and he wanted them to have as much time together as possible.

Chapter Thirty-nine

1988 – 1995

Chris decorated his large house in Bedford, New York, quite handsomely once it was finished. When his schedule allowed, he nested in his elaborate greenhouse with his collection of exotic orchids. As busy as he was, he attempted to have a domestic life, complete with plants, two playful cats and even a few friends. More than ever, he felt the need to anchor himself to something more solid than his constant traveling.

It was a brisk, October day and Chris was warming up for a run around the reservoir behind his house. Once he had finished stretching his legs, he walked down his long driveway and noticed that some new neighbors had moved into the small rental cabin across the road. There was a man in the front yard clumsily attempting to split firewood and Chris watched him while deciding whether to be polite then or later. *Damn, I'm all revved for my run,* he thought to himself. Just then, the neighbor looked up and waved and Chris walked over and extended his arm for introductions.

"Hi. I'm Chris Patalino from across the street." The new neighbor vigorously shook his hand as Chris added, "I hope you don't mind me saying so, but you look a little out of place trying to use that thing. You're bound to freeze to death this winter at the rate you're going if you don't cut your leg off first!"

"It's true! How observant of you. I was hoping someone would take pity on me and come to my rescue," the man replied and they both laughed. "I'm Scott Jensen," he said, switching the axe to his left hand so he could shake with his right. "My wife and I just moved here from the city where I didn't have much use for an axe." Just then, Scott's wife came outside to see whom her husband was laughing with.

"Hi, I'm Sara. It's nice to meet you. We just moved in today, but I have my kitchen completely set up and dinner almost ready. The rest of the house is a total mess! Would you care to join us for dinner, Chris?"

"Sure. Why not? I'm almost out of daylight for my run. Dinner sounds good." Scott and Chris gathered the firewood and carried it in. The sun had set and the temperature dropped considerably. Inside, their cabin was chilly due to poor insulation.

"Looks like we're going to go through a lot of wood this winter, Sara." Scott said, getting a cigar from his humidor. "With my lack of talent in the wood-splitting department, this is NOT good news! Bummer. Hey, do you smoke cigars, Chris? Sara unpacks her kitchen first and I unpack my humidor."

"Yeah, why not?" Chris answered getting one out of the box. "Tonight, I'll over-eat, enjoy new friends and smoke cigars. Tomorrow, I RUN!" Scott handed him the cutter and Chris snipped the end off before putting it under his nose to take a fragrant whiff. "I hope these are as illegal as they smell." Chris smiled and reached for the lighter.

"As a matter of fact, they are straight from Havana. I have a Cuban friend who gets them for me. He wants Sara and me to move to Cuba with him. He thinks we would fit right in and he wants us to start a business with him—probably smuggling cigars! Could be lucrative, don't you think?"

"We told him it's highly possible and to keep in touch." Sara interjected before Chris had a chance to respond. "We hate these winters and would gladly live in the Caribbean. Actually, Scott and I would rather go to St. Lucia. We've been there on vacation many times and we always threaten to buy one-way tickets every time we go." As Sara spoke about the islands, Chris noticed the silky, dream-like look on her face. Perhaps it was the wine. "In reality, I'm sure we'd face headaches with immigration and work visas on St. Lucia with it being a foreign country and all . . . but, *Gawd,* it's gorgeous. We can't seem to get enough of it."

"I know what you mean." Chris could relate to their affection to the Caribbean. He had visited the island of St. John many times. "Have you two ever been to the V.I.?"

"The V.I.? Where's that?"

"The Virgin Islands. They're about fifty miles from Puerto Rico. Parts of the islands are British and the rest are a U.S. territory. There is no paperwork hassle for statesiders. I've been going there on vacation for years. You should check it out and if you like it, and decide to move there, I'll have a free place to stay when I come down," Chris teased.

"Come to think of it, the use of our tropical guest room would be a fair exchange for some split firewood," Scott fired back.

Chapter Forty

Within the year, Scott and Sara had taken Chris up on his suggestion. They had vacationed in the U.S. Virgin Islands twice before falling head over heels in love with the quaint little island of St. John. Within six months of their decision to relocate, they had packed a container and shipped their belongings. The couple had meant it when they told Chris they wanted warm weather in their lives on a full time basis.

Island life was right up Scott and Sara's alley. The off-center lifestyle of the Caribbean agreed with these two zany characters. They laughed at the contrast and how much they never fit into the conservative New England life all the years they had stuck it out there.

One afternoon, the couple found themselves wandering around Mongoose Junction, an architecturally attractive shopping plaza made from local stone. The open-air mall featured an array of unique shops and Sara was especially fond of the bookstore Katie Barry was presently managing. The couple had started hanging out at the cafe attached to the bookstore and they developed an instant friendship with Katie. From the moment they met, the three of them were inseparable.

"I don't care what's going on over on St. Thomas this weekend. You have to come over for dinner on Friday night and laugh with us. I promise you, these two are a riot!" Katie told Mariah over the phone one evening. "I already told them you are coming, so you have to be here."

"First tell me what you're making for dinner before I commit," Mariah teased.

"I don't even know what I'm having for lunch today, much less what I'm going to make for dinner four days from now. Just get your ass on the six o'clock boat and I'll pick you up." Katie said.

"Yes, 'Madam Bossy'," Mariah joked. As promised, when she got off the ferry early Friday evening, Katie was at the dock to pick her up.

"Hi, Sweetie! Welcome to my island." Mariah nodded and gave Katie a kiss on her cheek. "We're going to pick up Sara and Scott on the way to my house. They're very excited to meet you. Of course, I've described you as a Goddess, so try to act like one."

"That's easy…it comes natural for us, Sweetie', you know that." Mariah replied, noticing that Katie had her blinker on and they had just passed her street. "It's great they live so close to your place."

"I agree. We've been having a ball together. I'm so glad you could make it tonight." Katie said, turning into their steep driveway. "Here we are."

"I'll go up and get them if you don't want to beep," Mariah offered. "Is it that house on the right?"

As if on cue, Scott came out the door with a wine bottle in each hand and Sara was behind him carrying a tray of stuffed mushrooms. "Hi, you must be Mariah. I'm Scott and this is my wife, Sara. Katie has told us so much about you. We're already bored with *her* so it's nice to finally meet *you*," he said with a laugh.

"Well, thank you very much," Mariah replied. "Scott, would you like to sit up front where there is more leg room?"

"No, thank you. Sara likes me to be crammed in the back seat next to her instead." His wife punched him affectionately in the arm and everybody chuckled.

"So Katie, what are you making for dinner? I've missed your cooking." Mariah asked. Katie had gone to a culinary institute years ago and her talent in the kitchen was the envy of friends and business acquaintances alike.

"Grouper with mango chutney, fresh asparagus and scalloped potatoes," Katie replied. She reached over and gently put her hand on Mariah's cheek. She knew grouper with mango chutney was Mariah's favorite.

"New best friends and grouper, all in one night! Well worth the boat ride," Mariah said. "Thanks for the invite."

"Ever since Katie told us about you, we have been playing match-maker in our minds," Scott blurted out. Sara nudged him to be quiet but it was too late. "We have a friend in Bedford, New York who is loaded with energy and he's a real go-getter. Katie tells us that pretty much describes you, too."

"It describes a part of me, for sure, but like all women, I'm mysterious and multi-faceted." Mariah said with a wink and Katie gave her a thumbs- up.

Well, you certainly have a mysterious tattoo on that index finger—that's for sure. Where did you get it done?" Scott wondered.

"That's no tattoo, my friend. It's Mariah's magic mark—her birthmark. This is one psychic lady!" Katie proclaimed.

"Really? Is this true, Mariah?" Sara asked.

"Katie likes to exaggerate," Mariah replied. "I have occasional insights, much like strong déjà-vu. I don't do readings or anything like that."

"Cool! We've never known a real-life mystic before. What a bonus."

The rest of night went on from there and Mariah was sorely disappointed when the ferryboat departure time interrupted their witty exchange. "I can't remember when I've laughed this hard," Mariah said, giving Scott and Sara a good-bye hug. Katie motioned frantically to her watch from the open car door before Mariah finally got in the vehicle. Her hostess dashed down the hill to the dock just in time for Mariah to climb aboard the final vessel of the night.

Throughout the following months, Scott mentioned his friend, Chris Patolino to Mariah hoping to spark her romantic interest. At one point, Chris had visited for a long weekend shortly after Scott and Sara had met Mariah, but something came up and Mariah couldn't make it over to St. John to meet him.

"When is this electrified, Italian friend of yours coming back?" Mariah asked Scott over the phone. "I promise to clear my calendar and come to St. John to make his acquaintance."

"He'll probably pack his bags as soon as I tell him what you just said." Scott replied.

Chris was more than a little curious about Mariah after all his friends had told him about her. He found himself especially intrigued that she was somewhat of a mystic. *How weird to have a star-shaped birthmark on her finger like a ring,* he thought to himself. He found himself daydreaming about this woman on St. Thomas and he pumped Scott for information about her every time they spoke over the phone.

"Just get your ass on a plane and come down here next weekend and meet her yourself. I'm tired of being your go-between." Scott teased one night while talking to his former neighbor on the phone. Then he started singing: "Matchmaker, Matchmaker make me a match, find me a find, catch me a catch."

Chris laughed. "I'm looking at my schedule as we speak, and I can clear some days after the 16th of this month. Get the guest-room ready! I'm coming down! I haven't been able to stop talking to this woman in my head since you told me about her. I've got to meet her before I make myself crazy."

"Crazier—you already were crazy. We'll see you soon, my friend."

Chapter Forty-one

1640

Jigonsasee heard through the village gossip that Giawiio had finally brought his white brother home with him. Like the rest of their family, she had been looking forward to meeting Samuel. The rain and wind had temporarily subsided so she quickly bathed at the edge of the cold, clear river, dressing in her favorite skins and moccasins before joining the rest of her family in their lodge. She looked down at her feet and across both arms. Her fringe and beads were all in place. The star-shaped birthmark on her index finger seemed to shine like a brilliant stone. Ordinarily, it was a dull color, but today it seemed like a priceless piece of jewelry. How strange! Instinctively, she rubbed it before entering their lodge. When she saw Samuel across the room, Jigonsassee stopped dead in her tracks. His eyes and smile were what gave him away. She knew he was unmistakably the man in her dreams.

"You must be Samuel. It is an honor to finally meet you," she said. "I am Jigonsassee, Giawiio's only sister." She looked over at her brother with overflowing love. All the people she cared for most in the world were safe and in her presence at that moment.

"I'm glad you had sense enough to come in out of the rain," she teased him and Giawiio smiled in reply.

"I am honored to finally meet you, Giawiio's only sister. Luckily, we weren't far from here when the winds started." Samuel stood up and took Jigonsassee's hand and kissed it. "Your brother talks incessantly, and most of the time it is about all of you." Samuel looked over at Giawiio and smiled. He felt relaxed, even with Jigonsassee in the room. The situation surprised him because he was normally shy around women. "I feel I have known you for lifetimes," he blurted without thinking what his words might mean.

I am sure that is true, Jigonsassee thought, but just smiled, and gave a little nod. As they ate dinner, the wind howled through the trees outside their warm, cozy lodge. It blew strong enough to rip weaker trees from their roots and hurl them in various directions. The pounding rain changed to snow as the temperature plummeted.

"You must stay with us until the storm has completely passed. It is dangerous to travel in this weather," Haywathna spoke in her concerned mother voice.

"I accept your invitation," Samuel replied with his hands held over his heart. These types of storms often made him feel unsettled and lonely, magnifying the lack of companionship in his life. He often fantasized about reaching his house during just such a storm to find his woman there to greet him with dry clothes, a roaring fire, a hot meal and a night of lovemaking. The dream was real enough—it just had not come to pass in this life—not yet. But right now, he was safe and warm with his new family and he felt truly happy. His lonely world was nothing to rush back to and he secretly wished the storm would rage on for days.

Eventually, Giawiio and his parents excused themselves and went to sleep but Jigonsassee and Samuel stayed up by the fire, talking into the morning.

"That is a most unusual symbol on your finger," Samuel said. "Is it a tattoo to signify that you are a medicine woman?"

"In a way, it does, but it is not a tattoo. I was born with it. Our chief believed it set me apart. I am the only woman in the medicine council, although we do seek the advice from females often, as our people have great respect for the wisdom the great spirits have bestowed upon our gender." Jigonsassee replied.

"It is quite remarkable the way it shines in the firelight." Samuel said.

Jigonsassee rubbed her finger and nodded.

For no apparent reason, Samuel took his watch from his vest pocket and popped open the lid to check the time. He recalled Giawiio saying how much she would appreciate the music.

Jigonsassee had never heard anything so captivating in her life and she closed her eyes as it played. When the music stopped, Samuel noticed her eyes were wet with tears.

"I am so very sorry. Did my watch make you sad?" he asked as she dried her eyes with her hands.

"It is rapture that moves me to tears," she said. "Not sadness. The sound is so enchanting. What do those markings on the face of it mean?"

"It is a clock—a measuring device for time. Much as your people use the shadow of the sun to measure time, this instrument does also, but with more precision," he tried to explain.

"Why is it important to know the precise time?" she asked him.

"It is not important at this moment. My uncle gave me this gift and I am in the habit of checking it throughout the day. It does not have much importance when I am in the woods, but when I am back in my world, it matters somehow," he told her.

Jigonsassee just smiled and nodded. The music it played would be reason enough to open it! Samuel handed the timepiece to Jigonsassee and she ran her finger lovingly over the waterfall etching. "This is most beautiful. I would like to swim in this waterfall," she said with a shy smile and he agreed. Eventually, they bedded down on opposite sides of the center fire and gazed at each other until they each fell asleep. Jigonsassee did not dream of Samuel that night. No longer did she need to meet him in the dream world. At last he had arrived in the flesh!

The weather took two full days to clear before Samuel was on his way. From that day forward, his Huron family welcomed him warmly each time he came to their village.

"You must stay longer the next time you come. I no sooner get accustomed to having you around and then you are gone again," Tekakwida teased.

Samuel would assuredly stay longer. He wanted to be with Jigonsassee as frequently as possible. He trapped with Giawiio more than ever and had many mink and beaver pelts to take back to his trading post. Samuel kept their Huron village well stocked with coffee, sugar, bullets, sewing notions and various items the Indian communities had grown to depend on since the white man introduced these things to their lives.

Chapter Forty-two

1995

It was a hurricane season to beat all others. Mother Nature raged across the Atlantic, causing residents throughout the Caribbean and along the east coast of the mainland to be glued to the weather station.

Chris didn't care about the hazardous weather conditions. He finally had his trip planned to the U.S. Virgin Islands to meet Mariah and he didn't want anything standing in his way. *Maybe she is the woman of my dreams. I've surely been through enough that weren't.*

In recent years, he had dated a few women and most of them wore him out emotionally. He longed to find someone who wasn't so needy. It had been ten years since his divorce and he was tired of the dating scene. He was ready to have a true mate in his life and he believed there was a partner out there who could compliment his world. Hurricane or not, he was going to the Virgin Islands to meet this Mariah woman.

By Thursday afternoon, Hurricane Louis was trashing the islands of St. Maarten and Antigua, and was heading straight for the U.S. Virgin Islands. It was packing one hundred seventy-mile-an-hour sustained winds, and the whole territory was hunkered down for the nightmare that seemed determined to come about.

Chris arrived just ahead of the storm warnings and immediately took part in the frenzied preparations on St. John. Scott gathered his tools. "First, we'll go over and help Katie cover her windows with plywood and then we'll come back here and do our house." Scott's usually jovial manner was replaced with a more somber mood and Sara was a nervous wreck. Chris did his best to add some comic relief, but they were too preoccupied with the impending doom to have their usual sense of humor.

"We'll go downstairs in the utility room just in case the roof blows off. It's next to the cistern and it's solid concrete." Scott was trying to sound reassuring but his delivery was shaky. "Don't fret, love. We'll be fine no matter what." Sara then brought down a few bottles of wine; candles; water; pillows; a deck of cards; the book she was reading and plenty of food to munch on. In her usual way, she turned their concrete bunker into a comfortable, cozy space.

Meanwhile on St. Thomas, Mariah, her children, and two of her friends were bunkered in the downstairs apartment of the home she owned. Fortunately, Mariah did not rent that unit out; instead she used it as her master suite. It had a living room, small kitchenette, den, bathroom and utility area. The upstairs apartment was where Jason and Emily had their bedrooms.

"Jason, take the artwork I have piled up next to the stairs down to the laundry room and Emily, take the dishes out of the cabinets, wrap them in sheets and blankets and put them in the tub." Mariah took their photo albums and other personal treasures, put them in plastic bags and placed them in the now-crowded laundry room, one of the two most protected rooms in the house. She was careful to leave enough space for herself and her children if in fact they needed to pile in there, as well.

Mariah struggled with preparations until she was totally exhausted. With so much left to do to insure their safety, she felt desperate enough to call her contractor, ex-husband. "I don't have the tools to secure my house correctly," she told Bill over the phone, feeling her request was more than justified. "Can you please come over and help us put the plywood over the windows?" The other end of the phone was awkwardly silent so Mariah pulled out the big guns. "These are your children too, Bill. You're a builder for Christ's sake."

Bill was no stranger to guilt trips, but he'd rather be on the giving end than the receiving.

"Come on, Bill. What do you say? Will you help us, please?" She hated to grovel, but she was frightened and desperate.

"I say you can *kiss my ass,* Mariah! You could have had us all under one roof as a family but you threw it away—remember? Figure it out on your own. It was your choice!" He slammed the phone down, enjoying the power he felt from spite.

Mariah hung up in a rage and vowed to not call him for anything in the future. She and her children borrowed some tools from a neighbor and battened down their home the best they could.

After spending twelve hours bunkered downstairs, Mariah, her family and their friends breathed a sigh of relief when Hurricane Louis veered ever so slightly to the north and the eye of the storm missed them by twelve miles. There were a few trees knocked over and electrical power and phones were out, but they were not nearly as decimated as their neighbors to the south in the Lesser Antilles. Reports of severe damage on Antigua and St. Maarten were on the airwaves and eventually in the papers. For days, the inhabitants of the U.S. and British Virgin Islands cleaned up debris, and worked toward getting their lives back to normal.

Mariah was curious to know how her friends on St. John were doing, but with no phones, she was out of touch. Days later,

Mariah saw someone she knew from the town of Cruz Bay. "Hey, Mark. How did you fare over in 'Love City?'"?

"Very little damage to report," he said. "Your friends, Scott and Sara are as mouthy as ever and your friend Katie Barry is fine, too. As far as I know, their homes are unscathed. We're in about the same shape as St. Thomas—but better, of course. After all, it is St. John!" Mark joked. St. John was well known for its elitist Hilton-Headesque attitude.

At last, Chris was able to get out on his cell phone and when he checked his answering machine in New York, he discovered he had an important shoot the next day. He called the airport, which now had working phones and discovered there was one flight leaving every afternoon to JFK. Quickly, he threw his belongings together, took the ferry to St. Thomas, a cab to the airport and was back in the Big Apple in a few short hours. Once again, a trip to the tropics had ended without setting eyes on the mysterious Mariah.

Within days of Hurricane *Louis,* the weather reports began alerting the island residents of yet another major storm, which was barreling right toward them—Hurricane *Marilyn.* It was a category one storm and was south by the island of Dominica, heading north, northwest at about eight miles per hour. It was packing sustained winds of eighty miles an hour, increasing in intensity as it moved toward the warm waters of the Caribbean. Many people had taken down their shutters from the previous scare, only to have to put them back up. Mariah and her son decided to board up again but not take as many of their personal effects to the utility bunker room as they did during *Louis.* The reports were that *Marilyn* wasn't going to be nearly as serious as *Louis* could have been. Similarly, many boat owners decided to stay with their boats rather than go ashore, as they had done the previous week.

Marilyn was churning ahead rather slowly, which wasn't a good sign. Once a hurricane's motion slows up, it usually picks up speed within itself and intensifies. When the storm passed through the Lesser Antilles chain and moved over the warm waters of the Caribbean, it became real trouble. *Marilyn* was upgraded to a category two.

"Don't be alone, Nance," Mariah told her good friend over the phone. "Come over here again and be safe with us. We've got plenty of supplies—it'll be fun." Nancy had been one of Mariah's guests at her storm-slumber party the week before during the *Louis* scare.

"No thanks. I'm going to do this one at home. I'm too tired to pack all my stuff again. I'll be all right, and we'll talk on the phone—as long as there are phones!" Nancy operated a vacation villa management business, and with more than a hundred houses to worry about securing, she was exhausted. Like the rest of the island, she was taking it much less seriously than the previous one, since all the reports indicated it would not be as bad.

Chapter Forty-three

After five, seemingly endless hours into the hurricane, Mariah and her children heard the unmistakable sound of glass breaking upstairs in her daughter's room. There was little doubt the shutters on Emily's picture window had blown off. The storm was raging full blast and it wasn't safe to go outside to deal with it. Just before the radio station's tower blew down, they heard a harried broadcaster reporting on their battery powered radio that winds were gusting over two hundred and twenty miles per hour! After the window broke upstairs, there was a huge slam against their house, in the same corner of her daughter's room and Emily burst into tears. Her room was being destroyed directly above their heads. "It's OK, honey. It's only stuff," Mariah said, trying to comfort her frightened little girl. Just then, the house shook as if it had been struck by a wrecking ball and there were more crashing noises upstairs. Emily screamed and Mariah felt a rush of panic.

"Jason, Emily! Grab the radio! Take that painting off the wall above your heads and put it in the laundry room. I think we'll be safer in the bathroom if the shutters blow off any more windows. Did you see if *Shadow* ran under the bed? I can't find him," Mariah asked. *Shadow* was their Siamese cat.

"No, he's behind the couch. Make sure you get him, Mom," Emily pleaded.

The three of them, plus *Shadow,* spent the remaining hours of the storm listening to the upper level of their home being ripped apart while they huddled together in the two small rooms. Water was dripping through the light fixtures and it became obvious the upstairs of their house was now open to the elements. While her children dozed, Mariah flashed on another time and place when she and a young boy were desperately looking through the dark clouds of smoke and dust for her husband. She heard mothers and children screaming in anguish. Then, the scene was gone. In its place, another image came into her mind of them huddled and chained down below of a wretched ship with hundreds of other frightened people. Cold ocean water splashed down on them from the open porthole above their heads and Mariah shivered. How real it felt! The vision evaporated as she wiped the drips of water from their leaking ceiling off her arm. She blew out the candle and drifted off to sleep, with her children and cat cuddled close by her side.

She was the first to awaken the next morning and she carefully untangled herself from her sleeping family. Quietly, she slipped out the door of her lower apartment to what looked like footage of Vietnam during the war. They had been bombed by Mother Nature's fury throughout the night and their beautiful island seemed all but destroyed. Palm trees, striped of their crowns, looked like enormous matchsticks. Telephone poles were either horizontal or gone, as were most roofs. Cautiously, she worked her way up the stairs to the remains of their home. Furniture and clothing were soaked with water, and broken glass was all over the yard. A few chairs from the dining room were up on the road and one was hanging from a branch of their huge tamarind tree, which had been stripped of all its leaves. The front door was ripped from it's hinges, and interior walls made of wood frame and sheetrock were gone. The crash they heard during the storm was the roof of their neighbor's house down the mountainside. It had lifted completely off, flown up the hill and assaulted the east corner of their house. The impact caused half of the exterior concrete wall to cave in, which in turn, caused their roof to lift.

Mariah was in shock and she wept silently while fumbling through the remains of what had been their home. The kitchen cabinets had no doors and broken dishes were everywhere. Pieces of palm fronds were imbedded in the walls, and a huge pond of water with waves rippling in the open air was now her living room floor. Mariah stood on the outside verandah and looked at the destruction, frozen in disbelief. When she turned around, she saw her crying children standing in the front doorway and she opened her arms to hold them close. The three hurricane victims held tightly to one another in their ruined house, on their wrecked island.

"It's going to be OK, you two. I promise. We'll put our home back together and we'll be all right." Mariah's voice quivered but her children barely noticed. They needed reassurance and they wanted to believe her.

As the day wore on, neighbors began to surface. Everyone seemed to be in a stupor. "Jason, go with the men and help clear the roads so we can get out of here," Mariah ordered. "Emily, you and I should check on any house that doesn't have people milling about."

"OK, good idea. Let me get my boots on. You need to wear some hard soled shoes, too Mom." Mariah looked down at her sandal-clad feet and smiled. "Here, wear Jason's extra work boots." Emily suggested. "There's jagged galvanized and broken glass all over the place."

Thankful that her daughter was thinking clearly, Mariah took off her rubber flip-flops and put on Jason's boots and the two of them walked down the ravaged path. Surprisingly, everyone was all right, even the residents in the roofless house below.

They had gone down to the room next to their cistern once their roof was gone.

"It's probably safe to assume the rest of the island is in as bad shape as we are, don't you think, Mom?"

"Yes, I'm afraid so, Sweetie." Mariah's voice was flat.

Jason went with the men to help with the clearing, and Emily helped her mother sweep out the small lake that now covered the family living room floor. The lower apartment was all they had to live in now and they needed to keep it as dry as possible. Mariah found some fresh batteries for their portable radio, and eventually found a station from Puerto Rico. According to the broadcast, the Army Corp. of Engineers, the Federal Emergency Management Agency, the Red Cross, and hordes of other government agencies had already arrived on the island. Within days, they flew in tanks and dump trucks with snowplows on the front and began pushing debris from the roads into huge piles. Clearing a path to the hospital and getting the airport in optimal working order were top priorities. It was a huge undertaking to maintain order and a strict curfew of six p.m. was made law to minimize looting. FBI personnel and federal marshals were flown in from the mainland to assist.

St. John and St. Croix had been spared the massive amount of destruction that St. Thomas suffered. Downtown Cruz Bay on St. John even had working phones, an oddity, because St. John was only a few miles away from the ravaged island of St. Thomas. Somehow they were spared the direct eye of the storm.

In spite of the minimal damage there, Scott and Sara's house was among the unlucky ones. The couple had weathered the storm in their downstairs utility room while their house was completely demolished above them. In the end, ninety percent of their belongings were wrecked, and they were now homeless. Thankfully, their landlord owned a small real estate office, which had a shower in the bathroom and a small kitchenette. He let them move into it since there wasn't going to be any business for a while.

Within a month, the exodus began and many people left the island. The bulk of the remaining residents were folks who had lived in the islands all their lives—or for so long they couldn't imagine where else they might relocate, despite the miserable conditions. Convinced the island would be restored and they would get their lives back, it was their hope that held folks together.

Chapter Forty-four

1995 – 1996

The mess around them was overwhelming at first and it seemed as though nothing short of heavy equipment could return the island to some sort of starting place. Jason took on the role as man of the house and organized the outside clean up. Together, Mariah and her children cleared functional paths in their yard, making several piles of what had been their household belongings.

Emily spent the first two days rummaging through the soggy remains of her bedroom. Much to everyone's delight, she found enough mementoes to recreate a new place of her own in what used to be their downstairs storage room.

The roads in Mariah's neighborhood were cleared over the next few days and many of the major island streets were drivable. By day five, Mariah, Jason and Emily were just short of stir crazy so Mariah loaded them in her Blazer to venture beyond their war zone. Her main priority was to see if her office on the east end was still intact. As they drove along, the stunned trio saw that the rest of the island was indeed, as destroyed as their north-side community. Hundreds of huge blue tarps with FEMA stamped in big white lettering were draped over damaged houses to serve as temporary roofs. Telephone poles and trees were heaped along the roadsides. Foliage was completely stripped from trees, and they looked naked and sad. Not a single section of the island had escaped the violent ravages of hurricane *Marilyn.*

"If we get to my office and it's destroyed, we're going straight to the airport," Mariah said without hesitation as they drove through the 'S' curves of the lagoon.

Jason and Emily were in shock and they nodded in agreement. As they rounded the corner and approached her office, Mariah held her breath. Miraculously, her building was unscathed! Filled with mixed emotions, Mariah came to the quick realization that she had a business to run, or at the very least, there was equipment to liquidate. She couldn't just fly away and leave her responsibilities, but oh, how she wished she could.

With all television and phones knocked out indefinitely, radio and print would be the only way to get information to the public. Mariah needed to find out if the *Island News* was destroyed, since they printed her publication on their press. If it wasn't, she was still in business. She figured they could limp along with cell phones and generators until the utilities were restored.

Glancing down at the gauge, Mariah saw that her SUV needed gas. There was a long line at the only operating gas station and it took forty-five minutes to inch her way up to the pumps. At least, her air-conditioned vehicle was one of the few places they were truly comfortable! After the hurricane, the air got oppressive, like a steamy summer day in the Louisiana bayou, and loaded with mosquitoes. Sitting inside her well-appointed vehicle made everything seem temporarily normal.

Meanwhile, in Chicago, Ron James was glued to his TV watching the weather channel throughout the night of the storm. He saw footage of the damage on St. Thomas and all he could think of was Mariah. During the commercial breaks, he made a list of emergency items and early the next morning, he grabbed one of his employees.

"Come on, we're going to Home Depot. When we get there, you start at one end and I'll start at the other. Here's half the list." He tore the long paper in two. "Get three or more of everything. Whatever Mariah can't use, she can share with her neighbors." Four thousand dollars later, Ron loaded his huge company truck, and headed to a nearby municipal airport.

He found a charter plane service willing to get the supplies to her as soon as the St. Thomas airport was officially opened. Ron was finally able to reach her on her cell phone and she started crying when she heard his voice.

"Oh, Ron! Everything is so destroyed! If I wasn't here to see it with my own eyes, I would never believe it," she said.

"I chartered a plane and filled it with supplies. They should be there in a few days. Try not to worry, Mariah." Ron did his best to sound convincing. "You are the strongest woman I have ever met. You can get through this. I know it."

"Ron, I'm so grateful for everything you have done for me," Mariah said through her sobs. Just then, her left index finger started to burn a little and she wedged her cell phone between her chin and shoulder so she could rub it. As she struggled to hear him through the static, she had a brief vision of the two of them bound and shackled on a ship. Water was pouring in a porthole above their heads and they were soaked with salt water and perspiration. In a second, the image was gone. "We've been through worse times than this together. You're right. We'll get through this too," she said with resolve.

Ron had no idea what worse times she was referring to, but he let her talk. The static on their connection was like a crackling, plastic bag. With all land lines down and many transmitter towers destroyed, cell phone companies were overloaded and service was poor.

"I'll be there in person as soon as I can clear my schedule. In the meantime, please know that you are in my constant thoughts. I know it's difficult to get through but try to call me anytime you need to—call collect—in the middle of the night. It's OK. I'm here for you." Mariah hung up the phone feeling that deep sense of safety Ron always gave her.

Before long, there was a financial boom during the rebuilding process while the insurance money flowed. New service people arrived daily on the island. Construction crews, electric companies from the southern states and huge barges of building materials were shipped down. The aftermath of *Marilyn* became a raw lesson of survival, one day at a time.

Chapter Forty-five

Chris Patolino was in touch with Sara and Scott through the struggling months of their rebuilding efforts. Two weeks after the storm, the couple found an unscathed house to rent, with an affordable price, located on the most remote point of St. John. The area was called, Coral Bay, or more affectionately, *Hurricane Hole,* due to its usually safe anchorage, but in the case of *Marilyn,* most of the boats that sought refuge there were either wrecked or sunk. The normally peaceful bay was now littered with sailboats lying on their sides, looking like beached whales. In spite of the neighboring destruction, Scott and Sara's new home had come through without a scratch.

In mid April, Chris received a call from his friends. "Greetings from hurricane hell," Scott joked. "Well, as much as we loved it here, we can't deal with this survival lifestyle anymore. As crazy as it sounds, we're ready to trade in our flip-flops for L.L. Bean snow boots and move to Maine. It's a radical choice, we know, but right now it seems appealing after what we've been through—snow and all!"

"I don't blame you. It must be hard for city slickers like yourselves to cope with it all," Chris chided. "I'll come down and help you pack what few belongings you have left. By the way, is your friend, Mariah still down there?"

"We saw her at the big Christmas Party she throws every year and we spoke to her on the phone in March, but beyond that, we're not sure what's going on with her. Katie mentioned the other day she heard through the grapevine that Mariah was trying to sell her business. When you get here, we'll call her. Maybe we can finally introduce you two."

Chris was not prepared for what he saw as he flew over St. Thomas a week later. It had been seven months since the storm and he assumed the island would be back together by then. He hadn't taken into account the Virgin Islands are twelve hundred miles from the mainland and everything needed for reconstruction had to be shipped in. Every rebuilding effort was bound to take longer.

Scott and Sara's yard sale was well underway when Chris got there and he rolled up his sleeves and helped load sold items into the purchaser's vehicles. But, by day two, he was anxious to get in touch with Mariah.

"Did you call her, yet? Give me her number and I'll call her myself." Chris' patience had expired. "If I wait for you, we'll be too old to enjoy each other."

"Give me the phone, you crazy Italian. Everything doesn't revolve around you and your social life, you know?" Scott teased. "We're trying to move in case you haven't noticed." He dialed Mariah's office and left a message asking her to meet them at a restaurant adjacent to the ferry dock. At four thirty that afternoon, she called back to confirm.

"Finally, this mysterious friend of yours will have a face as well as a name," said Mariah. Changing the subject, she added, "God, I've missed you and Sara! Now, you're moving to the great white north to become true Maniacs! You're going to freeze your asses off come winter. Don't you want to rethink this?"

"Sara doesn't want to stay through another hurricane season. She's had it. It takes her too long to collect the crap we haul around the world to have it ruined again in another storm," Scott kidded. "Once was enough, thank you."

Mariah arrived at the restaurant several minutes early. She recognized a group of people who were dining there and was chatting with them when her St. John friends walked in. Noticing them out of the corner of her eye, Mariah saw Chris and instantly felt a familiar connection. Within seconds, a vivid scene of the two of them in a northern landscape by a lake flashed across Mariah's memory and she was temporarily stunned. In the vision she was dressed in a buckskin dress with beaded designs on the sleeves and neckline. She smiled at Mariah and whispered, *"It is him."* The Indian squaw nodded and blew Mariah a kiss. She held up her left index finger, which bore the same star-shaped marking. Then, quickly, the image was gone.

Mariah took a deep breath and held onto the back of a chair for stability. The scene had been so real! The voice clearly audible! Mariah glanced out at the ocean and was surprised to see pelicans on the water rather than Canadian geese. She glanced down at her star-marked finger and shuddered.

"Well, enjoy your dinner," she said to the diners. "If you'll excuse me, my friends have arrived from St. John." Mariah walked toward the entrance of the restaurant and waved to a few more patrons. She gave Scott and Sara each a warm hug and a kiss. Impulsively, she gave Chris a hug, too and he blushed. Before they even sat down, their banter began.

"You sure know how to work the room, Mariah," Chris teased. "Do you actually know everyone here, or are you just pretending to be this popular?"

Surveying the room, she responded, "I don't know any of those people at the bar—yet! Give me half and hour though, and I will." Communication was her Gemini specialty.

"Hopefully, we will be more interesting company for you this evening." Chris said, gazing into Mariah's eyes and smiling. Chris' gleaming white teeth mesmerized Mariah. His smile jarred her soul's memory and throughout the evening, her mind wandered and merged between the thin veil of time and space to another lifetime.

For a brief moment, she saw them introducing themselves to each other in a cozy Indian lodge around a warm fire on a stormy night. In another glimpse, they were both in a field on a farm. She was muddy—he was extremely over-dressed. Later on, during the course of the evening, she saw them both in a big, sparsely furnished house in an unfriendly northern town with a French name. Mariah was used to her intuitive glimpses, but this night was more active than any she had experienced. She struggled to keep herself on solid ground while she drifted between the worlds.

"We have forty-five minutes to kill until the next boat leaves for Cruz Bay," Scott said, pushing his dinner plate out of the way. "Let's walk over to Duffy's Love Shack and have one of their weird, smoking cocktails. It's a young crowd, so the visuals are always intriguing, if you catch my drift," Scott said, winking at Chris. "What do you girls have to say? Should we go and sample the concoctions?"

"I like the visuals I have right now, thank you very much." Chris answered, staring at Mariah. "But sure, let's go across the street and check it out. Ladies, what do you think? Are you up for some weird after-dinner drinks?"

"Most definitely," Mariah replied. Duffy's was one of Mariah's advertisers and she always appreciated opportunities to patronize them.

"I knew you two would hit it off," Scott whispered to Chris as the foursome crossed the street. The girls were lagging behind, chattering away. "Sara and I always said that getting you two together would be like setting off an explosion." Scott laughed.

"God! Imagine me actually finding a woman who can keep up with me!" Chris remarked.

"Yes, God is good meh son," Scott said as he made a sign of the cross. Chris slapped his hand away and they both laughed.

Duffy's Love Shack was in the middle of a parking lot where people were drinking and dancing all the way from the bar to the asphalt. The two couples found a table that wasn't too loud and struggled to see the cocktail menu in the dim light of a citronella candle. Periodically, music from 2001: A Space Odyssey played and a waitress came out with a bizarre, smoking drink in a parrot shaped glass, and placed it in the middle of a table.

Scott and Sara shared a concoction shaped like a smoking volcano and Chris and Mariah enjoyed their novelty beverage from a plastic Godzilla. Before they had a chance to finish, the last horn of the night blew its five-minute warning that the final ferry to St. John was leaving. They paid the bill, and then dashed across the street to where Mariah's car was parked. Scott and Sara gave Mariah a hug and kiss and Chris took the liberty to do the same.

"Can I call you so we can get together again before I leave?" Chris asked as he held her at arms length.

"You better call me. We've waited too long to finally meet to have this be our only time together," Mariah replied with a wink.

"My flight home isn't until noon on Sunday, so I'll call you tomorrow and we'll figure it out." The three of them boarded the boat, and waved until Mariah disappeared from sight.

Chris gazed out over Lovango, Mingo and Grass Cays and the rest of the moonlit British Virgins beyond, while the ferry skimmed across Pillsbury Sound to St. John. He sat back in the seat with a peaceful expression on his handsome face. His curly dark hair bounced in the sultry evening breeze and he closed his eyes remembering the longing in Mariah's eyes.

"Why didn't you tell me she was such a unique almond color? She's very exotic," Chris said. "I want to touch her skin all night."

"I'll bet you do." Sara commented with a smile. "Someone in her family must have been black or Indian, maybe. I've never asked her. You two seemed to hit it off tonight, Chris."

"Yeah, we did indeed! It's strange. . . it felt like we were old friends getting together after being apart for a long time. She has a certain familiarity, yet I know I've never met her before."

"Maybe it's because you've heard us talking about her so much over the last couple of years, you feel as though you already know her," Sara suggested.

"Maybe, but it was more than that. As I watched her talking with her friends when we first walked in tonight, I had one of those déja vu moments I've heard about but never experienced before. For a split second, I saw her leaning over, explaining some sort of issue to a group of workers, and she was wearing a long skirt. Then the scene vanished out of my head and I saw her clearly standing by the table with her friends again. It happened in a flash. It was really weird." He shook his head vigorously.

"Yes, my Italian friend, you *are* weird, which is why we get along with you so well. What do you make of it, my man?" Scott asked.

"I don't know. Maybe I'm delirious with exhaustion from all the moving chores I've been doing since I arrived." Chris teased. "I'm supposed to be on vacation but instead I'm overworked and my mind is playing tricks on me."

"Yeah, that's probably it. Too bad, baby," Sara said without moving. Her eyes were closed and she was beginning to doze off. "Well, on the other hand, don't you think you should thank us for giving you such an interesting experience? If it wasn't for us, you wouldn't be able to tell a wild story like that."

"True." Chris mumbled as he closed his eyes. He let the hum of the ferryboat hypnotize him while thoughts of Mariah consumed his mind.

"That's a cool birthmark on her finger, don't you think?" Sara asked.

"Yes, it is. I've never seen anything quite like it before. It sure looks like a tattoo—it's hard to believe it's not. Sometimes, it appears to almost glow in certain light."

"Yeah—her sister's call it her magic mark. She's pretty magical, all right. We're really going to miss her." Sara mumbled. You could hear the regret in her voice.

That same night, Chris dreamed he was with Mariah in a mountainous area by a huge lake. They were camping in a cave fixed up like a cabin with a thatched bed. She was teasing him because he wouldn't bathe in the cold lake. When Chris awoke, he was amazed at how vivid his dream was and how it lingered in his thoughts throughout the day.

"I had a great time last night," Chris said to Mariah over the phone the next morning.

"Me, too. It's hard not to have a great time with Scott and Sara. And it's so nice to have finally met you." Mariah said.

He almost told her about his dream, but decided better of it. "There's a good-bye party for Scott and Sara in Cruz Bay on Friday night. I would love you to be my date. Katie also wants you to come. She misses you."

"I would love to be your date." Mariah replied. "It'll be fun seeing my St. John pals again. I'll be on the seven o'clock boat." Mariah hung up the phone and let out a joyous squeal. It was only Wednesday—Friday felt like an eternity away.

As the ferry approached the pier that Friday evening, Mariah gazed at the peaceful little village of Cruz Bay and was relieved all seemed well since the storm. She got off the boat and breezed toward the restaurant through a throng of curious, disembarking passengers. Across the street, she saw Chris standing by the rail on the deck where a long table was adorned with black balloons. Whatever winter clothes anyone had to offer as props to rib their friends about their northern destination were draped on the backs of chairs and hanging on hooks. Pictures of snow-covered scenery were pinned on the walls and Mariah later noticed they were locations in Maine. Katie had them enlarged from some calendars she had at the bookstore. Of course, she only chose winter scenes to emphasize the cold. She was pulling out all the stops, hoping to convince her friends to stay.

Chris' face seemed to beam brighter than the nearby street lamp when he saw her cross the street. He waited patiently while she greeted her friends, slowly working her way toward him. He had always been somewhat shy and he admired how she handled everyone in the crowd with such grace. By mid-evening, the party had faded to the background. As far as they were concerned, Mariah and Chris were the only two people left on the planet.

A reggae band was playing music at the docks. It was carnival time on St. John and Cruz Bay was keeping the beat. They danced along with the spirit of the party until Mariah had to leave. "Cinderella's pumpkin" was tied to the dock, once again blowing its last horn of the evening.

They walked hand in hand to the boat and as they kissed goodnight, Mariah could feel Chris' desire poking through his jeans. They laughed and kissed again. "Are you sure you can't stay over and leave early in the morning?" Chris tried not to beg. "I'm sure it's fine with Scott and Sara.

"I'd like to, but I can't. Not tonight. It's late and I'm a mom. I need to go home," she replied. "Let's all have dinner tomorrow night on St. Thomas. Then we'll send Scott and Sara on their way. You can stay overnight at my house and I'll drive you to the airport late morning. Didn't you say you had a noon flight?"

He replied, "Yes, I do, unfortunately," his voice dropping. Clearing his throat, he added, "It sounds like a good plan. Where should we go for dinner?" he asked.

"One of my favorite places on the island is Virgilio's, and I heard Sara mention she had always wanted to eat there," Mariah suggested.

"Perfect. What boat should we come over on?" Chris asked.

"How about the five o'clock?" Mariah asked. "That way, I can work a full day and attempt to catch up on some work. With all my daydreaming about you this past week, I haven't gotten much done." They kissed again, and she boarded the boat reluctantly. "I'll pick all of you up at five-twenty tomorrow afternoon," she said and blew him another kiss.

Saturdays were usually productive workdays for Mariah. Normally, it was the only time she could work without interruptions—but not this particular Saturday. It wasn't phone calls interfering with her concentration; it was fantasies that filled her overactive mind. Twice, she stopped her page layout completely. She flashed on a scene in an old fashioned Inn where she saw herself go willingly down the hall to the room of a man she loved. That man was indeed Chris. Forcing her mind to pay attention to her work, she tried hard to put the images to rest, but they would not stop playing in her head. Later, she saw Chris dressed in frontier clothing in a northern wooded place by the edge of a big lake. They seemed deeply in love, content with one another.

Finally, the clock stuck five! It was time to lock the office and pick her guests up at the ferry dock. Mariah pulled into the parking lot just as the boat was tying up to the pier. Chris was the first passenger to disembark. He ran down the ramp and the short pier to her vehicle, suitcase in hand. Scott and Sara lagged behind, giving the couple a few minutes alone together.

"I thought we would have a drink at my place before dinner," Mariah said once everyone was seated in her Blazer. "The view is worth the drive, I promise." Mariah had sold her wrecked house a few months before and found a rental in the same neighborhood overlooking exquisite Magens Bay and beyond to the British Virgin Islands.

"Sure, we haven't seen your new place, yet," Scott urged. He added, "Oh, I hope you don't mind, Mariah, I called Nancy earlier and she's meeting us for dinner tonight. We wanted to see her again before we left." Mariah expressed her delight at the thought of catching up with her long-time compatriot.

Later, when they arrived at Virgilio's, Nancy was already there, waiting for them.

"It's an honor to finally meet the man who has as much energy as Mariah!" Nancy said, reaching her hand toward Chris for a shake. "Scott told me you two were positively explosive together! I'm Nancy, Chris. Nice to have you St. Johnians' on beautiful St. Thomas for a change."

"Well, every once in a while we like to come over to the chaos of your island so we can appreciate the quiet of ours," Chris replied smiling at Mariah, who jokingly stuck out her tongue at his comment. "We do appreciate some things about St. Thomas, though." Chris took Mariah's hand and kissed it. "Like your restaurants, for instance."

"Oh sure, our restaurants, uh huh. I thought you were going to say that you appreciated St. Thomas for its women." Mariah leaned over and put her arm around Nancy and they both nodded.

Midway through their dinner, Scott nudged Chris. "Hey, stop hogging Mariah all to yourself. Sara and I will be missing her for a long, long time. On the other hand, I imagine you will be down here to see her more than you ever came to see us." There was an obvious energy around the couple and it was evident to their friends that love was in the air.

After they sated themselves with lively conversations and an assortment of Virgilio's specialties, they paid the bill and said their good-byes to Nancy. She promised Scott and Sara use of a tropical villa at a discount when the snow started to fall in

Maine. Mariah and Chris then drove Scott and Sara to the east end so they could ride the ferry to St. John for the last time before they flew off the island that following Tuesday. "I'll see you both in New York on Wednesday, right?" Chris asked. "Didn't you say you had more furniture in a storage unit in Brewster?"

"Yeah. Our crap is spread all over the globe—literally!" Sara said with a laugh referring mainly to the hurricane. "We're going to drive to Maine in a U-Haul, after you help us pack it." Chris caught her little joke.

"There's no way I'm going to help you load more stuff for this move. I just pulled yard sale duty for two days. Tell you what. I'll call you and say goodbye over the phone. It will be considerably easier on my back," Chris said, giving Sara a hug. Then he shook Scott's hand and patted him on the back.

"Sounds good. We appreciate your help, even though your motivation for coming was to meet Mariah. Don't try to deny it. We understand. Come and see us in Portland sometime, Mariah. We'll probably be down to see you by mid-February." Scott chided, "that will be about as long as I'll be able to take Sara's bitchin' about the cold." Sara slugged him lightly on the arm. They boarded the ferry just before it pulled away from the dock.

"Bye, you wild and crazy people. You know you're welcome to come and thaw out anytime. Keep in touch...I'll miss you," Mariah yelled over the boat's bow thrusters. Chris escorted her down the dock toward her SUV.

"I'm looking forward to having you all to myself. Let's get out of here," Chris whispered in Mariah's ear as she started the engine.

While Mariah drove to her house, Chris held her hand to his lips and gently kissed her fingers, sending warm, tingling sensations through her body. She glanced over at Chris and saw he had a peaceful, smile on his lips. He leaned over and kissed Mariah's neck as she was driving and squeezed her hand tighter as they traveled to the north side of the island. The eight-mile ride to her house seemed a thousand hours long.

Mariah realized they had the house to themselves for a limited time. Jason was due home later on that night. Mariah turned on her favorite music, and Chris headed for the couch. She took his hand and led him to her bed, instead. She had never been shy and she knew what she wanted. They only had a few hours before he would fly away and Mariah had to take the chance he might think her too aggressive. They lay down and immediately began kissing each other while removing their clothing. In their passionate frenzy, they forgot all about her son until they heard the front door unlock, open and slam shut. Mariah quietly got up and pulled herself together before going to her son's bedroom door.

"Goodnight, Jason, I love you," she whispered through the louvered door. "Did you have a good time, tonight?" Mariah started to mention they had a guest in the house, but decided to save the introductions for the morning.

"Goodnight, Mom. Yeah, I had an OK time. I love you, too," he mumbled, already half asleep. Mariah then got their futon mattress out of the hall closet and regretfully made Chris a bed on the living room floor. She hated to have to do it, but she could not allow him to spend the night in her room with her son now home. Once Chris' bed was set up, Mariah went back to her bedroom, closed the door and climbed into bed. Chris, in preparation for possible introductions had already gotten dressed. The couple lay on her bed and groped at each other attempting to be quiet.

"It's 3:15 am." Chris eventually whispered in her sweet smelling ear. "I'm going out to my own bed so you can get some sleep."

"OK. We can try it. Goodnight you delicious thing," she whispered. Chris went into the living room alone and attempted to fall asleep but Mariah's bedroom door wasn't closed all the way. He could see her laying in her cozy bed, so soft and inviting. He crept back in to cuddle with her and she instantly curled her body into his like a spoon. Within seconds, Chris could tell by her breathing she had fallen into a deep sleep. He held her for a few hours and just before dawn, he unwound himself so as not to wake her and returned to his bed in the living room in case her son got up early.

When Mariah opened her eyes an hour later, she saw Chris' silhouette through the blinds on the sliding glass doors, which led out to the verandah. He was watching the colorful sunrise splash over the neighboring islands. Mariah lay in bed watching him for a few moments before getting up. She wished she wasn't driving him to the airport in a few short hours. Mariah got dressed quickly and went out to greet him. It was 6:00 am, already a beautiful day in her Caribbean neighborhood. Chris held her tightly in his arms. It seemed so unfair having to leave in a few short hours after waiting so long to finally meet her.

They ate breakfast on the deck and talked incessantly about life in New York, the Virgin Islands, growing up in an Italian household and being a single parent. Jason didn't wake up until shortly before they had to leave for the airport.

"Mom, why is this bed on the floor and who is that guy on the porch?" he yelled from the kitchen while getting himself a glass of juice.

"He's a friend of mine who needed to sleep on St. Thomas so he can catch his plane this morning. Why don't you come out here and I'll introduce you," Mariah answered back.

Jason came outside with his sunglasses on, extending his hand when Chris reached out to shake it. "Nice to meet you," he growled with suspicion.

"I'm driving him to the airport on my way to the marina. Remember I told you I was going sailing for the next three days with my girlfriends?" Mariah asked.

"Yeah, I remember," her son said. He nodded to Chris before walking to his room. Jason was eighteen years old, and very protective of his single mother. Chris understood and smiled at Mariah. Jason eventually left the house, surfboard in tow and headed for the beach and Mariah drove Chris to the airport. As they pulled up in front of the terminal, they exchanged business cards and phone numbers.

"I'll call you the next time I'm here," Chris uttered. He knew the words fell well short of his emotions. It sounded like some line he would use in a bar. He gave Mariah a final good-bye kiss on the lips before heading to the first-class check in.

"You better call me before that," Mariah said, walking toward him. "Have a good flight home. Be safe." She gave him one last kiss on the cheek and got back in her vehicle to drive out of the airport. His business card was staring at her from the console. Impulsively, she picked up her cell phone and dialed his number.

"Hi, I just left you at the airport, and you are already haunting my mind. I'll be back from my sailing trip in a few days and will look forward to talking to you then. I'm not sure how much mileage we can squeeze out of our brief romp last night, but I'm feeling greedy for more. Call me Wednesday evening if you feel the same." Mariah pushed the 'end' button on her phone and let out an excited yelp as she drove to the dock to meet her friends.

During the three days of sailing, Mariah swooned and giggled and drove her friends just short of crazy.

"You're disgusting," they kidded her. "You're acting like a school girl!"

"Yeah, get a grip on yourself, for Christ's sake!" Katie added jokingly. "Actually, girlfriend, Chris is the perfect man for you. Who else is going to keep up with you? At least you both have a lot of spark. That's bound to come in handy when a relationship needs a jump start." The girls agreed.

"When I met Chris, I remember wondering who he reminded me of?" Katie said. "It wasn't his features so much as his energy. But, after about ten minutes in his presence, I connected him to you!" Katie kissed Mariah's hand. "Even though he lives far away, do it girlfriend. It's only a three-and-a-half-hour flight from JFK and you're there—or he's here! Distance keeps it all romantic!"

When she got home, there were three messages from Chris, all of them wanting her to come for a visit. He remembered her speaking of a wedding she planned to attend in Manhattan, but he couldn't remember the date. The longing in his voice soothed her doubts. She played the messages a few times and later that evening, she returned his calls.

"The wedding isn't until mid-September, and it's barely July. I doubt we can stretch our groping the other night that far. If we don't meet up soon, I'm afraid I might lose interest," Mariah teased.

"I can't let that happen! Why don't you come next weekend? We can go to the city one day and play in the country at my house for the rest of the time. Can you get away from Thursday to Monday?"

"Yes, but I'll be struggling with patience more than scheduling. I assume you're worth the wait," she teased.

"Let's hope so. We'll help each other through it," he joked.

She landed at JFK nine days later and was greeted by a limo driver who held up a large black and white sign with her name on it. Due to a TV taping, Chris couldn't be there himself so he explained where the hide-a-key was and told her to make herself at home when she arrived.

Ironically, both vehicles pulled into the driveway at precisely the same time. Chris tucked his Suburban in the garage and nervously unloaded groceries while the limo driver got Mariah's bag. As she took in the image of his house from the window of the limo, her left index finger started to throb. She rubbed it quickly as the driver opened her door, and helped her out.

"Hey! How are you?" Chris called out, behind the bags of food. "I had no idea we would finish as early as we did. I could have picked you up after all."

Mariah walked over to him and gave him a big, passionate kiss. "Actually, I enjoyed riding in the limo. It made me feel like a rock star," she said, tossing her hair from her face. "Aren't you going to invite me in? I'm dying to see this place."

"Of course I am. Where are my manners?" Chris said, feeling more relaxed. "Won't you please come in?"

"My pleasure! Tip the driver and let's leave this driveway at once."

"Good idea." Chris agreed, reaching for his wallet.

Mariah was amazed he lived in such a large house. The design was architecturally stunning, and was constructed in the post-and-beam style with massive oak beams and high, cathedral ceilings. As she peered into two sparsely furnished guest rooms, Mariah had a subtle, lonely feeling, but she only smiled.

"It's amazing! You must feel like the King of the neighborhood with all this space."

"King Patolino—absolutely!" Chris said with a nod. "When I designed this house, I was married, but by the time I finished it, I wasn't. It was supposed to be filled with kids and noise. I'm still hoping that will happen." He told her the short version of his divorce story. As he spoke, it was apparent he also had wounds of betrayal.

As she listened, she knew they could help each other heal, if they dared.

The next morning they awoke to stormy weather, but by mid-afternoon the rain stopped and Chris took Mariah for a walk in the woods. "Let's swim in the reservoir and wash off this mud! " She loved to swim and even with the stormy weather, she thought the reservoir looked inviting. "I don't ever get a chance to swim in fresh water on St. Thomas."

"Are you kidding? That water will be freezing after all this rain!" Chris said.

"I know! Think how refreshing it will be!" Mariah yelled, so she could be heard above the spillway. Chris shrugged and gave her a little smile. They stripped out of their clothes and jumped in. As they swam, Chris remembered the dream he had about them sharing this same experience the night he had met Mariah. The memory filled him with wonder and warmth.

They awoke the next morning to clear, blue skies and wasted no time going to the Big Apple. There was a Smithsonian exhibit at the old New York Coliseum and a showing of paintings and sculptures of fairies at the Frick Museum that they both wanted to see. Mariah loved fairies and was delighted Chris appreciated them, too.

"Wasn't that fabulous?" he asked Mariah when they left the museum. There was a street vendor on the corner selling Italian ice and Chris motioned for two.

"God, yes! I was swept away by it. I thought I recognized a few of the fairies in the beginning of the tour, but I'm not sure. It's been a long time since I've see them up close," Mariah said.

"Yeah, sure you did. Are you on a first name basis with these fairies?"

"No, actually, we were never formally introduced." Mariah replied with certainty.

Chris was teasing but he immediately realized Mariah was not. *Does she actually believe in fairies?* He wondered, but decided to leave the comment alone. He glanced at her finger and the star appeared to be shining like a beacon.

"Let's walk through Central Park and see the street entertainment. I love the dancing and the drumming on the plastic paint buckets! Oh, and the puppet shows, too! New York is a trip!" Mariah stated enthusiastically

"That, it is, my love." Chris said, kissing her fingers. "A walk would be nice after all that standing on the marble floors at the Frick." The day was clear as crystal and Central Park was full of people enjoying the fresh air. They walked by Wolman skating rink and ended up by the Boathouse where they paused to watch boats piloted by giggling girls, rowing along the river.

By late afternoon, they were ready to retreat to the country. They retrieved Chris' vehicle from the underground parking lot and headed north to the suburbs. As they traveled along the Merritt Parkway, songs played from a favorite CD.

"I just got this *Squeeze* album and every time I hear this song, I think of you," Chris said grasping her hand across the console. *"This summer, I'm so in love with you."* He smiled as he sang aloud. Mariah was starting to feel the same way.

Chapter Forty-six

1641–1643

It took less than a week for Jigonsassee and Samuel to fall deeply in love. Samuel trapped around her village more often so they could spend time together. Since meeting her, he had been home to Coteau-du-Lac only twice. He stayed just long enough to check his trading post, see how his employee was fending in his absence and re-pack clean clothes before returning to her village. Samuel's heart was now with Jigonsassee and his material world held little importance in comparison.

His store was doing well and the profits increased steadily. Truth be told, he was much more comfortable in the woods, away from people and Samuel was delighted he could rely on his manager, Mr. Stark to hold things together. The Trading Post was Samuel's security and because of it, he was able to do the two things he loved most—trap, and be with his Huron lover.

When Jigonsassee was young, she often begged Giawiio to take her with him on hunting trips and sometimes he appeased her. Giawiio was not only her brother—he was also her best friend. It was only fitting that he would be the one to bring her the love of her life. Now she had Samuel to go on explorations with. Since he was forever seeking new trapping grounds, they would go for days, sometimes weeks, trapping until they had all the pelts they could carry.

Once, they went to the mountains west of the Hudson River and found themselves in a huge lake region. They hiked south, past St. Regis Falls and climbed to the top of Rice Mountain. From there, they looked into sweeping valleys, surrounded by the majestic Adirondacks. Lakes were plentiful as far as their eyes could see and Jigonsassee was in awe of the Great Earth Mother's beauty. She raised her arms and gave thanks and praise for the moment. Samuel smiled when he heard her singing. Jigonsassee was absorbed in ritual, carried away by the power of spirit and she did not hear him approach. As he watched her, he felt the power of that same energy. It stirred all the way to his feet, through his arms and out the tips of his fingers.

Somehow, Jigonsassee had released a bound up part of Samuel. This spiritual freedom was uncharted territory for the otherwise controlled man. His world was bigger and his life felt more complete.

He was amazed the first time he and Jigonsassee made love. He had experienced sex several other times and expected it to be similar—pleasure for ten minutes followed by an overwhelming eagerness to get up and get dressed. But with Jigonsassee it went far beyond the physical and he wanted to stay in bed with her and snuggle into their old age. Their souls, as well as their bodies, united in a timeless recognition. Samuel now knew the power of love and he could see beauty in everything. He could hardly remember his life without Jigonsassee and it was as if she had always been with him.

The abundance of beaver, mink and otters within a three-day journey from the Huron village astonished Samuel and he marveled that he and Giawiio had not stumbled on that treasure trove before. Perhaps the reason stemmed from the fact that they were on the northern edge of Mohawk territory and the Hurons had a healthy respect for the aggression of the Mohawks. They were not a tribe to be taken lightly, yet whenever Samuel and Jigonsassee were in that vacinity, they saw no one.

Lake Placid was their favorite body of water in the area. It was surrounded by the Adirondack Mountains and was indeed placid and freezing. But the frigid temperature didn't bother Jigonsassee as she dove in each day to bathe. Samuel, on the other hand, inched his way into the water, gradually numbing his lower extremities. "Come, Samuel, dive in at once. It is not as cold when you do it that way."

"I am doing just fine going in slowly, thank you very much. The shock from that cold water could give a person a heart attack!" he exclaimed. "I cannot believe you can tolerate it. When I am trapping alone, I usually heat water and wash myself with a sponge. I hate cold water!"

"Well, then, get out and heat your bath water. Just because it is my preference to wash that way, does not mean you have to do it, too," she was matter-of-fact. Jigonsassee was already out of the water, dried off and dressed. "I will get some kindling for a fire," she told him as he inched himself further in the water.

As Jigonsassee gathered an armful of small, dry twigs, she stumbled upon a small cave by the edge of the lake. Most likely a bear had claimed it. It was roomy inside and the back wall had a natural ledge, helpful for storing supplies off the ground. Jigonsassee got an idea and headed back to their camp to find Samuel still standing thigh deep in water.

"I am willing to bet you can no longer feel your legs! You are a funny man, my love." Jigonsassee kidded. She reached for a warm blanket, holding it open for him as he got out of the water. Once his teeth stopped chattering, he built a fire. "I found a home for us on the edge of the lake." Jigonsassee said excitedly. "It is around that bend. Put your boots on and let me take you there."

"All right. Hand me that big log next to your foot, please. I want to get this fire roaring so we can cook breakfast as soon as we return." He put the log on the bed of coals and after he had filled their big cooking pot with water, he positioned it evenly over the fire. Jigonsassee smiled. She knew he was going to bathe his own way when they returned. They went around the bend and she showed him the cave. "Is this not perfect? We could stay warm and dry in here all winter if we chose to."

"I only hope it is not occupied at the moment." Samuel said picking up a clump of bear fur from the ground.

"No, the bear is gone, but we need to get our scent in it soon if we want to use it when we come here. After this next moon, he will want to return for his winter's sleep."

She cleaned out the cave and reinforced the roof with pine boughs and various underbrush piled high with leaves. She again layered it with more pine boughs until the covering was strong and thick. She built a bed in the same manner and put it by the back wall of the cave. Each time they returned to the lake, they had their own cozy retreat that they hated to leave when it was time to go.

There was a peaceful, passionate ease in their togetherness. Each of them felt solid in themselves and their relationship was a compliment to their lives. Jigonsassee was the soothing balm that Samuel's heart had been aching for—and he was hers.

"Since Jigonsassee has come of age, most of our warriors have wanted her, but she would not choose any of us," a brave from the village told Samuel one night as they smoked by the fire. "It is you she wants to lay with. It hurts our pride to be passed over, but we honor you as her choice and our brother. Here, smoke."

Samuel took the pipe and inhaled deeply. He appreciated their acceptance.

Jigonsassee was swept away with blissful love and she relished her time with Samuel. He was independent and she was amazed that he could accomplish so much without the support from his birth family. She was independent too, but she understood the value of her villagers. By contrast, Samuel had always been a loner, his own man. Being around his determination and energy was addictive for Jigonsassee, and she found herself craving his presence whenever he was away on his own.

Chapter Forty-seven

1995 – 1996

Every other weekend, either Chris flew to St. Thomas or Mariah flew to New York. Between visits, they spent endless hours on the telephone. Professionally, they continued to work in order to keep their business lives running. But being with each other was a priority. Whenever they were apart, Chris and Mariah ached to be together and it was worth whatever it took to make it happen.

Mariah was amazed at how comfortable she felt with Chris. She wondered if her deep inner satisfaction had anything to do with *Sam*, the imaginary mate she had conjured up at the Royal Hawaiian bar two months previously while on vacation with Katie. How else could she have requested such specifics about her lover if she didn't already know him in her soul?

During a peaceful romantic evening when the two of them were alone, Mariah told Chris the story about *Dan* and *Sam*. He leaned back in his chair, folded his arms across his chest and listened while looking deep into Mariah's eyes. "Well, you might as well start calling me *Sam* right now, because it's *me,* baby! I'm your guy. I heard you calling out to me all the way across the world."

Over the years, Mariah learned to not expect much but rather take things as they came. She and Chris cared deeply for one another but she also felt they did not need to stick to each other like glue. She was relieved that she didn't need to be the one to keep it all together. Chris was an active participant in their relationship and they each felt a deep trust, in spite of their physical distance.

Over time, the American Airlines ticket agents at both airports got to know each of them by name. For the most part, when they visited each other, they stayed home and played house together. It didn't matter where they were, as long as they were together. Mariah was thankful that her children were older and settled into their own daily routines. Jason was eighteen and working a full-time job with a dive shop and Emily was attending boarding school on the mainland. Mariah was experiencing a freedom as an adult she hadn't known since before she was married.

Over time, the back and forth vigil got tedious for them both. Eventually, something would have to give and decisions would have to be made. Chris' business was based out of New York City and he couldn't relocate to the islands.

"Didn't you tell me that at one time you had considered selling your business and moving off the island?" Chris asked one night after they had gotten into bed.

"Yes, I thought about it for a while. I love Hawaii, and I considered moving there but it's too far away. I wanted to live somewhere out of the threat of hurricanes. At one point, I thought about the mountains of North Carolina. The kids and I have been going there on vacations for years and we love it there. That was our plan anyway, but you know how plans can change with life." Mariah said with a wink.

Chris snuggled next to Mariah and held her close. "Yeah, life has a way of changing even the best of plans." He felt the urge to suggest she and Emily move in with him, but changed his mind. For some reason, the timing didn't feel quite right. "You've certainly changed my life for the better," he said instead. Mariah curled herself into Chris' warmth and relaxed into the safety.

Prior to meeting Chris, it would have never occurred to Mariah to move to the northeast. While it did have a quaint charm, it wasn't a place that called out to her. The area felt too conservative for someone as free-spirited as Mariah. She was used to wearing brightly colored sarongs and dainty sandals and couldn't imagine herself sporting an all black wardrobe. Nevertheless, a powerful attraction was drawing Mariah to New York. It was the magic of Chris Patalino.

Chapter Forty-eight

1643

"I want to show you my home, Sassy. And you must see my big store! It sits at the end of the town's main street and you can read my name above the door from several blocks away," Samuel boasted, sticking out his chest. "It is filled from floor to ceiling with every object imaginable." His voice was nostalgic. "Will you please come and see it and spend some time with me there?"

"Of course I will. Your home has been a mystery to me since I met you. I want to see it," she said with a sincere smile. Jigonsassee had not been to a white man's village before, and she welcomed the opportunity to see one.

It took the couple five days of steady travel to arrive at their destination, and she then realized what Samuel went through every time he came to see her.

When they arrived in Coteau-du-Lac, the white people stared at Jigonsassee as if she were on display. As they proceeded down the street in his wagon, not one person spoke to them or gave the slightest gesture of greeting. She felt shunned and confused by the obvious lack of welcome.

"Do you not know these people? They must know you, yet they do not greet you," she whispered in Samuel's ear. Her treatment in Coteau-du-Lac was quite different from the hospitality extended to a stranger who entered her village.

"Sssshhh. They will think you are gossiping about them. My people prefer to be formally introduced. They do not know who you are." Samuel added, "That is how things are done in civilization."

"Well, I have learned to be more civil than this!" She sat up in her seat, held her head high, and began smiling and nodding at the people walking by. Not one of them returned her gestures. Finally, Samuel grabbed her arm to stop her from waving. "Let go of my arm," Jigonsassee commanded, pulling free from Samuel's grasp.

"I am sorry," Samuel said, letting her arm loose, "but you are embarrassing yourself." Jigonsassee jerked her arm free.

"I have nothing to be embarrassed about. Perhaps it is you who feels shame," she said, folding her arms across her chest for the remainder of the ride down Main Street. Samuel was humbled by her words and had no appropriate response. In his heart he knew she was right.

He lived on the edge of town by a narrow creek and Jigonsassee gasped when they came upon his house. She never imagined it would be so large. As she walked around, she tried to picture herself living there, cooking in his kitchen, and planting her garden in his backyard. She was amazed by the huge, cooking fireplace. "What is this symbol here?" Jigonsassee asked as she pointed to a star-shaped design made of seashells below the mantle. "It is just like the mark on my finger!"

Samuel nodded, smiling at his true love. "It is a design I made long before I knew you. A man traded those shells for supplies at my store and I saved them. He said he got them at the edge of the ocean, which is the biggest of lakes." Jigonsassee nodded. She had heard of the ocean and had herself found shells along the banks of the St. Lawrence River.

She found the artistic shell design most attractive, but overall, she thought his house was cold and unlived-in. However, when she went upstairs to his bedroom and saw his big feather bed next to yet another fireplace, she could not wait to climb in.

"What luxury to have this big bed all to yourself!" she exclaimed. She was used to sharing both fire and sleeping spaces in her lodge with her family. Samuel's bedroom was the only room in the house where she felt truly comfortable. Overall, the spirit of the Samuel she knew was not present in this building. He seemed to not belong to it.

They spent two long months together in Coteau-du-Lac and Jigonsassee began to feel like a prisoner. She wasn't used to waiting for an escort to take her places but Samuel insisted. He hoped to shield her from further public scorn.

Jigonsassee loved Samuel and she wanted to be with him, but she was a misfit in his town. The few times she did go out by herself, people stared at her and pointed. As the days passed, she longed for her Huron family and the beauty of nature in her village. It was dusty in town from the traffic of the wagons and it was hard to see the surrounding green hills. She was unhappy being so caged in.

She did not belong in his world and as she observed Samuel's life, she was convinced he didn't belong to it either. He hardly knew his neighbors and he had no social life. Samuel told her about the Christmas holiday, and how the townspeople came together in celebration. But Jigonsassee could not imagine the goodwill he boasted about if the ones participating were this cold and unfriendly throughout the rest of the year.

Samuel was a recluse in Coteau-du-Lac and while it was practical for him to build his life there, he seemed much happier in the woods. Jigonsassee struggled to understand how white people could be so detached from one another, yet live so close together physically. Her village was a large, loving community and she grew up believing home was where your heart was. Samuel believed home was where your bank account grew. Now, his heart was with her and he wanted her to reside with him in Coteau-du-Lac.

"I got word from your family today," Samuel said during dinner one night. "They said to hurry back. A trapper friend saw Giawiio a few days ago."

"I miss them," she answered with sadness in her eyes. "Your business thrives in your absence, Samuel, and Mr. Stark is a good man. You say that often. Why can we not live in the village with my family and friends who love us?" Jigonsassee pleaded. "Could you not continue to trust your manager while we live with my people?"

"Stark is a good man, for the most part, but for all I know, he may be skimming money for himself when I'm not around. For a while, I told myself I did not care if that was the price to be with you, but I do care, Jigonsassee. I need to devote more time to the store. After all, it is our security."

Jigonsassee listened but did not understand how a store could be a person's security. Samuel wanted her to marry him and live in his house.

"This is difficult for me," Jigonsassee said one night after dinner. "I have things on my mind and I need you to hear me." She exhaled slowly and cleared her throat. "In my village, women are respected. Since I have been here, I have observed that a white women's purpose seems to be about child bearing and chores. But Huron men honor all women. Among my people, it is the mothers who choose the chiefs and the mothers who can remove them if they fail in their duties. Huron women have great value in the community."

Samuel fidgeted in his chair, but said nothing. He knew what she was leading up to and wished the situation could be different. Jigonsassee took a drink of water and continued.

"Women have no voice in this place. They are not encouraged to have opinions or express them, if they do. Huron men seek the opinion of women and truly believe the Great Spirits bless women with a deeper wisdom in certain matters." Jigonsassee took another gulp of water and a deep breath.

"You know I am a healer in my village and my people respect me." She looked at Samuel and he nodded. "These things give me purpose and joy. But, my medicine would not be respected in this town, Samuel, and you know it. I am invisible here and my spirit withers and starves. I speak the truth." Her dark brown eyes were swimming in tears.

"Whoosh," was all Samuel could utter. He didn't want to hear anymore of what he already knew. Pushing himself up from his chair, he got up to take a walk by himself.

The thought of living in Coteau-du-Lac, with the smug, cultural attitudes of the white people was a dark thought indeed. Jigonsassee cried herself to sleep as she pondered whether or not there could ever be a solution to this dilemma. She loved life with her people and being cut off from them was like some one pulling her heart out through her skin. The paradox was that when she and Samuel were apart, she felt the same way.

Chapter Forty-nine

1996

Mariah's business still had no prospective buyers even though it had been on the market for over six months. "Your precious publication will survive without its 'Mommy', I promise you." Katie advised her. "You must know somebody on St. Thomas who could manage things in your absence."

"Well, I do know someone, but I don't feel confident about it." Mariah said. "Call it ego, but I don't feel secure leaving my *brain-child* in someone else's hands." Mariah felt that most small businesses needed an on-premise owner. It was her energy that made her business soar. "I've worked hard these past ten years and a manager is not going to care about it the way I do."

She struggled with this decision for weeks. If she and Chris were going to have a life together, she would have to be the one to make the bigger change. Having two women in his house after living alone would be a huge adjustment for Chris, but beyond that, his life would remain the same. The only thing familiar for Mariah and Emily in New York would be each other.

Moving there went against every liberated woman's creed: "Never relocate for a man—keep your life in your own control... Don't make life-changing choices with your heart—use your head! Remember the hell of divorce and learn from it. Set yourself up in your own house with your own equity, so no one can tear your life apart again."

Mariah's decision involved more than just turning her business over to someone else. It was about relinquishing a part of her identity. Her self-sufficient life was being threatened now after struggling to feel safe on her own. The thought of moving to suburban New York and into Chris' house made Mariah feel vulnerable and claustrophobic.

During this time of emotional volley, she had a dream of herself in a lovely house on a tropical plantation. There was a handsome, dark haired man whom she loved and he was inviting her to join him in a far away place. The struggle was much like her present situation except in the daydream, they were both saddened because she refused to go with him. *"Trust your heart,"* she said profoundly, looking straight into Mariah's psyche. *"Vulnerability is the way to intimacy. The more you try to control your life, the less life you will have to control."* With that she winked and disappeared up a foggy path into the mountains. When Mariah awoke, she wrote every detail of the dream in her journal. She referred to it over the weeks, as she continued to weigh her choices.

Since getting to know Chris, she had been in a free-fall of love, withholding nothing, and she had been truly happy. But now, fears of security, power and control were rearing their ugly heads. Why were these issues back on her plate? Mariah thought she had conquered these demons. Were these genuine, intuitive red flags, or was she being silly?

While driving home from her office one night, she heard Gladys Knight singing over the radio: *"I'd rather live in his world, than live without him, in mine. . ."*

"Damn love songs!" she said out loud to herself as she turned it off. "If only it were that simple!"

Chapter Fifty

1643

Jigonsasee and Samuel remained in Coteau-du-Lac for two months. Her presence made his house a home for the first time and Samuel was settling into a blissful domestic routine he had never known before.

"It is an entirely different experience for me, Tom," he told his manager one day while unpacking inventory at the trading post. "Remember when I used to stay in here and work well into the night?

Tom nodded. *I hope he's not implying that I am supposed to stay late and work with him.*

"I realize I was stalling because a dark, empty house was not something I was anxious to return to. But now," he paused, "I can barely wait to go home and see my Sassy." He chuckled aloud at her new nickname. "That is what I call her, *Sassy*."

He is in love with that Indian squaw, Tom thought, relieved his boss' strange new attitude did not have anything to do with work.

"As soon as I approach the path to my door, I am greeted by the delicious aromas coming from my kitchen, and all the lanterns are lit. There is actually life in my house now, Tom!"

Samuel exclaimed. "What a difference! I know she is nearby when I smell lavender and sandalwood." Samuel knew he was gushing like a schoolboy, but he couldn't help himself. He wasn't embarrassed by his happiness. "I enjoy having her there to greet me." Samuel put his hands over his heart as if to prevent the love from pouring out. "It is an incredible feeling, Tom. I used to stay up late working on any project that came to mind in order to avoid prolonging the endless nights in my bed alone. But now, I can hardly wait to go to bed with Jigonsassee."

Tom Stark patted his boss encouragingly on the shoulder. "I know what you mean, Samuel. A good woman can make all the difference in your life. I was married to my Christina for twenty-eight years and not a day goes by that I do not ache for her." Tom was a recent widower. He took a deep breath and let it out with a sigh. "I miss our talks and our laughter…hell, I even miss our fights!" Tom laughed, adding, "I especially miss her beside me in bed—especially, during the winter. Sleeping with Christina was like sleeping with mink. She sure kept me warm."

Samuel was delighted with their conversation. Tom had worked at the Trading Post for over ten years but they had never shared their innermost thoughts like this before. *I cannot imagine not having Sassy in my life,* he thought, realizing his manager's loneliness.

As Tom continued to unload the rest of the deliveries, Samuel daydreamed about domestic bliss. He loved to wrap himself around her body and fall into a deep, peaceful sleep. He envisioned dark-haired, laughing children swimming in the cold clear water of Lake Placid with their beautiful mother—his Sassy.

"My life is so complete with her." Samuel told Tom. "Everything I have worked for is starting to make sense and I now realize my ambition was for Jigonsassee, all along. I simply had not yet met her." Tom nodded. "I can afford to give her anything she wants," Samuel added.

"Well, Sir," Tom said taking off his black, clerk apron. "I am pleased for you. You deserve every happiness in this life." He put on his heavy coat and scarf. "I am heading for home now, sir. Good-night." Tom lumbered off to his empty, dark house, missing his Christina all the more.

If only Jigonsassee shared the same domestic happiness that Samuel felt. He wanted her to be his wife and move to his world, and with all her heart, she wanted to marry him. However, the thought of placing herself in his unfriendly world made her panic.

She walked around his house and tried to imagine her feminine touch, but it was difficult to see beyond his things. "This is Samuel's house, his world. Please help me!" she cried to the heavens. "I do not want to disappoint him, but I cannot hide my feelings." Daily, she pleaded with her spiritual guides, hoping they would reveal a workable solution. Jigonsassee realized she had to tell Samuel she could not live there permanently, but finding the courage to do so was becoming more difficult with each passing day.

"I was thinking we could turn the extra downstairs room into a nursery, when the time comes," Samuel said with a glint in his eye. The room was currently full of traps, snowshoes and other outdoor equipment. "I want you to do anything that pleases you with this place, Sassy," he said. "This is your house too." Samuel added, looking into the future.

If it is truly my house, can I take it apart and rebuild it in my village? She wondered, but dared not say it aloud.

I cannot bring our children up in this cold, unfeeling place. Our babies would be treated as outcasts here. My children need to be brought up knowing they are unique and valuable, she declared silently to herself.

Samuel would not admit his hometown was unfeeling and lacked community. He couldn't risk challenging what he'd worked so hard to establish.

Jigonsassee was the brunt of vicious jokes—she was the local freak, the Indian slut. Could Samuel be her whole world? Could their love be enough of a life for her?

As the weeks passed, he could see the dullness in Sassy's eyes and he noticed the slower pace of her stride. Until recently, she walked with bounce to her step but now, she moved much like a sleepwalker. Deep in his heart, he knew the reason for the change in her but he refused to face it. Although he felt a deep, accepting love and sense of communal family with the Hurons, which he did not feel with his own kind, he was unwilling to live the Indian life. It was not how he had been raised. White people lived according to their financial standing—and that was that.

Ironically, after years of trapping animals, Samuel was now the one trapped by his own foolish, social rules. He was blinded by his own rigidity and could not see how very out-of-touch he was in the place he called home.

Chapter Fifty-one

1996

Mariah was frozen in indecision. Although there was no urgency in altering their long distance situation, she knew it was only a matter of time before geographical distance would become an issue in their relationship. Eventually, she would have to hold her breath and jump if having a life with Chris was what she wanted.

When she and Katie put their declarations into the universe that moonlit night on Waikiki Beach, she meant it. Mariah knew Chris was her life's gift.

Their situation would resolve itself if it was meant to be. When she was in the love flow, everything felt wonderful in her life. It was only when she gave fear audience, her joy was extinguished. It happened every time she let her over-active, protective mind run amuck.

Chapter Fifty-two

1643

Jigonsasee had to speak her mind and it had to be that night. She and Samuel were too close to have this wedge between them. After dinner, Jigonsassee sat him on the front porch, held his hands, and looked into his sky blue eyes, directly to his soul.

"Samuel, I want you to describe me before I came to this place," she said, hoping he would be honest with her.

"You were sure of yourself," he said without hesitation. "Your life had purpose and you stood tall and confident. Thoughts and ideas flowed from your voice like a river, and I could see and feel energy all around you." It was easy for him to list her qualities. "There was usually a smile on your beautiful face. You sang all the time and wanted to make love every chance we could."

Jigonsassee's eyes moistened as he spoke. His sensitivity touched the deepest part of her and she struggled to find her voice. "Now, please describe me since I have been here." She hoped he would continue as honestly.

"You are quiet now and your river of energy has run dry. You perform your daily chores but there is no joy in your actions." Samuel took a deep breath and exhaled slowly. "I have not seen your happy smile in over two months and I truly miss it." He took another breath. "You have little sense of purpose here and I have noticed your posture is now limp rather than straight and confident as it was before." He paused at the reality of his words. The battle of stubbornness and flexibility raged between his ego and his emotions. "Lately, you are disinterested in making love and I can see you are not happy." Samuel's posture had also drooped and his eyes looked sad. "It grieves me to say it out loud." Tears streaked down his troubled face.

"I love you, Samuel. You do know that?" Jigonsassee asked with a smile. He nodded affirmatively. "I longed for you and have waited for us to be together all my life." She reached out, took his hands into hers and kissed them both. "You are the man of my dreams and the soul partner I belong with. I know this." She took her right hand and patted her heart in confirmation. "You are happy I am here with you and I am glad I make your home a better place. I want to bring you contentment, Samuel, but I can no longer do it here. This place is for white men and their women, who can somehow exist in a place where they have little importance." The raw honesty of the statement made her uncomfortable. She got up and walked across the room.

"I have no place here. We can be together in many other places, but this town does not receive me." Jigonsassee paused a moment. "It is my belief you do not belong here either. When you are in my village, you have inner peace and it shows in your eyes." She looked at his face and it confirmed what she had just said.

"I know you feel a new contentment in your home since my arrival, but it is not the same for me. Your choice seems to be to stay here and live, and I respect that. Please know that I want to be with you for the rest of my life, but it cannot be here. I am sorry to disappoint you, Samuel, but I must speak my mind so you understand that my recent unhappiness is not about you, but about this place." Tears rolled down their cheeks, and he crossed the room to hold her.

It was true. Samuel had no personal life in his town. But he was one of the wealthiest men in the area and he felt a responsibility to his race. He could not take off and become an Indian husband, relinquishing what he had strived for. It was not the way he saw the picture of his life and it certainly was not the life his uncle Jean Pierre had groomed him for.

"I understand what you are saying, Sassy, really I do. I have witnessed the unwelcome attitude of the townspeople towards you, and wish very much it were different. Coteau-du-lac is simply not ready for the diversity you bring it, but I believe it can change, if you dared to remain and make a difference," he said, putting the onus on her.

"It will take many more generations before people of different races can live together without prejudice. My life's purpose is to be with you and raise our children in a place where we can all be happy. It is not to change mankind's stubborn ideas," she said.

"Well, perhaps I am just as stubborn, Jigonsassee, but I cannot live in your village as your husband. I need my world, in spite of its prejudices," he said, throwing up his arms. His frustration made him pace the room in hopelessness and fear.

"I honor your decision, Samuel. I will not ask you to change your mind. You are a man of insight, and I respect you. It brings me great sadness to ask you to take me back to my village as soon as you are able."

"Fine! As you wish. We can leave the day after tomorrow. I have an arrival of furs from Nova Scotia that need attending to, but once I inventory them, I will take you home. Do you think you can survive a few more days?" Jigonsasse was amazed he could switch moods so drastically.

During the next few days, they hardly spoke. Samuel performed his chores with an air of martyrdom and insisted on doing hers, as well. He was aloof and distant and Jigonsasse's heart felt as though it would crack in two.

"Can I do anything to prepare for our trip?" she asked. *He will not even let me help him,* she thought. *I shared my feelings and he rejects me. I do not understand.*

"I have everything under control," he said in a huff. "We will be on our way soon enough,"

Their five-day journey was miserably quiet. It was mid-September, but the air already had a harsh bite. Perhaps it was more the mood than the weather. Jigonsassee found herself reaching for her wrap as they walked along the river. "It is unusually cold for early autumn, is it not, Samuel?"

He grunted and shrugged, avoiding eye contact. She attempted to converse with him when they made camp each night, but Samuel would not participate. He checked his watch with impatience. *It never seemed to take this long, even when I was jumping out of my skin to see her again,* he thought. Jigonsassee found comfort hearing the music from the watch, but it also made her weep as she realized it might very well be the last time she would hear it. This trip had once been joyous for Samuel. Now it was a funeral march to bury their relationship in a grave of stubbornness.

When they reached the Huron village, her people came and greeted them with Giawiio leading the pack. "We missed you both very much," he told Samuel. "It has not been the same around here without my sister and brother. We have been telling Samuel-and-Jigonsassee-stories for weeks now, trying to imagine your lives. Come, my brother, tell us. Share our pipe."

Samuel put on a polite, stern face. "Well, Giawiio—I thought our lives were wonderful but apparently, your sister did not. I would love to stay and smoke a while, but I need to get back to my store and attend to things. It probably seems unnecessary to you, but it is quite necessary to me," Samuel replied without dismounting his horse.

"You must stay for a while. I have missed you, my friend," Giawiio said, gesturing for Samuel to get down.

"No, really, I cannot, Giawiio," Samuel put his hand up to stop Giawiio from pressing him. "Good bye, Jigonsassee," he said and leaned down from his saddle to pat her on the shoulder. "Now, you have everything you want." His coldness broke her heart.

She reached up and held his hand, "No. That is not true. I will not have you. I love you, Samuel, and will long for your return."

"There is nothing to reconsider," he spat, jerking his hand away. "You made your decision. Clearly, your people are far more important to you than I am. I hope your life will be as fulfilling as you want it to be," he said as he turned his horse around and rode off. Jigonsassee cried softly as she watched him gallop over the hill, out of sight.

"Come." Giawiio said to his sister. "Let me hold you." She collapsed in his open arms and sobbed. "He will be back . . . he is my brother . . . he loves us." Giawiio mumbled, patting Jigonsassee on the back, holding her close. She curled into his embrace, and gently rubbed her index finger, which burned like fire.

That night Jigonsassee dreamed of Samuel. He was far across a great divide, yet she knew it was him. When she called out to him, he did not respond even though his name echoed off the walls of the canyons: Samuel...Samuel...Samuel...

Then the familiar vision of a woman appeared. Indeed, it was her own reflection—yet this person was not a Huron. What was she saying? "*You both must be true to yourselves. It takes lifetimes to learn to trust in love. He will learn and so will you.*"

Jigonsassee shifted to her side, pulling her buffalo pelt up and over her shoulders. She continued to dream about her Samuel until the morning doves interrupted her sleep.

Chapter Fifty-three

1996

Chris knew he wanted to marry Mariah within a month and a half of meeting her but the rules of his New England upbringing prevented him from proposing until they had known each other a respectful six months. Wanting her for his mate was as clear to him as the waters of Lake Placid, the very place they went on vacation shortly after they first met.

Mariah felt energized in the cool northern mountains again after living at latitude 18° for so many years. The area reminded her of Idaho and she felt a peaceful sense of home. Chris had made reservations at a lodge in the Adirondacks on the shore of Lake Placid. They had a charming cabin made of local river stones and a shake roof. Along the front of the house was a long porch adorned with classic green-plaid-cushioned Adirondack chairs and a hanging wooden swing. The front door was four inches thick and made from quarter-sawn oak with three large ornate iron hinges. The door handle was also wrought iron and its smooth curves beckoned a person to come inside.

Mariah melted at the sight of the massive fireplace and the king-sized feather bed that was draped with a hand-stitched, locally made patchwork quilt. Outside their door, across a short stretch of lawn, was the lake, framed by dense, tree-covered mountains. The woods smelled fresh and familiar to Mariah as she remembered her days in Idaho. Each morning, the water was covered with hundreds of Canadian geese honking through the misty fog. By mid-day, flocks of trumpeter swans joined them, gliding gracefully on the mirrored surface of the lake. And when the dusk settled in, Chris and Mariah took their wine on the porch and listened to the loons serenade them with their wobbly northern lake songs.

On their second day, Chris and Mariah filled a daypack with light provisions and headed for the trailhead behind their lodge. The path started along the lake and followed the shoreline for a mile or so before it climbed to the crest of the mountain. As they rounded the bend before the ascent, Mariah noticed a small cave against the embankment. She felt strangely drawn to it. Suddenly, she had a glimpse of herself making a bed from pine boughs. The image streaked through her memory as fast as lightening. Mariah turned to look at Chris and knew it was familiar.

"I want to check this out," she said, climbing to the mouth of the cave. Mariah went inside and saw a natural ledge along the back wall and remembered thinking it would be handy for storing supplies. She was sure they had been there before but Mariah kept silent. She didn't want Chris to misunderstand her.

The trail was steep with several switchbacks all the way to the top of the mountain. Chris was delighted that Mariah could keep up with him and because she could, he felt even more assured she was his life partner. After eight miles of climbing, the breathless couple finally reached the summit and the view left them speechless. Saranac Lake was to the south and the northern tip of Schroon Lake was visible to the southeast. Looking north, they tried to see Lake Champlain, but layers of purple mountains hindered their view. Mariah held up her hands and closed her eyes, allowing tears to flow. The rapture of their surroundings took her breath away. All she could do was weep in awe of her life, which was overflowing with blessings. Chris was swept away too, but he was more composed than Mariah. As he watched her take in the scenery with such deep emotion, he felt more deeply in love with her. Mariah looked at him and saw his tears. There were no words as they drank in the tranquility of the late afternoon light.

They had several more miles to hike down before dark so the couple gathered their belongings and started their descent. Walking downhill was faster and they found themselves back in their cabin in a little more than two hours. Mariah collapsed on the feather bed and Chris took off her boots and started filling the double Jacuzzi.

"Come and soak with me, love." Chris said, lighting the candle on the windowsill. "We earned it!" Mariah slid off the bed and dragged herself to the ecstasy of the steamy, massaging jets of the spa.

Their cabin was stocked with extra blankets. The following day, they took one and spread it over the lawn. After their grueling hike the day before, the couple decided to spend the afternoon relaxing in the sun.

"Come on, Sam. Let's take a swim. The water will feel good on our tired muscles." Mariah was already standing and had extended her hand to help Chris up. "I can't believe we hiked twelve miles yesterday, can you?

"When I feel my thigh muscles twinge like they are right now, I believe it. What I can't believe is that you want me to swim in that icebox with you?" he teased, reluctantly taking her hand. Together, they headed toward the water's edge. Mariah dove right in while Chris gingerly inched his way into the freezing water. When they got out and dried off, Mariah began thumbing through one of her favorite books, by Dr. Clarissa Pinkola Estes. It was a book of legends and stories passed down through generations by various cultures. Each story had an archetypal message that Dr. Estes translated. Mariah's favorite one was called, *Skeleton Woman.* It taught how commitment-phobic most of today's society is and how afraid we are of the life/death/life cycles in life, especially in relationships. The author explained that until we accept this cyclical concept, we couldn't experience true, deep love with another person. It had been several years since Mariah had read the story, and she underlined certain things throughout the chapter. Chris wondered what would cause her to write in a hard cover book.

"What are you reading? Is it private, or will you share it with me?" he asked.

"No, it's not private, although it is very special to me. I would love you to read it." Mariah replied, as she passed him the book. "Here, it starts back a few pages, and goes to page one hundred sixty five. Excuse my notes, I hope it won't distract you."

"No," he said. "It'll be interesting for me to see what you found so important."

Mariah handed Chris the book as she got up to take another swim. As she dove into the lake, Chris dove to the depths of the soul, where Skeleton Woman lived. At one point, he took a quick break from his reading to look at Mariah who was once again lying next to him.

"Can I borrow your pen and take a few notes of my own?" he asked.

"Of course you may. It's beautifully written, don't you think?" Mariah asked.

"Yes, it is." Chris replied.

Mariah had no doubt he was the one she had requested that moonlit night on Waikiki.

Six months later, Chris was on St. Thomas for Mariah's annual business Christmas party. It was the biggest party of the year on the island and women were in wardrobe crisis for weeks, preparing for the big event.

Early one Friday afternoon, Chris and Mariah had lunch at Zorba's restaurant on Government Hill in downtown Charlotte Amalie. It was a beautiful day, and Mariah longed to get out of town and head straight for the beach. Her party dress was a champagne color with a low-cut back, and she wanted a tan. Chris, on the other hand, wanted to go shopping on Main Street.

"Are you sure you want to face that chaos on such a glorious afternoon?" she asked him before realizing it was probably his only chance to get his holiday shopping done. Before Chris had a chance to answer, she began bragging about the great stores the island had as they walked down the hill towards the duty-free zone.

"When de las time you bin shoppin in Charlotte Amalie? We got new stores wid cool, island tings in dem, meh son.' We kin go to da beach t'morrow. No problem, mon." Chris laughed at her West Indian dialect.

Suddenly, Chris stopped walking, and took Mariah's hand. "I don't want to shop for my family. I want to go to some jewelry stores so you can pick out the ring of your choice. I want to marry you, Mariah."

She was stunned. Chris looked deep into her eyes and waited for her response. "Of course I'll marry you. I love you. If it's one thing we have on St. Thomas, it's jewelry stores! Move over tourists, we're going shopping!"

Chris traveled back to New York three days after the party but returned the day after Christmas. Mariah and Chris booked a sailboat charter to the British Virgin Islands for four days, for the whole family. It was important for Jason and

Emily to spend time with Chris since, he was going to be their stepfather.

Emily had decided not to return to the states for the rest of her sophomore year because she missed her island home and her family. Since moving off the island was imminent, Mariah gladly agreed to have her daughter return for the rest of her school year. Emily would be in a new school in New York, soon enough. When school got out, she and her daughter would move to Chris' house. Jason had plans to attend the University of California in the fall and was going to fly west after the wedding. Chris and Mariah decided on an August twenty-ninth date and Mariah and Emily planned to move to Bedford a month before the wedding.

Fifteen years of Caribbean life were coming to an end and Mariah was filled with many mixed emotions.

Chapter Fifty-four

1644

The spark was gone in Jigonsassee. It had been five months since Samuel rode off with his indignation. They had each chosen their own worlds over each other and the entire village grieved the loss of Samuel's presence along with Jigonsassee. Samuel was the only brother Giwaiio had ever known; their bond was strong and difficult to let go of.

"AyAy AyAy. Come to me my brother. Let go of your fears and feel our love for you." Giwaiio cried in chants while he was out trapping, hoping Samuel would hear him and appear as he had so many times before. A new, white Frenchman came to their village to gather pelts and trade for material goods, which sealed the fact; Samuel was not to return.

Occasionally, there was talk about the days when Samuel was with them, the jokes he told, and the special gifts he brought to the village. It was shocking how quickly he became legend, being referred to as a point of history. When Jigonsassee heard the tales of Samuel, all she could do was weep.

"We are concerned about your daughter, Tekakwida," the medicine man said one day to Jigonsassee's father who was seated in the meeting lodge. "She is too thin and she seems to have lost her insights for cures. There was another outbreak of a plague up river, and she needs her strength to resist it. She must stop all her racing about, helping everyone else. See that she rests. I do not want her walking about the village," he said emphatically as he got up to leave. "This is serious, my friend. I fear she has lost her will to live."

"I agree with you," said her father. "Her mother and I are quite worried about her. Giawiio hovers over her constantly, but she refuses to listen. Her heart is broken and she needs time to heal. I will force her to rest."

Within two days, Jigonsassee got sick. Her resistance was low and her willingness to fight was gone. After days of hallucinating from the high fever, she surrendered like a willing prisoner.

"She is leaving us, mother." Giawiio sobbed as he watched his sister struggle to breathe. Her family knew she was dying. They witnessed her steady decline over the months since Samuel had ridden off. Haywathna sobbed quietly and nodded to her son.

In feverish delirium, Jigonsassee hummed the tune from Samuel's watch. It gave her comfort in her last hours. "Giawiio, if you see him, tell him I never stopped loving him. Promise me, brother," she pleaded with eyes wide open.

"Of course I will tell him. Let go now, little sister. There is no pain where you are going." Giawiio held his sister's hand, humming the tune from Samuel's watch in his wobbly, grief filled voice. The tears flowed from his bloodshot, brown eyes.

"I am tired," she faintly whispered. "I must go now…" Jigonsassee loosened her grip on her brother's hand and quietly slipped into a coma. He looked down at her ring-shaped birthmark. It seemed brilliant in color, much like a valuable stone. By daybreak, she had passed to the other side.

Jigonsassee was only twenty-six years old when she died.

Chapter Fifty-five

1997

Mariah moved out of her rented house and into an apartment below her office. It was filled with some of her special things and it gave her comfort rather than staying at a hotel when she was on island for business. The rest of her belongings were packed and shipped to New York. She devoured the sights and smells of her island as if she were leaving it forever. While she was glad she had made the choice to marry Chris, she was fearful of such a big change in her life. She had not lived on the mainland for over fifteen years and wondered how she would cope with the suburbs.

Mariah had doubts not only about herself, but also about her daughter. Her children had grown up on the island and had little experience with stateside life, save for summer camp and the occasional trips for vacation. Emily was already an emotional handful as she groped her way through her teenage years. Mariah worried that going to yet another school in a completely different environment on top of adjusting to having a stepfather was going to put her into a tailspin.

Mariah's friends had a huge going away party for her—complete with a betting pool, taking odds on how long she would last in America! As she danced and laughed with her friends, she was filled with sadness at the thought of leaving and she wondered how she was going to function without them.

She moved north right before the fourth of July and Emily planned on following around the first of August. Her best girlfriend's family invited her to stay with them for a month and Mariah knew it was important to Emily to have more time with her friends. The wedding was not until the twenty-ninth of August so mother and daughter would have a few weeks to get their bearings and shop for a dress once Emily arrived.

Mariah felt like a kid in a candy store when she first got to New York with so much to see and experience. Each afternoon, after scouting the area to learn her way around, she would come back to Chris' house and take a nap. The new schedule surprised her, since she wasn't one to sleep during the day. The enormity of being a single parent and owning her own business had caught up with her. She hadn't realized how tired she was from it all until she stopped. Adjusting to the pace of the northeast was no easy task for someone who had spent her last fifteen years on a Caribbean island.

Before she knew it, a month was over and Emily was about to arrive in her new home. Mariah was filled with mixed emotions about her new location, but never once faltered in her love for Chris. This was his home and she was determined to try to make it hers and her daughter's as well.

"Sweetie, can you please draw me a map to JFK so I can pick Emily up next week? I can't bear to have the limo pick her up. I want to be there to greet her. Although knowing Emily, she would probably love riding in a limo! Perhaps we'll do that another time."

"Sure, hon. Remind me later and I'll do it after dinner. I wish I could go with you but I have a shoot in New Jersey and won't be finished until well after dark."

"It will be good for me to find my own way. It's always been a policy of mine to familiarize myself with the airport locale. You never know when you might need to make a quick getaway!" Mariah laughed at her own joke but Chris didn't think it was all that funny.

On the day of Emily's arrival, Mariah headed south to JFK, map in hand. Her cell phone was charged and Chris was ready for a call if she got lost. Emily's plane was a few minutes late so Mariah bought her daughter a welcome bouquet of flowers, hoping to soften her entry to this strange, new world. Emily was bold enough to express her unhappiness about moving and Mariah was filled with anxiety about her upcoming marriage with a disgruntled teenager in tow.

Emily was indeed in a surly mood, and sulked in the car the whole way to Bedford. Mariah even tolerated playing the dance hall rap music her daughter loved on a local radio station, but Emily was unflappable.

"Sweetie," Mariah said, "let's take a few days to get you situated and then we'll go down to the city and go shopping for a dress. How does that sound?"

"Fine. Whatever you say, Mother."

Oh, boy, Mariah thought to herself as she glided the car toward the exit ramp.

When they finally went to the city to shop, Emily's mood was much better. She loved the city and had a great time scouring the many stores. After trying on several dresses, they decided on a long dress with a cutout back design and a long chiffon scarf that lay loosely around the neck. Mariah stared at her beautiful, grown-up daughter when she came out of the dressing room modeling her gown. She experienced one of those scary moments all parents have the first time they see their children as adults. It gripped Mariah's heart like a vise as she reflected on how fast their lives were changing. All she could do was exhale and smile at her stunning "Maid of Honor."

Chapter Fifty-six

1644

After leaving Jigonsassee at her village with her people, Samuel could feel the life drain from his body. He walked around like a shell of his former self. His house lacked the lovely ambiance it had offered during those brief, beautiful months when she had lived there. He had lost several pounds because he couldn't muster up the energy to prepare food for himself. Even his work was unfulfilling. Samuel had saved a considerable amount of money; he owned a profitable business and a stately home but none of it held any importance now. His world was an empty place with no joy. After eight grueling months of living completely alone again, Samuel finally came to the only sane conclusion there was—he could not live without his "Sassy."

He put some pork and beans in a crusted pot, the same exact dinner he had prepared the past three nights. It hung on the spit over the fire, and was hot in minutes. As he sat down to eat, Samuel saw his reflection in the oak-framed, beveled mirror on the wall by the table. For the first time in months, he stared at his appearance. The circles under his eyes were the size of silver dollars and there were deep groves along both sides of his mouth and a few long wrinkles in his forehead. His hair was grimy and it lay flat and matted to his head. Several months before, he had stopped shaving regularly and now, his face was covered in stubble. He looked years older than he really was and it shocked him to realize this.

"Jigonsassee, you used to mix lavender into the soap when you washed my hair," he said out loud, staring at himself while running a hand through his greasy hair. "Then you dried my head in a fresh, clean-smelling towel," he was mumbling now, remembering yet another lovely memory of their time together. "'Let me brush your hair away from your face so I can gaze at how beautiful you are.' That's what you used to say to me," he could barely speak for the sobbing.

His eyes were a dull grey, not at all the sparkling turquoise they had once been and his shoulders were slouched over. Samuel hardly recognized the person looking back at him.

As he stared at his bedraggled image, he realized what he must do to save himself. Getting up from his chair, he began pacing back and forth across the room.

"I must go to her and BEG her to take me back." He walked up to the mirror and spoke to his sorry reflection. "I need to tell her I will gladly live in her village . . . hell, it is the only place I ever felt real love and acceptance beyond my Uncle Jean," he was all revved up and he started to shout. "I am a FOOL to have turned down the opportunity to live with such enlightened people! What is the matter with me?" Her people were more evolved than any white person he had ever known. She had taught Samuel a connection to the spirit world and he now understood that he was clinging to a worldly sense of security.

"HOW COULD I HAVE THOUGHT THAT ALL THIS, COULD REPLACE THE LOVE OF MY LIFE?" he held his arms wide open. "WHY DID I FORGET HOW EMPTY MY LIFE WAS BEFORE SHE CAME AND FILLED IT

WITH LOVE?" He crumpled to his knees on the bare, chestnut floor and curled up in a fetal position and wept. Soon, the gift of sleep brought him some relief and in a few hours, when he felt cold, he dragged himself upstairs to his lonely bed and tried to continue sleeping through the night.

The next morning, as was his usual habit, Samuel opened his watch to check the time, but this time, he was struck with a clever idea. He would have the inside cover of the watch engraved with: *Je t'aime pour tout ma vie—I will love you all my life.* Then, he will go to her village, take her into his arms and give her the watch as a symbol of surrender to his material way of life! *She loves this watch,* he thought to himself as he placed it in its original blue embroidered box to take to the jeweler. What a grand idea!

Samuel packed his supplies with new energy and headed toward her village with an excitement he had not felt since he first met her. He was truly happy for the first time in months and he sang out loud while traveling along. When a perfect rainbow appeared on the second day of his journey, he dismounted from his horse and gave thanks to the Great Spirit for a sign of new beginnings. Traveling into the dark of night was not something he normally did but Samuel broke his own rule on this special trip. He stayed focused and the light of his love illuminated the wary path.

On the morning of the fourth day, he reached the Huron village but not without searching. The Indians had moved their camp since the last time he was there. Giawiio was just coming out of his lodge carrying a large bundle of furs and was the first to see Samuel ride in. Dropping the furs, he ran to Samuel who had already leaped from his horse and was headed toward his Indian brother with outstretched arms. They embraced tightly and patted each other on the back. "I have missed my brother these many moons," Giawiio told him. "I had grown to accept that you were gone from our lives forever."

"I have been a foolish man, my friend. How could I have ever thought a life without Jigonsassee, you and the rest of my Huron family would be a life worth living?"

Giawiio looked down at his feet and kicked the pile of furs he dropped before looking into Samuel's hopeful eyes. "My sister is no longer with us in the flesh, my brother. She passed two moons ago from the smallpox. After her stay in your village, she returned to us with a defeated spirit. She was always the one to help us combat disease, but this time, she was the one who contracted it. We believe she could have fought it, but she seemed content to surrender. She told me she welcomed the peace of death, rather than life each day with the pain of her broken heart."

Samuel froze in disbelief. Jigonsassee, dead? How could that vibrant, strong, spiritual woman be dead? She was in the medicine council; she knew the herbal remedies better than anyone. Samuel's mouth fell open, and his eyes stared, deep into his brother's soul.

He lowered himself to the ground and moaned with abandon. His heart had been broken all the months they were apart, but now, it was shattered beyond repair.

Haywathna came out of their lodge and saw Samuel lying on the ground, wailing in mourning. She covered her mouth with her hands and cried as she watched him rock back and forth, jabbering. "Jigonsassee, my Jigonsassee, oh my love. I am so sorry... sssoooo very sorrrrrry—God, I beg you to take me to her. PLEASE—TAKE ME THERE!"

Haywathna sat down and took Samuel's limp body into her arms as if he were a small child. She let him cry until he could cry no longer. She smoothed back his hair and wiped away his tears.

"My daughter loved you more than anything else in her life." Samuel sat up and looked deep into Haywathna's compassionate eyes as she spoke. "She was never so happy as she was with you." Jigonsassee's mother paused, remembering her daughter's eyes brimming with love and her beaming, happy smile. "Samuel, my Son—this time, you let fear rob you both of happiness, but I know you will be together in another life well beyond what we can see. I believe this is true."

Samuel nodded in shame and Haywathna only smiled at him. She did not want him to blame himself for her daughter's death. "No person should live with guilt unless he takes a life and even then, there are circumstances that allow." Samuel clung to her and they sat there for a long while. "We are to learn these valuable lessons in life—this is why we are here."

"Stay here with us. We can heal one another." Giawiio stated. He had never seen Samuel so distraught and he was worried about his brother. They needed each other now.

Words were scarce during the new few weeks but hugs were plentiful. Tekakwida was taking the loss of his daughter hard, but he was genuinely glad to see Samuel again. They took several long, quiet strolls through the remaining wild flowers and Samuel felt his genuine love and acceptance.

On the day he was leaving to go home, Samuel had a vision. As he and Tekakwida came around the bend in the river, he saw Jigonsassee bathing. She was naked in the water and he heard her singing. Samuel watched her get out of the water, tossing her long hair back and forth to shake off the water.

"Did you see her?!! Oh my God—it was her!" Samuel turned to Tekakwida excitedly. "She was right over there," he said running to where he had just seen her splashing in the shallow water. He looked around in every direction, hoping to get a glimpse of her again.

"No, son. I did not see her this time, but I know she will show herself from time to time. I am happy that she appeared to you. She is not far away, my son. You can rest in that." Samuel nodded and felt satisfied by that, if only for the moment.

That afternoon, Samuel's Huron family gathered round, loading him with provisions enough to last far beyond the five days it would take to get home. The whole village took turns embracing Samuel before finally letting him go.

"Do not be a stranger, my brother. Come often and stay with us," Giwaiio said as he walked Samuel to his horse. "You will always be part of our family."

"Thank you, brother," Samuel said, shaking Giawiio's hand. "Send a messenger to my trading post for whatever provisions you might need. From the bottom of my heart, I appreciate you all for accepting me and not blaming me for our loss. Perhaps in time, I will stop blaming myself."

Tekakwida nodded and smiled. "This situation is bigger than you, my son. All of our departures are in the hands of the Great One. You must let go and look forward to spending the afterlife with our beautiful Jigonsassee. She is already waiting for you."

Samuel smiled in agreement and tipped his hat to the people he loved most. He then mounted his horse and rode off to face his empty world.

Chapter Fifty-seven

1645

It took Samuel eight days to make the trip back to Coteau-du-lac. He traveled slowly and stopped often to stare into the wilderness for long periods of time. He was in an emotional fog and could not believe his sweet Jigonsassee was truly gone.

"Why was I so stupid?" he shouted at the mountains and they echoed the question back to him. When Samuel finally arrived home, he dragged himself into his dark, lonely house and sat down at his kitchen table. He looked around at his utilitarian home like it was the first time he had ever seen it.

"I HATE this house!" he shouted, suddenly realizing the truth. He had never truly felt at home there. He slammed the door and kicked over the table. It crashed up against the wall, breaking the beveled mirror in a million pieces. Leaving the mess behind, Samuel climbed the stairs to his room and crawled into bed. Sleep was the only refuge from his miserable grief.

Over the next several days, Samuel went through the mechanics of his business life, but he had no interest in any of it. There was a large inventory of furs at the Trading Post so there was no reason to go out and trap. He considered going anyway just to be alone, but he could not seem to muster up the energy. Samuel no longer cared about anything and had slipped into a deep depression. Within a few weeks of his return, he realized what he must do.

With a renewed sense of purpose, he packed up his house, leaving only the stove; his bed; the kitchen table, and a chair or two. Samuel then brought the rest of his meager personal effects to his Trading Post to be sold. Summoning his manager, Thomas Stark, to a meeting, Samuel informed him that he would be leaving for a long time. Wishing to elevate Tom to an official partner in the Trading Post, he got out a piece of paper and began to write:

"I, Samuel Fontaine, being of sound mind," he smirked at the statement and went on, "assign fifty percent of this business, Fontaine's Trading Post, to my faithful manager, Thomas Stark. All transactions must be taken up with him in my absence and he is to conduct the operation of this establishment in the manner to which he sees fit." Then he signed and dated the document: Samuel de Fontaine, September 22, 1645. "Tom, please sign this right here below my name and put the date next to your signature," Samuel said handing over the quill. When Tom had done as he was asked, he handed the paper back to Samuel.

"Well, sir, I appreciate your vote of confidence and I am honored to be partners with you. I am dedicated to this store—you know that. There has never been one day that I was not proud to work here. Thank you very much." Tom reached out his hand, and Samuel shook it, smiling at his new partner.

"There, that's done. I should have made you my partner a long time ago, but I was too greedy to have thought of it until now. I apologize for being so inconsiderate, Tom. You've been a conscientious employee and I have appreciated your loyalty all these years, even though I never expressed it to you." Samuel never believed Tom was dipping into the till. It was just an excuse to justify his fears. "I will be heading north for a while, so I need you to hold down the shop, partner," Samuel said patting Tom on the shoulder. "Of course, you will need a raise in pay now that you have more responsibility and you will receive half of the profits as well."

Tom Stark stood next to his new partner with a big grin on his face. This was a stellar day!

"Where are you headed, sir, if I might ask? As you know, we have enough furs to last us through spring, what with those new suppliers from Newfoundland."

"I am taking a trip, probably headed north—nowhere in particular—just north. I will be leaving tomorrow, so please, go by my house and help yourself to anything I left behind that you might need." Tom nodded. It sounded as though Samuel might be liquidating his belongings and he wondered why, but said nothing.

When Samuel left the store, Thomas put the document they had just signed in the cast iron safe in the back room and began to unpack the boxes of Samuel's things so he could price them. At the bottom of the first box, Thomas discovered Samuel's watch. He held it and studied the carved waterfall on the front cover, since he had never really seen it up close before. When he opened the lid, he noticed the inscription on the inside cover. "Samuel loves this watch. He must have put it in here by mistake." Thomas said aloud to himself, putting the watch in his pocket. Immediately, after closing the shop that evening, he went over to Samuel's house to return the watch. He knocked on the door and Samuel ushered him in without a word. "Sir, I found this in one of your boxes. You didn't mean to have it sold with the rest of your things, did you?"

"Yes, Tom, I did. It was going to be a gift for Jigonsassee, the love of my life. You remember her, don't you? Hell, everyone in this damn town probably still gossips about her." Samuel took his pipe from his top pocket and filled it. Patting down his other pockets to feel if he had any matches he turned to Tom. "Do you have a light?" Tom already had the match out before Samuel was done with the question. "Thanks," Samuel said after he had taken a long drag. "How could I have expected her to live in this God-forsaken place?" Samuel shrugged. "I had the watch engraved for her and I went to her village to beg her to take me back. I wanted to give it to her as proof I had given up my rigid ways. I was ready to live anywhere she wanted, as long as we were together." Samuel took the watch, opened the lid and the music began to play. "Jigonsassee loved this music. She cried the first time she heard it," Samuel said as his own eyes filled with tears.

"Anyway," he said snapping the lid closed, "I am a fool, Tom. I let the most precious gift God has ever given me slip right through my fingers because of my stubborn pride. I loved her very much, but I was too late. When I returned to her village a few weeks ago, I found out she had passed away. Her stamina withered away because I kept her here to please myself! When she got back to her village, she had no resistance to fight illness. I broke her heart, Tom...I broke both of our hearts." Samuel sat down on one of the remaining chairs in his empty kitchen, set down his pipe and clung to the watch. He was visibly shaken and he looked up at Tom with eyes filled with grief. He was touched by Samuel's sorrow.

"She did not want to live anymore. I practically killed her, Tom. I stripped her of her will to live when I left her village eight months ago, and rode off with my pride. Perhaps I will find a way to forgive myself while I am up in the north woods." He took his pipe and packed down the tobacco with his thumb. Tom took out another match and lit it for him. Samuel nodded in appreciation. "I really do not know what else to do at this point."

Thomas Stark listened with compassion as his new partner spoke. He approached Samuel and put his arms around him and Samuel held tight to his new friend and sobbed. Tom handed him his handkerchief. "Do not go worrying about one little thing. You just go and reflect on things and regain your own inner strength." Tom stood up and pulled Samuel with him so they could face each other straight on. "You listen to me, Samuel Fontaine. Do not do something foolish like starving yourself or nothing like that. You hear me? We have a prosperous business to run here, and you have plenty to live for, even though you cannot see that right now, you will in time."

"Yes, I suppose you are right, Tom," he replied half-heartedly. "Thank you for hearing me out and being here to take care of things." Samuel walked his partner to the door. "Sell the damn watch. It should bring a good price. I do not want it anymore," he said. "Good night, partner." Tom nodded and walked out the door. "I will see you in a few months." Samuel yelled to Tom who had already reached the street.

The following morning, Thomas Stark put the watch in the safe next to their partnership document. *He thinks he does not want this now, but one day, he will. That music will soothe his soul as he remembers his uncle—and his woman.*

Chapter Fifty-eight

1645

The air got colder, the farther north Samuel traveled. It was mid-September, and there was no indication of an Indian summer. He had already awakened to frost, eight mornings in the last two weeks, and he was delighted he was in for a very cold winter. There were moose, deer, caribou, mink and beaver around every bend but he had not brought his traps. His trapping days were over. Samuel had no need for possessions where he was going. His only goal was to join Jigonsassee, and he believed it would take a freezing winter to achieve this end.

He built a small lean-to beneath a hill, next to a creek. "It reminds me of the cave we had at the lake, although it is not as warm, which is perfect, since I plan to peacefully freeze to death," he confessed aloud.

For a little more than a month, he fished or snared rabbits for food. Sometimes he fasted, not eating at all. He lost weight rapidly and his hair grew craggy along with his beard. He laughed when he caught a glimpse of his gaunt reflection in a small pond beyond his camp. "I look like a hermit," he proclaimed. "Which is exactly what I have become!"

Often, he would ramble out loud to Jigonsassee. "How do you like my hair these days, love? I need you to take care of it for me. Did you see that rainbow? I tried to sing and dance and offer praise, but I cannot do it like you. You did everything so perfectly. . . I have been trying to remember the way the tune from the watch sounded, but I keep leaving out a section of the melody. I will close my eyes and listen for you to sing it to me. . . go ahead, I know you know it better than I do. . . well, you can do it when I see you . . . I love not having any traps. It is as if the animals want to be with me. I woke up yesterday and there were three beaver waddling to the creek from my direction. I think they were watching me sleep . . . . did you see them?. . I miss you, my love . . . do you miss me? . . It is getting colder and I am getting weaker, I can feel it. It should not be long now, Sassy . . . please welcome me in the next life. . . I love you so much . . . I can hardly wait to hold you."

Samuel became emaciated and his mental capacity was greatly diminished. He wandered around his camp, having conversations with himself, Jigonsassee, and his uncle. Each day, a pack of wolves situated themselves on the edge of the clearing near his camp. Samuel knew they were waiting for him to die so they could feast on what was left of his skinny carcass. He appreciated their patience and recalled various conversations over the years about wolves being vicious. He howled out loud at the absurdity of man.

"We talk with such authority on things we know nothing about," he preached to the wolves, as they cocked their heads and stared at him. "It is true. Most white men think they are smarter than animals. The Indians know better, but the white men do not. But, you wolves have the right idea. You live with each other, in a family pack." Samuel walked closer to the beasts. They had been sitting, but they got up as Samuel came toward them. He stopped fifteen feet in front of them and began his monologue again while the wolves silently watched. "I was invited to live with my Huron family and be part of their pack, but I turned down the opportunity. I felt safety and warmth when I was with them, but my pride kept me from choosing a life with my mate and our family . . ." Samuel closed his eyes and took a few deep breaths before continuing his speech. "I was too foolish to realize the value of the pack." He felt tired so he sat down on a nearby log. "Why would you want to eat me anyway? I should think my meat would taste bland and my texture would be too tough. I do not suppose I could talk you out of it, could I?" He laughed at his own question.

The wolves were bored with his speech and went off into the deep woods. They would check on Samuel the next day, as they had many times before.

As Samuel got closer to the wildlife, he observed animal-human similarities, as well as their differences. Humans were the only animals with an ego and this inflated sense of ourselves clouds our instincts. Samuel decided he much preferred living with wildlife than with the unfriendly humans in Coteau-du-lac. As cold as it was in his lean-to, it wasn't as cold as it was in that unfriendly, frigid town.

The wolves moved in closer each day but were polite enough to not smack their lips when Samuel was looking. It was now late December.

"Merry Christmas, Jigonsassee my love," he mumbled. Samuel tried wiggling his toes, but he had no feeling in his legs. He had severe frostbite, and his toes were turning black.

"Ha! Look Jigonsassee, I am getting dark skin like you." Samuel lay down on his bed of thatch, staring up at the stars. "Actually, your skin was like rich chocolate mixed with milk but mine is turning a greenish shade of black. It does not hurt, really—it does not. I cannot even feel it. I need to sleep now, love." He lay quietly, barely breathing. For several minutes, he did not close his eyes. Samuel stared into the cosmos, and he became more numb with every minute. As he gazed at the starry Canadian sky, he smiled at his upcoming destination.

"It is getting warmer and brighter! My legs are tingling." Samuel took a few shallow breaths before his death rattles. "I'm starting to feel whole again. I think I see you. . . is that you, my beautiful Sassy?" Tears were streaming down his face. "It is you! I prayed you would be the one to greet me. I hoped we would be together again."

They embraced tightly and looked into each other eyes.

"Welcome, Samuel, my precious love." Jigonsassee said as she tenderly kissed him on the lips. "I missed you every day."

"I missed you, too. Oh, my sweet Jigonsassee. Please forgive me."

"Of course I forgive you, Samuel—I love you."

In December 1645, at the age of twenty-nine, Samuel de Fontaine closed his eyes for the last time with a contented smile on his gaunt, bearded face.

Chapter Fifty-nine

1997

Married in New York. The phrase sounded like a title of a sitcom. Once again, Mariah felt herself in a "TV show life." Dating Chris and flying back and forth to each other's places was one thing, but living full time in Bedford, NY was quite another. The challenge of domesticity and maintaining an enduring love was before them. The wisdom of *Skeleton Women* was echoing in her head as she waded through this transition of her life.

Mariah felt like an alien on a cold and unfriendly planet. *There aren't even any black people around here,* she thought to herself one day while taking a walk around the reservoir. "I miss my mixed family in the islands," she yelled to the trees as she kicked wet leaves beneath her feet.

But that was then, and this was now. As she chopped the cilantro for the fajitas she was preparing for dinner that night, she turned to face Chris. "I need to find some kind of worthwhile work to do up here, babe. Until I sell my business on St. Thomas, it will be hard to commit to anything full-time, but I could do some kind of freelance thing, as long as it was flexible." Mariah wiped her hands with the dishtowel that hung on the oven door handle and faced her husband. He had not realized she was crying. He got up to hug her.

"I think you should do whatever you want to do, Mariah." Chris held her tightly, wishing he could be the balm she seemed to need. "I so much want for you to be happy here, Sweetheart."

Mariah struggled to find a sense of place in Chris' world. She was in a color-free zone and she stuck out like a neon sign with her dark skin and bright, cheerful clothing. *I thought I was ready to move off island, but I am not sure I'm cut out for this,* she thought many times during this transition.

Every seven or eight weeks, Mariah flew to St. Thomas to straighten out problems at her business, which suffered in her absence.

Ron had decided against buying her out but a year later, a buyer finally came along and Mariah was able to sell her publications. After the initial wave of relief had passed, Mariah found herself mourning the loss of her creation. Her grief was more for the loss of the life she had. She struggled with the lack of identity in this new life she had chosen.

Chris noticed her quiet moods and could see she was different from the light-hearted island woman he used to know. Mariah made an effort to fit in, but it was futile. She didn't blend and the problem was made crystal clear to her at a ladies social gathering she attended less than a year after her wedding.

An invitation had been sent to her for a potluck party at one of the neighbors' houses for that upcoming Friday evening. Mariah prepared a fabulous curry chicken dish with fresh mango and papaya, sprinkled with coconut and garnished with star fruit, which she placed along the edge of the platter. She dressed in her favorite sarong with a pink, silk, tank top blouse, and her yellow sandals. The stargazer lilies were blooming in their garden, so she picked one, put it in her hair, and walked to the party.

The hostess greeted Mariah, looked her and her platter over and gestured toward the center table where she could put her dish. Mariah noticed the frozen quiches from the designer grocery stores, the macaroni salads and several bowls of chips and mild salsa. There was even a green Jell-O mold with canned fruit. *I thought only old grandmothers made these,* she thought, putting her striking contribution on the table along with the rest. There was classical music playing in the background as well as a television, which was on in the family room. "CNN Money Line" competed with conversations about PTA, carpools, dance recitals and the summer houses on the Cape. Mariah got through the usual introductions but could think of nothing more to say to this room of wealthy housewives who had never had to work for a living.

"Well! Now we can be labeled an 'equal opportunity' neighborhood. We have our very own *ethnic*!" said a woman who had been gossiping loudly since she had arrived. She took inventory of Mariah's outfit and asked, "Is that early Bohemian, dear?" The party ladies giggled. "What exactly do you call that type of *thing* wrapped around your waist?" The ladies laughed and Mariah smiled.

"It's called a sarong. I'm glad I could help balance out your community." Right then, she struggled with deciding whether to leave or stay, but impulse took over and Mariah went to the table and picked up her untouched platter. She was too uncomfortable to stay where she didn't feel welcome. "Balance is a good thing. Goodnight everyone. Thank you for having me. I really must be going."

No one made an effort to stop her and they bid her farewell. Once she got down the street, she started to cry. She chastised herself for not trying harder to make friends, and knew her tears were because she was homesick. She missed her old friends and she felt very much out of place.

Katie Berry was Mariah's lifeline during this hard adjustment time, and the two girlfriends spoke on the phone almost every day.

"Oh, Sweetie! I'm so glad you're moving here! I need you. I'm not exactly winning popularity contests up here," Mariah said lightly, even though she was dead serious.

"And it's not likely you will, either," Katie replied. "I understand this conservatism after growing up in Bryn Mawr, which doesn't mean I like it, mind you. Open friendliness is not the general theme in these northeastern towns," she explained. "Mostly, people in those suburbs socialize with their own economic and racial kind. I know you don't relate to that." She paused a moment so Mariah could absorb what she was saying. "It's largely segregated and probably always will be. Look, Mariah, you've been to England. Think of the British and how formal and proper they are."

"What does that have to do with anything?" Mariah wondered.

"Well, you're in the *New* England area now, Sweetie—it's similar. Do you see what I'm trying to convey to you, my kooky, spiritual daughter?" she asked.

"I suppose so. Thanks for clearing that up for me, Great Wise One!" As usual, her good friend had cheered her up.

Katie had decided to leave St. John after living in the tropics for twelve years but was undecided where to relocate. With Mariah living in New York, she figured it was as good a place as any to re-enter the mainstream. "I swore I would never live in the northeast again when I left Pennsylvania, but who knows? Perhaps I can do some good up there. There are lots of people in that area who could use a little therapy, don't you think?" Due to her interest in hypnosis, Katie had changed her career and was now a licensed hypnotherapist.

"Most definitely," Mariah replied. "Look at it like you are entering the Peace Corps. It's so easy to get lost in all this material wealth. Maybe you can help people get back on track with what's truly important in life."

Katie smiled at Mariah's comments. "It's funny—I wanted to join the Peace Corps when I was younger. Who knew I would do it in the richest country in the world—America! This way, I don't have to get all those bothersome shots or buy one of those ugly vests with all the pockets in them," she said and they both laughed. "Well, my mother is three hours south of you and my son and his wife are three hours north, so it's a convenient locale to my only family.

Katie was thrilled they would have each other's support during their adjustment period and Mariah was relieved she was finally going to have someone she could relate to in the area.

Mariah made it clear to her husband that none of her discomfort was about him. He hated that his new wife felt so unsettled since he loved where he lived and couldn't relate to what she was feeling. After all, he had grown up in the northeast and was used to the lifestyle there. Plus, his professional life took him to fascinating places and when he returned home, he enjoyed the quiet his rural neighborhood provided. If some of the women in the area were snobs, it had never come to his attention.

Mariah was adaptable and strong. Her life had taken her through difficult adjustments and this was just one more. She needed to figure out a way to live there and still have a life of her own.

Overtime, she began working for various Caribbean based companies on a freelance basis, which gave her the opportunity to travel to the islands regularly. With her frequent island visits to look forward to, Mariah gradually began to feel more like her old self again.

Chapter Sixty

1999

In early October, Chris had a two-day camera shoot in Montreal, Canada that he was very excited about.

"Mariah, I want you to come with me and my crew so I can show you where my cousins used to live. It's amazing up there," Chris said, clearing the dinner dishes from the table, being careful to not drop Mariah's favorite wine glasses. "Have you ever been to Canada?"

"Yes, western Canada—a few times, but never Quebec. Montreal has always intrigued me. I've heard it's a beautiful city—and oh, so *French*," she added. "Thanks for the invite, Sam. I'd love to come."

A week before they flew to Montreal, Mariah had three very significant dreams. In them, Chris was alone in the woods during the winter months and he eventually froze to death. The image was disturbing enough that Mariah shared it with her husband.

"We aren't going to be in any freezing woods when we go to Canada, are we, Sweetie?" she asked.

"No, why?" he wondered. Chris had experienced her mystic ways and Mariah sometimes unnerved him with her intuition.

"I've had three dreams this past week and in each of them, you freeze to death in the north woods," she said, emphatically. "But the odd thing is that you seem content about it—like it was your choice, rather than an accident." She looked into Chris' eyes and quickly saw the two of them in an Indian village saying goodbye. Mariah could see she was crying. Chris was being supremely stubborn and he wouldn't get off his horse. As quickly as it appeared, the scene was gone. Mariah let out a long sigh and dabbed at her eyes.

"Hey, come here," Chris said, opening his arms to hold her. "I certainly do not choose to freeze to death in Canada or anywhere—thank you! It must have been some other guy who looks just like me."

"Yeah, sure. It was probably that other handsome man named, *Sam*," Mariah said, teasing him. "Just promise me you won't go wandering off the beaten track while we're there."

The video crew rented a mini-van at the Montreal airport and drove to their hotel. Chris and his team began their shoot the next day, while Mariah toured the Museum of Archaeology and History. The area completely fascinated her, and Mariah was curious to learn more about the early days of New France, as it was originally called. That night, the entire group had an exquisite dinner of duck a la orange at Chez Julien on Rue Union, just around the corner from the TV-shoot. Throughout the evening, Chris spoke tenderly of his childhood.

"My cousins and I would float along the St. Lawrence River with their canoes even though we weren't allowed to go in the water without a parent. I would be the fur-trapper and my cousin would be my Indian friend," he mused. "We pretended we knew the best places to trap. We even had hats for our costumes—him with a feather and me with my coon skin." His crew laughed and poked fun at him, making Indian noises with their flat hands tapping on their open mouths.

Later that night, Chris told Mariah he wanted to find the town. "It's pretty there. My cousins lived above the river. Maybe we could have a picnic." His voice sounded nostalgic.

"Sure, let's do it. I want to go there almost as much as you do," Mariah said. "The whole area is fascinating to me. I learned about the early days of Quebec today, while I was at the Museum. I think it's adorable that you used to play fur-trapper and Indian games here when you were a little boy," Mariah said.

"Right now, we can play our own fur-trapper—Indian game. I'll be the fur trapper, and you can be the beautiful Indian woman who wants to try out a white guy," Chris laughed as he grabbed his wife and pulled her back against the pillow.

"Sounds good to me. I obviously like to mix things up." Mariah giggled, and pulled back the covers to climb on top of him.

Chapter Sixty-one

The couple awoke around eight the next morning and enjoyed a light breakfast of strong coffee, croissants, cheese and melon. Chris got out a map to plan their day. While he drank his coffee, he noticed Mariah was a bit groggy and not her usual perky, morning self. "How did you sleep, Love? You must have had a bad dream," he said as he studied the names of the surrounding towns on the map. "You were tossing and turning all night and hoarding the covers," he added with a chuckle. "I kept trying to cuddle up to you but you would have none of it! And I was so cold. What a bed-hog—geeez!"

"As a matter of fact, I did have a bad dream. It was the same one I had right before we came here—the one where you froze to death in the northern wilderness. It's weird I caused you to be cold while I was dreaming about you freezing to death! I'm sorry for robbing the blankets as well as your sleep," Mariah said apologetically.

"You didn't rob me of my sleep, Sweetheart. I was snuggled in next to you and I slept like a baby—a perfectly *safe* baby," he added with a wink. Then, attempting the French language, he said a few of the names out loud: "St. Barbe; St. Zotique; Coteau-du-Lac; St. Chrysostome." He was adept at changing the subject when he felt the need and Mariah dropped it without further comment.

"I'm not sure, but I think Coteau-du-Lac is where we used to go. Let's head in that direction and maybe it will jar my memory. We hardly went into the town since everything to do there cost money, and we never had any," he said with a laugh. "We mostly hung out at my cousin's house. Our parents played cards and drank beer while the kids disappeared to places we weren't supposed to go," Chris said, smiling.

"We can find a little cafe, have some lunch and then browse the antique shops, if there are any," Mariah offered. The idea seemed to put her in a more upbeat mood and Chris nodded in agreement. They both appreciated antiques.

It took forty minutes to get there. They drove southwest, along the St. Lawrence River through gently rolling farmland and Chris thought it looked somewhat familiar. As they cruised along the highway, he glanced at his wife who was looking out the window with a concerned look on her face. She was clutching her jacket close to her body.

"Honey, are you still thinking about me freezing to death up here?"

Mariah nodded and looked at her husband in fear. "I know it's weird, but I feel cold all of a sudden, especially on the right side of my body. . .the side facing *north*." Mariah folded her arms in her lap and continued to shiver. Her index finger began to throb and she rubbed it until it stopped.

"Sweetheart," Chris replied in his calmest voice, "It's not even close to freezing out there and we are heading west, not north. Believe me, I'm toasty warm right now, all the way to my soul." He took her fisted hand and kissed it lightly. He could feel the love and concern from her and it warmed him more than the car's heater ever could. "It's all right." Chris said with a smile and

Mariah returned it with a brief nod. He knew her intuition was keen but there was absolutely no danger of either one of them freezing in the Canadian wilderness. At least, not on this trip!

They pulled into town, and found a convenient parking lot to leave their car. It was at the beginning of the main street, which seemed to be where the majority of the shops were located. Holding hands, they strolled down the sidewalk where they saw numerous signs for antique and consignment shops all waving like colorful flags. Mariah eagerly pushed up her sleeves in anticipation. She made a conscious effort to leave her foreboding behind.

Chris saw a wooden Indian on the sidewalk in front of a store across the street and hoped it was a tobacco store. He felt the urge to smoke a cigar, so he excused himself, telling Mariah he would be back in a few minutes. Once inside, he realized it was primarily an antique shop, but there was a display case in the back filled with Cuban cigars. *At least in Canada, I won't have to feel like a criminal for smoking one,* he thought to himself.

As he looked down the street savoring his cigar, an eerie feeling started spreading through him like a chill from an open window. Suddenly, it seemed as though he was watching the scene in a movie rather than standing there in real life. The street was about seven or eight blocks long and at the end of it, facing Main Street, was a big wooden building. Although he couldn't quite make it out, there was obviously some sort of name above a large set of double doors. He crossed the street and poked his head into the store where he had left Mariah.

"Take your time, Darlin'. I'm going to head down the street to the big building facing up the road," he told his wife. She nodded and waved her hand.

"That's the old Trading Post," the store clerk told them both. "It's the oldest building in town and one of the few that still operates as the original business."

Mariah and Chris smiled at the man who was obviously proud to be sharing this bit of his town's history. "OK, Babe. I'll be along, eventually." Mariah said.

As Chris headed down the street toward the Trading Post, the cold eerie feeling persisted. His peripheral vision became clouded, adding to the movie set atmosphere. The few blocks he walked were a blur. He felt like he was moving in slow motion and he tried to stay focused on his destination. He stared at the name above the big doors. He still couldn't quite make it out, but the closer he got, the clearer the letters became. In big white, somewhat chipped, but still visible lettering, was the name: FONTAINE. Chris froze. His mouth went dry, his arms went limp and he dropped his cigar on the sidewalk. FONTAINE... Fontaine... Fontaine! Why was that name ringing in his ears?

A young woman who was crossing the street saw him standing with his mouth open. "Are you all right, sir? You look like you just caught your wife in bed with your best friend," she said with a chuckle.

"Yeah, thanks," Chris mumbled without looking at her. His head was spinning. As he looked down Main Street, he saw people of another time period dressed in colonial garb, traveling in horse-drawn carriages. He envisioned himself up on a big ladder, leaning against the building with a bucket of white paint. He was busily painting the letters spelling, FONTAINE. A clerk in a black apron was directing him.

He could hear the clerk's voice, "Sir, you might want to make the 'F' a bit bigger than the rest of the letters." Indeed, the 'F' was bigger. "He called me sir," Chris said aloud to himself. There was no ladder or clerk anywhere to be found.

He looked up the street to see if Mariah was on her way but there was no sign of her. Chris took a deep breath and went inside the Trading Post.

Inside the shop, the ceiling was twenty feet high with exposed post and beam construction—his favorite type of architecture. There were big ladders on tracks with wheels against the tall walls so employees could reach the upper storage shelves. Extra inventory of the merchandise available at eye level was kept up above. Chris remembered coming up with the idea of those ladders with wheels. The floors boards were a wide-planked, honey colored chestnut that gave the place a warm feel.

Those boards were so heavy when we laid 'em down. . .still a bit green, but I couldn't wait for them to cure any longer. . .needed to get the doors open before Christmas. Chris smiled, recalling the day. The boards creaked with a sound so soothing it was like hearing his grandmother sing as she cooked his favorite meal. The main sales counter was made of quarter-sawn oak, and it had thick, beveled glass for the display case underneath.

"That glass was expensive. . .it took three months to get it here from London," he said out loud. He walked over to the sporting goods counter, looked up and saw the old twelve rung, gun-rack hanging on the wall. He remembered the day 'ol Jeb de Mornay brought it in to sell...*said he just didn't need that many guns anymore. I paid him for it on the spot, 'cause I needed it for a display rack.* "How could I know that? This is crazy! What is this place?" Chris said

Chris was caught up in his reverie and didn't hear an older gentleman who wore a black apron come up behind him.

"Can I help you son? I'm a little hard of hearing and my English isn't as good as my French, so you'll have to speak up. Were you asking about a certain gun?" he asked. Chris whirled around and gasped when he saw the gentleman standing there in his black clerk apron. "Are you all right, boy?" he asked again. "You look as if you've just seen a ghost"

"Yes, I'm all right. No, actually—I'm not! I'm a bit dizzy. Can I sit down a minute?" Chris mumbled. "Do I know you? You look very familiar to me."

"Well, no, I don't think I know you, son. You don't look familiar to me at all. Are you from around here?" the clerk inquired.

"No, I grew up in Connecticut, but I used to come to this area when I was a young boy. I had relatives who lived around here, but we never spent much time in town. They lived about fifteen miles out in the country on a small farm," Chris answered.

"People tell me I have one of those common faces. That's probably it. Hell, I've never been to Connecticut. Never really been anywhere, except Montreal a few times. Once upon a time, my six times great grandfather used to own this store and my family has kept it running as a trading post all these years. Going on three hundred, last time I added it up. Amazing, when you think about it," the clerk boasted.

"Incredible!" Chris got up and stretched. Talking to this man was helping him get his center of gravity again. Chris walked over to the display case and ran his hand across the oak. The eerie feeling came flooding back. He envisioned himself sawing that wood and sanding it down before adding the linseed oil. He was proud of how well they had held up all these years...

"OK—BREATHE," he told himself out loud. "A few deep breaths will help...breath in and out," Chris said, willing himself to snap out of this time warp. It was like listening to a radio that was double banding between stations. One moment, Chris was tuned in to his immediate surroundings, the then, another scene came flooding through his memory.

"You look like you could use a cold drink of water," the clerk said not waiting for a reply.

While the man went to the back room to get the drink, Chris looked beyond the workmanship, and stared into the case itself. On the top shelf, surrounded by old cuff links, broaches and other vintage jewelry, he saw a beautiful gold pocket watch with a waterfall etched on the cover. He froze again, hunched over the display case, staring at that watch with his mouth wide open.

"Son, what is it? Do you want to see something in that case?"

"Y e s, pleeeasse," Chris answered, his voice wobbly. He had begun to sweat, his hands shaking. "T h a t . . . w a t c h. May I see that watch, please?"

"But, of course. Let me get the key," he said pulling a long strip of rawhide with several keys tied to it out of a drawer. "Here we go," he said as he unlocked the sliding glass. "Now this is a very precious item," he said. With gentle care, he handed Chris the watch. "I recently found this in the antique safe we have in the back room. I believe it belonged to the original owner of this very store," the clerk added.

Chris held the watch like it was a priceless jewel. "It's OK, go ahead and open it," the old clerk suggested. "It plays the most beautiful tune."

"I know," Chris replied, without opening it. "My woman loved the music so much, it made her cry the first time she heard it." Chris' own eyes welled with tears. He took both hands and smoothed back his hair. "What the hell am I talking about?" Chris said aloud, rubbing his eyes on his shirtsleeve. He wondered if he was having a nervous breakdown.

"Son, I'm not sure what you mean by that. Maybe you've seen a replica of that particular watch somewhere before. Anyway—open 'er up, let's hear that tune," the old man said, rubbing his hands together in anticipation.

Chris opened the lid and the music started to play that all-too-familiar melody. He was not able to control himself and he started to cry. The clerk was moved by his reaction, and put his arm around Chris' shoulders. "It's OK, young man. You go ahead and feel what you're feeling. Sometimes we get sentimental about things, don't we?" The man led Chris to a chair and patted him on the back, trying to comfort him. "That really is one special watch, isn't it?"

"Yes sir, it is," Chris replied as he pulled a handkerchief from the pocket of his jacket. He turned the watch over in his hand to look at the back, then flipped it to the front and opened it again, which started the music. He carefully angled it to get a closer look at an inscription on the inside lid. The message was in French, but it was signed, *Sam*.

Chris pointed to the engraving. He tried to pull himself together enough to ask who Sam was. "What does this say? I don't speak French," Chris asked in a weak, voice.

"It says: *I will love you all my life.* The original owner of this Trading Post was named: Samuel de Fontaine—that's why it's signed, *Sam*."

"Are you a Fontaine then? Was that your relative?"

"No, I'm a Stark. My ancestor was partners with 'ol Samuel de Fontaine."

Chris looked at the inscription on the lid of the watch. He remembered there wasn't enough room to put the whole name: *Samuel*, so the jeweler shortened it to *Sam*. "Who was the inscription for?" he asked the clerk.

"Well, the way I recall my great grand-daddy telling the story, it went something like this: Samuel de Fontaine owned this here store. He was a young, ambitious man, who made his fortune trapping furs, and establishing this business. It was the only successful store in these parts for many years. Now, this was back in the mid 1600's mind you! Anyways, on one of his trapping jaunts, Samuel de Fontaine got friendly with the Hurons and he fell in love with one of their squaws. He brought her here to Coteau-du-Lac, hoping she would agree to stay and marry him. But the townspeople were horrible to her, and she couldn't see herself living in a place where she didn't belong. Anyhow, Samuel, being a stubborn, proud man, wouldn't agree to move to her village so he brought her back to her people. But, he was miserable without her and he decided he wanted her back in his life. A few months later, Samuel got the idea to have the watch inscribed for her. He was going to give it to her as a present and tell her he was willing to live with her, anywhere," the clerk said, with a little cough. "Do you mind if I drink the rest of this water? My throat gets scratchy when I talk so much." he said.

"Go on, please. Help yourself. This is a fascinating story." Chris encouraged him.

"Yes, it's a romantic tale, to be sure. Now, where was I? Oh, I remember—Samuel took the watch and headed out toward her village. He had missed her very much, and was looking forward to their reunion. But, when he got to her village, he discovered that she had passed away. Don't that beat all?" the old man asked. "It was probably the smallpox—that did a lot of folks in back in those days."

"It's awful. It hurts just hearing about it," Chris said, covering his heart with his hand as he looked up at the man.

"Do you want to buy that watch, son? It's three hundred American dollars, but I feel I should let you have it for two hundred and seventy-five. You seem to have a special attachment to it."

"Yes, I do. I want to give it to my wife. We got married three years ago and this inscription is exactly what I want to say to her every day. Ironically, her pet name for me is *Sam*," Chris told the man.

"Well now, isn't that a coincidence?" The man fell out of his story telling mode. It was time for business. "Will that be cash or charge?"

"Charge. Is Visa OK?"

"Sure, we take all the plastic. Got to nowadays," he said with a little smile. "I have the nicest little box to put it in, too."

As Chris signed the slip, the clerk stared at the signature and was speechless for a minute. "That's the damnedest thing," he said out loud, rubbing the grey stubble on his chin.

"What's that?" Chris asked.

"Well, it's your handwriting—it's real familiar. You sure you've never been up here before?"

"No, sir. My handwriting is atrocious. I feel sorry for anyone who writes this badly," Chris said with a chuckle.

"I agree! That's why I remembered it," he let out a laugh of his own. "Wait! I remember where I saw it. Hold on a minute! Don't leave," he added as he creaked across the old floorboards to the back room. He was gone for a good ten minutes, but Chris was so enthralled with his surroundings and his new watch, he didn't notice the wait.

"Here it is," the clerk said waving a legal size piece of paper. "I might be old, but my mind is still sharp as a tack," he said, tapping his temple with his index finger. "Now, look at this document I found in the old antique safe. It was sitting next to that watch you just purchased. This here is the original document Samuel de Fontaine drew up, making my six times great grand-daddy, fifty percent partner in this trading post. Don't his handwriting and yours look alike?" he asked as he put Chris' signed credit card slip right next to the document by Samuel de Fontaine's signature. How strange! Chris couldn't disagree. He then signed: Samuel de Fontaine, and there was no mistaking it, it was exactly the same signature. "Now, that is downright spooky—especially since you have such an attachment to his old watch and his old building!" Chris nodded as he stared at the signature. He couldn't speak.

Scratching his beard again, the clerk then said, "I remember the rest of the story now that we're talking about it. Samuel de Fontaine came back from the Huron village completely devastated. With his woman now dead, he felt more alone than ever. My granddaddy said he blamed himself. Said that if he had gone to live in her village she would have been able to fight the plague. Anyway...where was I? Oh, yeah, the document! Samuel cleaned out his house of all his personal effects and brought 'em over here to the store and told my great grand-daddy to sell it all off. He claimed he didn't want his things anymore, and for my grand -daddy to go over to his house and take anything that was left.

Oh, by the way, did you know Samuel de Fontaine's house is right on the edge of town? It's the Town Hall now, so it has been converted to offices, but the original structure is the same. Anyway, 'ol Samuel wanted my kin to sell all his stuff, because he was headed for the north wilderness to try and mend his broken heart. He didn't even take his traps. Those are them, hanging on the wall across from the gun rack. I use 'em for decoration."

Chris got up, walked back over to the sporting goods area and looked up at the old traps. The leather strap on the beaver trap was still ripped. He remembered that he was going to put on a new one but he never got around to it. He rubbed his eyes and tried to focus.

The old man continued with his story as Chris shuffled back across the room. He clutched the watch to his heart and sat back down on the stool. "Truth was," the clerk went on, "Samuel was going up there to die. He wanted to be with his woman. Ol' Samuel froze to death up there. Some trappers found his body, half eaten by wolves.

Anyway, my six-times great grand daddy put his watch in that old safe back there, along with this document. I reckon he thought maybe Samuel would want it when he came back. Samuel's uncle had been some big muckety-muck in these parts back then, and had given the watch to him originally. Samuel de Fontaine never returned, and that watch never made it out of the safe until I found it a few weeks ago. I got a hold of an antique safe cracker to open that old thing up. He specializes in opening older safes without ruining their antique integrity. Imagine that . . . specialized burglars gone professional!" Laughing, the clerk slapped his knee, delighted at his own joke.

Chris looked more closely at the document. The handwriting was exactly like his—barely legible! The eerie feeling he had been experiencing all day got stronger and he started to sweat and shake again. "I'm sorry I'm such a basket-case," Chris said. "Could I please have a copy of this document?"

"Sure, I suppose so. They have a copy machine at the Town Hall, and since that's the place I told you was Samuel de Fontaine's house, I figure you probably want to head over there. Make two copies of it, if you don't mind. It's always good to have an extra copy of special documents," the clerk said.

"No problem. Glad to. I'll be back shortly. If my wife comes in here, please tell her where I am. She's dark skinned and very beautiful. You'll know her immediately," Chris smiled.

"Sure thing, son. Tell Gladys—she works the front desk there at the Town Hall—tell her that, Jean—that's me—said 'hey.'" The clerk had a gleam in his eye at the thought of Gladys getting his little message.

"Of course. I'll be back shortly."

Chris looked up the street to see if Mariah was anywhere in sight. Once again, the street looked like a movie set: dusty, dreamy, the clatters of horses' hooves clicking down the road. He longed to tell Mariah what he was experiencing. "She believes in all this weird stuff," he murmured as he walked out of the store. He briefly thought about tracking her down, but the need to see Samuel de Fontaine's house took precedence.

Chris started down the street, behind the Trading Post—about the equivalent of three blocks—and he instinctively turned left into the back entrance. There was no sign indicating the structure was the Town Hall, but Chris was positive he was in the right place. He walked around the side by the chimney bricks and got down on his hands and knees. The bottom brick had the letters S.F. carved into it. He remembered doing that when he built the chimney. "I have entered the Twilight Zone," Chris said to himself as he got up, heading for the door. There was a plaque on the wall that read: House of Samuel de Fontaine, originator of the Trading Post. 1615–1645.

He went inside and saw that Jean's description had been correct. The house had indeed been converted into modern offices. Then he noticed the plump receptionist.

"Are you Gladys?" Chris asked and the woman nodded. "Jean, down at the Trading Post says, 'hey.'" Gladys giggled, and blushed. "Where is your copy machine?

"It's in the next room, right by the fireplace," she told him.

He started to go in, but stopped in his tracks. As he looked into the room, the movie in his head returned. This room had been the original kitchen; it still had the old soapstone sink under the window and crude shelves once used for housing dishes. Next to the window was a big walk-in fireplace. As Chris entered, he remembered laying every brick. There were a few small seashells stuck in the mortar, forming a star design in the center of the mantle. *When those shells came into the trading post, I thought they were beautiful, so I kept them. It was fun putting them into the design.* He could see the back of his Huron woman cooking over a huge black pot, which hung in the middle on the spit. Just then, Gladys came around the corner and saw him standing there, gaping at the fireplace.

"They don't make 'em that big anymore," she said. "Did you need some help with the copy machine, sir? The copies are fifty cents—Canadian, that is. You're American aren't you?" she asked.

"Yes, this time I'm an American," Chris answered her. "Thank you for offering. I need two copies of this document, please. Here's the money." Chris handed her a handful of change. "Thank you. I'll be back to get the copies in a minute. I want to look around this old house, if you don't mind. Is it OK to go upstairs?"

"Sure, this is a public building. Make yourself at home," she told him. If she only knew just how at home he was!

Chris went upstairs and opened the first door on the right. There were only two rooms on the second floor: one was his bedroom and the other was going to be a child's room. He sat down on the floor in front of the fireplace in his old room and hugged his knees to his chest. His breathing was uneven as he rocked back and forth. He started to sweat again.

"Geez! What is happening to me? I'm really losing it," Chris whispered to himself. "I need Mariah. She'll know what's going on."

Chapter Sixty-two

1999

Mariah had been in every antique shop along Main Street. Worn out from her shopping, she headed toward the Trading Post. As she walked, her legs started to feel weak, and her pace slowed. Just ahead, she saw an oversized planter with a wide edge, so she sat down to gather her wits.

"Maybe I'm faint from spending too much money," she chided herself. Taking a few deep breaths of the crisp autumn air, she looked up and down the street and then over at the Trading Post. That all too familiar déja-vu feeling Mariah had experienced so many times in her life began creeping over her now. Sights and sounds of the modern day were blended into the dated foreground before her. Mariah's eyes started to itch from the clouds of dust the horse-drawn carriages were stirring up from the dirt road.

She saw herself—and a man who Mariah recognized as Chris—sitting side-by-side on a horse-drawn wagon traveling down the street, toward the Trading Post. She was dressed in decorative Indian clothing. Her outfit was light brown in color, made of tanned animal skins. There was beautiful blue and white beaded handiwork on the modest neckline and on the loose edges of her long sleeves. The same beaded pattern was repeated on the tops of her boots. Chris was also dressed in frontier clothing, rawhide pants and fur-lined boots as high as his knees. He went into the store, and she waited outside in the wagon. Curious pedestrians passed by, staring and pointing at the beautiful Indian woman. They mumbled rude comments knowing full well they were within earshot of the squaw.

Mariah rubbed her eyes. Instantly, the scene flashed back to the present. She had not experienced a past image that strong since she was in Martinique several years back.

Ten feet down the sidewalk, two women were gesturing toward her and Mariah heard them gossiping.

"She looks like a Negro, it's true, but she's not quite dark enough. Maybe she's an 'Injun.' Lord knows, there are enough of 'em still around. My Billy had one as a substitute teacher the other day. Imagine that, an educated Injun!" The women giggled, as they passed by the planter. Mariah thought about tripping the one with the bigger mouth but decided against it. Instead, she made a little Indian noise with her stiff fingers patting her open mouth. Both women let out a gasp and scuttled quickly past, clutching each other for support.

Feeling proud of herself, Mariah stifled a laugh, even though she felt a pang in her heart at their scorn. Mariah took a deep breath and looked around, hoping to see Chris. She then stared at the name FONTAINE above the doors of the Trading Post. She remembered knowing someone by that name but couldn't quite picture who it was. That was the store Chris said he was going to so she got up, gathered her purchases and went inside. Hearing the door open, the old clerk came out from the back room, wiping his chin with a napkin.

"Oh, pardon me," he said, "I was just having a few bites of lunch in the back room. You must be that handsome young fellow's wife. He told me you were beautiful and he was right. You are a pretty one, ain't you?"

"Why, thank you, kind sir," Mariah said, with a little bow. "Is my husband still here?" she asked, looking up at the architecture. "I'll bet he appreciated this old building—he loves post and beam construction."

"As a matter of fact, that man of yours did have a certain affinity to this place. It struck him real familiar like. Actually, he's over at Town Hall. Told me to send you over there."

"Um, yeah, I feel it too. I've never been up here before—but somehow, I know this place. For me, it's more the outside storefront than the interior. Maybe it reminds me of a scene I saw in a movie," Mariah mumbled as she continued to look around.

"Could be," the old man said. "Your husband got all clammy and teary-eyed over it. It was like he'd spent a lot of time in this store—like he remembered it somehow."

"Really? How do I get to your town hall?" Mariah asked anxiously.

"Go past this building about three blocks, then go left. Can't miss it," he told her.

"Thank you, sir. If my husband and I miss each other, please tell him to sit tight and I'll be right back. Is it OK if I leave these parcels here for a few minutes?" she asked before dashing out the door.

"Oh, sure. Put 'em over there by the counter."

Mariah's heart was beating fast, even before she began running down the street. She was used to these flashback experiences, but could imagine how disturbing it would be for someone who didn't understand what was happening. "He's probably freaking out right about now," she said aloud to herself.

Gladys was humming at her desk when Mariah came bursting in. "Oh my! You startled me," she said with her hand over her heart. "Can I help you?"

"Yes, ma'am. Please, excuse me. I'm looking for my husband. He's medium height—dark wavy hair, pearly white smile. Is he here?"

Gladys smiled and pointed to the next room. "He went upstairs to look around. He seemed extremely curious about this old house."

"I'll bet. Is it OK if I go up and find him?"

"Sure. Like I told him, it's a public building. Help yourself. Go through that room there and you'll see the stairs," Gladys said, gesturing for Mariah to go on up.

As Mariah walked through what had been the kitchen, she became weak in the knees, again. She saw herself cooking in that fireplace, using a big iron kettle. There had been blue dishes on the shelf that now held reams of copy paper. She walked to the soapstone sink and ran her hands over the smooth, rounded edge. She saw herself washing in it as she looked out the window and remembered daydreaming about her home and her own people as she worked. Just then, her birthmark finger started to burn so she turned on the faucet and let the cold water wash over it.

Tears rolled down her cheeks as she felt that same longing—then and now. CHRIS! She was so caught up, Mariah forgot about finding him. She turned off the water and dried her hand on her shirt and ran up the stairs, two at a time. She flung open the right door at the landing and saw her husband sitting on the floor in front of the fireplace, rocking back and forth. In his hands was a small blue box.

"Hi, babe." She sat down and gently put her arms around him. "Are you OK?" She wanted to share her recollections, but could see that Chris needed a minute to pull himself together. He laid his head on Mariah's shoulder and continued rocking. She ran her fingers through his hair several times to soothe him and within moments, his breathing became more even. She touched the beautiful box. "What did you buy?"

Chris sat up, looked at her and smiled. "I bought you a present, Sweetheart. I hope you like it." Mariah could see he was shaken to his core.

"Well, that was thoughtful of you, Sam." Mariah put the box over her heart with both her palms, cradling it gently. Looking into her husband's deep blue eyes with an intensity that went back into the folds of time, Mariah pursed her lips together and blew gently in his direction. With her eyes swimming in tears, she opened her gift. There lay the watch on its cotton bed, the gleaming waterfall, shiny and familiar. She picked it up and turned it over, studying the carvings on the outside shell. Mariah had been to that very same waterfall in Martinique—she recognized it immediately.

"It's beautiful, don't you think?" Chris asked eagerly. Tears were streaming down Mariah's face and all she could do was nod. "Open it," Chris urged through his blurred vision. Mariah smiled and opened the lid, anticipating what she would hear when the music began to play. They gazed deep into each other's eyes and listened to the tune all the way through. Mariah then noticed the engraving inside.

"It didn't used to have this inscription. When did you have this done, Sam? What does it mean?"

Mariah's comment did not go over his head. They were on the same wavelength.

"It's French. It says: *I will love you all my life.* Samuel de Fontaine had it engraved for his Indian woman, but when he went to her village to give it to her, he discovered she had passed away. I've got to tell you the whole story, Honey. You're not going to believe it," Chris said, excitedly.

Mariah nodded. "Of course, I'll believe you. This was your watch, Chris. I remember it . . . especially the music, but the last time I saw it, there was no engraving. And this was your house—your feather bed was against that wall," Mariah said pointing to the window. "I loved sleeping in here with you next to this big fireplace. Just now, when I came through what used to be your kitchen, I saw myself cooking and washing in that old sink. This was your house, Chris. You were Samuel de Fontaine."

She watched Chris' reactions as she spoke. The confidence in her voice gave him assurance that what he had experienced during the past hour was real. "I spent time here, Sam, but it was your home, not mine. As I was coming down the street to the Trading Post to find you, I heard some women gossiping about me. They were trying to guess if I was a Negro or an Indian and, as I listened to them, it brought back the scorn I felt when I was here—in this town, with you—in another lifetime." Mariah put her hand squarely on his shoulders and looked him in the eye. "I've always known that you and I were old souls. We probably knew each other in the Caribbean, as well."

"You've always said that and now, I think you're right, Baby. This has definitely been the weirdest day of my life! You're used to this metaphysical stuff, but I'm not." Chris said, letting out a sigh. "Damn! What an amazing situation!" They got up and headed downstairs to get the copies Gladys had ready for them. The personable civil servant smiled at the couple as she gave them the papers.

"Here you go. Now, you tell that Jean Stark to come on down here himself and make his own copies next time." Gladys' cheeks were flushed and she acted shy all of a sudden.

"Yes, ma'am. We will," Chris said as they started to leave. "Bye now. Thanks for the tour of my old house."

Gladys stared at him for a moment, then shrugged off the strange comment.

As Chris closed the door behind them, Mariah heard Gladys whisper under her breath, "Kooky Americans."

Mariah laughed and held Chris' hand as he took her around the side of the house to show her where he had carved his initials in the bottom brick of the chimney.

As they strolled back to the Trading Post, Chris explained what had happened to him earlier as he walked down the street toward the store and once he was inside. The color was beginning to return to his face, and as he continued to relay what he had been through, he was filled with gratitude for having Mariah back in his life.

She picked up her packages and waited while Chris gave the clerk his copy of the historic document.

"Mr. Stark," he said, "I want to thank you for such a fascinating afternoon."

"Sure, son. You come back again, sometime. I'll try to dig up some more information about those times for you. There's still folks that live around here who had relatives back in 'ol Samuel Fontaine's time. Could be there's more to tell." Mr. Stark shook hands with Chris and patted him on the back. He winked over at Mariah. "You take care of that pretty wife of yours, you hear?"

Chris smiled at him. "Yes sir, I will—you can be sure of that! We will visit again someday, and I want to thank you for being so kind to me today. Samuel Fontaine's watch is finally in the hands of its proper owner."

Mr. Stark shrugged and gave a little wave before going back inside to tend to Chris' former business.

The couple sat on the curb in front of Fontaine's Trading Post soaking up the warmth of the late afternoon sun. They were quiet for several minutes before Chris turned to face Mariah. He took her hands in his and looked deep in her big brown eyes.

"I will love you all my life, Mariah, just as it says in this watch. It was meant to be given to you years ago and I'm honored to have been given another chance to do so."

Mariah took her watch from the blue, embroidered box, opened the lid and the music began to play. "Well, Samuel de Fontaine, I am honored to finally receive my priceless gift. Thank you, my Love." The couple listened to the intriguing tune play all the way through. "God, I've always loved this music."

The End

About the Author

Raised in Fort Lauderdale, Florida, Donna Pagano has been a resident of St. Thomas, Virgin Islands, for more than two decades.

The author spent her college years studying forestry in the frosty climes of the Montana wilderness. Her passion for nature was rivaled only by a growing interest in publishing.

To that end, she accepted a position with a small independently-owned newspaper—the Mountain Trader. That experience became the foundation for her initial career goal: to one day establish a publication of her own.

By the late 1980's, that dream became reality when she founded two popular tropical newspapers and a tourist publication in the U.S. Virgin Islands.

Delighted by the ability to provide freelance writers with byline opportunities, some for the first time, she felt a growing need to find her own voice in the world of writing.

Eight years ago, she sold the publications in order to devote full time to crafting novels. *Merging Lives* is her first book. A second novel: *Connected Souls,* is already in the editing stages.

The mother of two grown children and grandmother of two youngsters, she is married to director of photography and filmmaker, Tony Pagano.

Made in the USA